"This book is a gem, or rather, like the city of Toledo, it is a jewel box. Each chapter, each digression, each detour is a delight . . . A hymn to a lifelong love affair with Spain. It will stand comfortably alongside Borrow, Starkie and Brenan as one of the great books about [Spain]" TRISTAN GAREL-JONES, *Observer*

"Nooteboom turns out to be a wonderful guide to Spain and all things Spanish . . .With a northerner's hunger, he feasts on the heat, colour, darkness, religiosity and primitiveness of the place"
Economist

"His prose is as sturdy as a good Rioja, and equally delicious"
SARA WHEELER, *Mail on Sunday*

"With this immensely attractive book, Cees Nooteboom joins a select band of writers . . . who have the rare ability to evoke the soul of a nation. No one with a feeling for Spain should fail to read this book" EUAN CAMERON, *Daily Telegraph*

"The erudition, ambition and resonance are reminiscent of Claudio Magris's magisterial *Danube*. But the voice – and, as he has rendered it, the territory – is Nooteboom's own"
Independent on Sunday

"Warm-hearted and impeccably scholarly"
STEVEN POOLE, *Guardian*

"Nooteboom's style is directness itself. Its clarity allows him to convey a multiple layering of experiences, and yet seem to be travelling light" RUTH PAVEY, *New Statesman*

"His descriptions of the cathedral and city of León are outstanding and leave one impatient to set off by the next train"
PATRICK MARNHAM, *Punch*

CEES NOOTEBOOM was born in The Hague in 1933. He is a poet, novelist, and author of several travel books. He has journeyed through much of the world; making his first voyage as a sailor to earn his passage from his native Holland to South America, he has been travelling ever since. His first taste of international success was the Pegasus Prize for *Rituals*. More recently, following the success of *A Berlin Notebook*, Cees Nooteboom was awarded the German Order of Merit. In 1993 he won the Aristeion European Literature Prize for his novel *The Following Story*, which was also shortlisted for the International IMPAC Dublin award 1996, and which confirmed his prominence in contemporary European and world literature. His books have been translated into many languages.

INA RILKE has translated a wide variety of art-historical literature, and is the translator of *The Following Story* and most recently *The Virtuoso* by Margriet de Moor.

Cees Nooteboom

ROADS TO SANTIAGO

Translated from the Dutch
by Ina Rilke

THE HARVILL PRESS
LONDON

For Simone

First published with the title *De omweg naar Santiago* by Uitgeverij Atlas, Amsterdam, 1992

First published in Great Britain in 1997 by
The Harvill Press, 2 Aztec Row, Berners Road, London N1 0PW

www.harvill-press.com

This paperback edition first published in 1998

5 7 9 8 6 4

The acknowledgments on page x constitute an extension of this copyright page

Cees Nooteboom asserts the moral right to be identified as the author of this work

A CIP catalogue record for this title is available from the British Library

ISBN 1 86046 419 X

Designed and typeset in Sabon at Libanus Press, Marlborough, Wiltshire

Printed and bound by Mackays of Chatham

Half title illustration by Chris Corr

CONTENTS

ACKNOWLEDGMENTS

The publisher gratefully acknowledges the support of the Foundation for the Production and Translation of Dutch Literature

All of the photographs copyright © Simone Sassen, 1992, with the exception of those reproduced by courtesy of the following archives:

Arixu Mas, Barcelona, for pages 68, 73, 76, 79, 92, 121, 134–6, 145
The National Gallery, London, for page 69
EFE News Agency, Madrid, for page 221

Map of Spain drawn by Reginald Piggott

Grateful acknowledgement is made for permission to reprint the following copyrighted material:

Excerpt from *Blood of Spain, the experience of civil war*, by Ronald Fraser, reprinted by permission of Penguin Books Ltd
Excerpt from *Don Quixote*, by Miguel De Cervantes, translated by J. M. Cohen, reprinted by permission of Penguin Books Ltd
Excerpt from *Islamic Spain 1250 to 1500*, by L. P. Harvey, © 1990 by The University of Chicago, reprinted by permission of The University of Chicago Press
Excerpt from *Antigones*, by George Steiner, 1984, reprinted by permission of Oxford University Press
Excerpt from *Spanish Romanesque Architecture of the Eleventh Century*, by Walter Muir Whitehill, Oxford University Press, 1941, reprinted by permission of Oxford University Press

LIST OF ILLUSTRATIONS

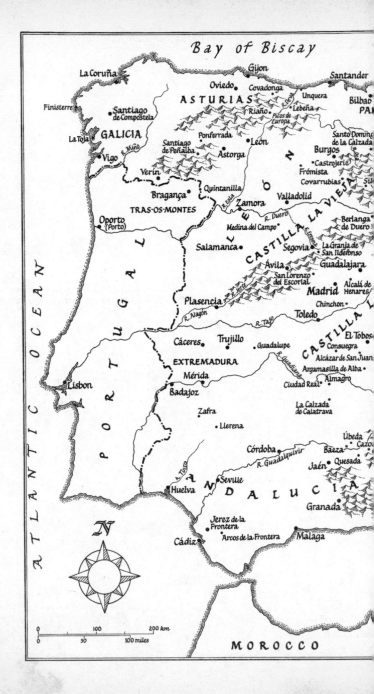

Readers with an interest in following the
Author's route should refer to either the
Michelin road maps of _Spain_, or Collins
single sheet map of _Spain and Portugal_.

FRANCE

San Sebastián • Biarritz
Irura • Rentería
VASCO
Pamplona • Roncesvalles · PYRENEES · Perpignan
Puente · Sangüesa · Iguacél
la Reina · R. Aragón · Jaca · Boltana
ogroño · Soś de Rey · San Juan
· Católico · de la Peña
Calahorra · Uncastillo
· Acín · Huésca · Vic
Tarazona · R. Gállego
Soria · Zaragoza
· Veruela · Fraga · Barcelona
Daroca · CATALONIA
Burbágena · Olite · Tarragona
· Alcañiz
NUEVA · Monreal del Campo
· Albarracín
· Teruel · BALEARIC ISLANDS
· Cuenca · MENORCA
LA MANCHA · MALLORCA
· Valencia · (MAJORCA)
R. Júcar
· Albacete · Cocentaina · Denia · IBIZA
· Villena
MURCIA · Elda
· Novelda · Alicante
· Cehegín
· Murcia
· Vélez Blanco · Mediterranean Sea
uéscar
· Vélez Rubio · Cartagena
Almería · ALGERIA

SPAIN

ROADS TO SANTIAGO

I

Through Aragón to Soria

Finding Spain ~ Making for Barcelona
Dalí's melted watch ~ Veruela
A brief history of monasticism

IT IS IMPOSSIBLE TO PROVE and yet I believe it: there are some places in the world where one is mysteriously magnified on arrival or departure by the emotions of all those who have arrived and departed before. Anyone possessed of a soul so light feels a gentle tug in the air around the Schreierstoren, the Sorrowers' Tower in Amsterdam, which has to do with the accumulated sadness of those left behind. It is a sadness we do not experience today: our journeys no longer take years to complete, we know exactly where it is we are going, and our chances of coming back are so much greater.

At the entrance to the cathedral in Santiago de Compostela there is a marble column with deep impressions of fingers, an emotional, expressionistic claw created by millions of hands, including my own. But it is already a distortion to say "including my own", for in grasping that pillar I have never felt the emotion that comes after walking for more than a year to arrive. I was not a man of the Middle Ages, I was not a believer, I arrived by car. If you disregard my hand resting on the marble, had I never been in that place, the claw would still be there, eroded in the hard stone by the fingers of all those people now dead. Yet, by laying my hand in that hollow one I was participating in a collective work of art. An idea becomes visible in matter: that is always wondrous. The power of an idea impelled kings, peasants, monks to lay their hands on exactly that spot on the column; each successive hand removed the minutest particle of marble so that, precisely where the marble had been erased, a negative hand became visible.

I am thinking these things on board a ship sailing at a leisurely pace

Cathedral of Santiago de Compostela

towards Barcelona, very early one July morning. I shall rent a car there and drive straight across Spain, or in a loop, to visit Santiago for the third time in my life. It will not in my case be a pilgrimage to the apostle, rather to an earlier, shadowy self, the recapture of a past passage. In search of what? One of the few constants in my life is my love – a lesser expression will not do – of Spain. Women and friends have vanished from my life, but a country does not run away so easily.

When I first went to Italy in 1953 I was twenty years old, and I thought I had found everything I had ever, unknowing, been looking for. The Mediterranean brilliance hit me like a bolt of lightning; the whole of human life was enacted on a single, fabulous, public stage against a careless backdrop of thousands of years of sublime art. Colours, foods, markets, clothing, gestures, language: everything seemed more refined, more vivid, more vibrant than in the low-lying northern delta I come from, and I was bowled over.

Spain after that was a disappointment. Under the same Mediter-ranean sun the language struck me as harsh, the landscape as barren, everyday life as coarse. It didn't flow, it wasn't pleasant, it was obstin-ately ancient and out of reach, it had to be conquered. I can no longer think in those terms. Italy is still a delight, but I have the feeling – it is not possible to talk of these things without resorting to an odd, mystical terminology – that the Spanish character and the Spanish landscape correspond to what in essence I am, to conscious and unconscious things in my being, to what I am about.

Spain is brutish, anarchic, egocentric, cruel. Spain is prepared to face disaster on a whim, she is chaotic, dreamy, irrational. Spain conquered the world and then did not know what to do with it, she harks back to her Medieval, Arab, Jewish and Christian past and sits there impassively like a continent that is appended to Europe and yet is not Europe, with her obdurate towns studding those limitless empty landscapes. Those who know only the beaten track do not know Spain. Those who have not roamed the labyrinthine complexity of her history do not know what they are travelling through. It is the love of a lifetime, the amazement is never-ending.

From the ship's rail I watch the dusk settle over the island where I have spent the summer. The approaching night steals into the hills, everything darkens; one by one the tall neon street-lamps come on to illuminate the quay with that dead white glow which is as much a part of the

Castillo de Valencia de Don Juan, Léon

Mediterranean night as the moon. Arrival and departure. For years now I have been crossing to and fro between the Spanish mainland and the islands. The white ships are somewhat bigger than they used to be, but the ritual is unchanged. The quay full of white-uniformed sailors, kins-folk and lovers come to wave goodbye, the deck crowded with departing holiday-makers, soldiers, children, grandmothers. The gangplank has already been raised, the ship's whistle will give one final farewell that will resound across the harbour and the city will echo the sound: the same, but weaker. Between the high deck and the quay below a last tenuous link, rolls of toilet paper. The beginnings flutter on the quay; up at the rail, the rolls will unwind slowly as the ship moves away, until the final, most fragile link with those staying behind is broken and the diaphanous paper garlands drown in the black water.

There is still some shouting, cries wafting back, but it is already impossible to tell who is calling out and what their messages signify. We sail out through the long narrow harbour, past the lighthouse and the last buoy – and then the island becomes a dusky shadow within the shadow that is night itself. There is no going back now, we belong to the ship. Guitars and clapping on the afterdeck, people are singing, drinking, the deck passengers are settling down for a long night in their steamer chairs, the dinner bell rings, white-jacketed waiters cross and recross the antique dining room under the earnest regard of the king of Spain.

The television screen in the lounge is showing blurred, shadowy images from the real world, but hardly anyone is watching. The passengers are postponing the moment of going to sleep, they hang around on the decks, drink until the bars shut. Then the very last, carousing song dies away and all you can hear is the slap of the waves against the hull.

The lone traveller goes to his cabin and lies down on the small iron bunk. He wakes up a few times in the night and looks out through the porthole. The vast surface of water sways in a slow, glistening dance. There is mystery and danger in the immense and silent element as it lies there with only the sluggish undertow disclosing that so much goes on hidden in the deep. The ivory chip of moon appears and disappears in the satin waves, it is at the same time sensual and frightening. The traveller is a city-dweller, unaccustomed to that vast and speechless sea of which his world now suddenly consists. He draws the skimpy curtain across the porthole and switches on a toy lamp by the bed. A wardrobe, a chair, a table. A water carafe in a nickel bracket attached to the steel bulkhead, a glass upturned over the neck. A towel marked *Compañia Mediterránea* which he will take with him tomorrow, along with the tumbler decorated with the flag of the shipping company. He already has quite a number of these towels and glasses, for he has made many such crossings.

Gradually he surrenders to the roll of the ship, pitching in her mighty mother's dance and he knows what it will be like. In the course of the night he will really fall asleep at last, then the first light of day will stream in through the unavailing curtain, he will go up on deck and stand with the other bleary-eyed passengers to see the city slowly approaching – looking improbably lovely in the early sun which will cast a light, golden, impressionistic veil over the horror of gasworks and smog, so that it will seem for a moment as if we are heading towards a hazy, gilded paradise instead of the uncharitable buffers of an industrial metropolis.

The ship glides into the stone welcome of the harbour. She is dwarfed by the towering cranes. The swell has ceased, this water is no longer part of the sea, and on board too the communal spirit has gone.

Everyone is wrapped up in his own affairs, in the expectation of what is to come. Down in the cabins the stewards are stripping the bunks and counting the number of towels missing. On the dockside it is already hot.

To make time melt strikes me as a peculiarly Spanish occupation, and nowhere has time been melted so handsomely as on the decaying, snail-like blob of Dalí's watch. As I wait for my car, I unfold the *Mundo Diario* and read the letter the ailing painter has written to his people to explain how ill he is *not*. The signature under the typed statement (letterhead: TEATRO MUSEO DALÍ) is shaky, but still familiarly distinctive – the letters of the magical name subsumed into a drawing of a Quixotic horseman, the lance thrusting bravely forward into the blank space of the paper. Poring over that signature, I think how Spanish Dalí's appearance is, how easily his self-made image will be absorbed into the national panopticum alongside pancake-frying Teresa of Avila, the nuns' corpses strung on the gallows of the Civil War, the garrotte, and Philip II languishing in the dungeon that is his own palace. Shutting my eyes, I can see the painter, the two pencil-sharp points of his moustache aimed like antennae upwards into the ionosphere to receive rarefied, coded messages incomprehensible to all other moustaches. STATEMENT FROM DON SALVADOR AND DOÑA GALA DALÍ reads the heading with majestic simplicity – no addressee specified.

"We are pleased to bring to the attention of all . . . the sincere hope of the undersigned artist . . ." – and more such dignified phrases give the letter the aura of a bulletin, issued at the palace gates when the king is known to be dying. Bitter earnest or is it black humour, you never know, but in any case "the undersigned artist" makes it known to his people that he has already set to work on a new painting. When it is finished it will go to his wife, and anon she will pass it on to the museum. On the inside page the signature is repeated, considerably enlarged. The newspaper editors have submitted it to a Professor Lester. It is not explained who this is, but in these parts if someone does not have a Spanish-sounding surname and has no first name at all it means that whoever he is need not be taken too seriously. The professor advises Dalí to take great care between 4 and 19 November, for at this time the planet Pluto and the star Lilith – the black moon – are in conjunction in the sign of Cancer, and this spells trouble above Cadaqués, where the artist lives.

He can escape disaster by travelling to Greece, where it is safer for Taureans at this particular time.

My route takes me through Zaragoza, by motorway from Barcelona to Soria, to old Castile, Castilla la Vieja. I see the town lying in the distance like a vision, shimmering in the heat. This is where the true Spain begins, the *meseta*, the high plain of Castile, empty, scorched, as huge as an ocean. Not much can have changed since the thirteenth century, when the principal sheep farmers joined forces to secure free passage of their flocks from the drought-ridden prairies of Extremadura to the green pastures of the northern cordillera. *Soria pura, cabeza de Extremadura* is the motto in the city's coat of arms. This is where the kingdoms of Castile and Aragón met the Muslim south. All over this region, transected by the River Duero like a line of defence, rise the ruins of once mighty fortresses whose sturdy contours still dominate the landscape. Berlanga, Gormaz, Peñaranda, Peñafiel, they all take on the colour of the dry soil as they lie there, sprawled and menacing on the low ripple of hills. Like dismantled, empty shells, the vast carcasses of extinct beasts – that is how they rule over the bare land and the low, unprepossessing villages in which churches and convents preserve the remembrance of former glory. In their sculpted calligraphy they evoke the memory of vanished Arab rulers. Time really did melt in this place, and then solidified for ever. The traveller sees the map growing emptier as he proceeds. There is nothing to tell, he feels lost in a well of centuries, set upon by ruins. The hot wind rolls with him over the plain, and he will encounter few beings on his way: Soria is the most deserted province of Spain, the population is still trickling away, there is no livelihood to be had there.

I seek refuge from the heat in the monastery of Veruela. It's like slamming the door on the plain behind you and stepping into a different, cooler, world. Oak trees and cypresses, the gentle lapping of water, rustling leaves, shade. There is no one to be seen, no cars belonging to other visitors, nothing. In Italy one often has the feeling that all the treasures are out on display, the eye is inebriated by what it sees, the great cornucopia is drained of its contents, there is no end to it. In Spain, and especially in these parts, one has to make an effort. Distances have to be covered, conquests made. The Spanish character has something monastic about it, even in their great monarchs there is a touch of the anchorite: both Philip and Charles built monasteries for themselves and spent much time in seclusion, turning their backs to the world they were required to govern. Anyone who has travelled widely through Spain is accustomed to such surprise encounters, and indeed anticipates them: in the middle of nowhere an enclave, an oasis, a walled, fortress-like, introverted spot, where silence and the absence of others wreak havoc in the souls of men. That is how it is here. I have walked under all the quarterings of Ferdinand of Aragón's coat of arms and the simpler, mitred arms of the archbishop of Zaragoza and of the abbot of the monastery. I am standing in the courtyard and have tugged the bell, but there is no response. I go back to the coats of arms and stare up at them, but they have lost their meaning. I can see, but am blind to what I see. There must have been a time when people "read" these symbols the way I read a traffic sign. I know that those quarterings indicate lineage, that they speak of couplings in remote Spanish castles which yielded knights and ladies, all of whom, rowing down the long rivers of their blood, are fused in this Ferdinand. Something like that. Marks of power and heritage trying to tell me a story in a language I can no longer under-stand. The arms are surmounted by a hat with twenty tassels, held up by two minute angels whose defiance of the force of gravity does not appear to exact much effort. Cardinal or archbishop? I can't remember. I stand there and look, and what I hear is what the early settlers in the twelfth century heard. I am inclined – accustomed as I am to so much more noise than they ever knew – to call that lack of noise "nothing", but after lingering a while I begin to distinguish all those nuances of nothing which together make up the silence, all those early, non-existent noises, the hum of distant insects, the slow wingbeat of a pair of doves, the wind in the poplars.

I pull once more on the bell and hear unhurried footsteps. Leather on stone. A monk opens the door. He tears a ticket off a pristine booklet and indicates the monastery with a vague wave: go ahead and take a look. He doesn't come with me, he doesn't speak. I wander around. The late Romanesque façade of the abbey church is decorated with a row of frail columns lacking a base. Not touching the ground, supporting nothing, they simply frame the semi-circular arch through which I enter. The coolness of the garden contrasts with the heat of the landscape, the coolness of the church contrasts with that of the garden, it is almost chilly where I am now. The thick walls of a church prevent the outside air, the ordinary air, from having its way. Suddenly I am standing before an arbitrary structure made of stone; its mere presence alters the quality of what little air has managed to come in. This is no longer the air wafting in poplars and clover, the air that is moved this way and that in the breeze. This is church air, as invisible as the air outside, but different. Church-shaped air, permeating the space between the columns and, deathly still, like an absent element, rising up to fill the pointed vaulting constructed of rough-hewn blocks of stone. There is no one in the church. Enormous columns rise directly from the paved floor, the position of the sun casts a strange, static pool of light through the oculus somewhere on the right of the church. It's a little ghostly. I hear my own footsteps. This space distorts not only the air, but also the sound of each step I take – they become the steps of someone walking in a church. Even if one subtracts from these sensations all that one does *not* in fact believe in oneself, then there's still the imponderable factor that other people do believe, and especially have believed, in this space.

The notions one might entertain about architectural purism, which invariably arise when someone tries to put an office block up next to a seventeenth-century canal house, do not function in this sort of space. The exterior of the building is Romanesque, the cross-vaults are Gothic, the tomb of Don Lupo Marco is a masterpiece of Renaissance art, the sacristy door is particularly exuberant baroque, but still the eye does not balk. All those mad, baroque angels set against the rough, irregular thirteenth-century stonework, fan out and up like rampant ivy, to form the entrance to the purest Cistercian chapterhouse: low, clear and still. Since I am alone I try my voice out loud to hear how the monks must sound – the discreet Gregorian chant, which takes flight, I dare suggest, high and tremulous, to and fro over the tombs of the abbots in the floor and then returns to me unimpaired. Set in one wall is the thirteenth-century tomb of the Lord of Aragón, Don Lope Jimenes. He reclines against the wall, *in* the wall, not on his back but on his side, though that curious position has not the slightest effect on the folds of his robe. The young, almost feminine head lies on a stone pillow, the left hand rests on his heart, the right clasps the hilt of a great sword. Two griffin-like creatures, one holding a small human face between its predatory claws, crane their necks, their beaks wide open in soundless fury. You see the noise, you don't hear it, but by seeing it you can hear it. That effect is achieved by the angle of the open beaks, the shape of the cavity shows you the sound, a high-pitched and terrible cry. Someone, once upon a time, must have felt great sorrow at the death of this knight. He is no less dead than we will be one day, but the grief over his parting has gone on for seven centuries, with unabating intensity chiselled in stone.

I try to imagine what it is like in this confined space when it is peopled with monks, but the point of a chapterhouse is that one is not supposed to be there at all. I am permitted to visit the place only during such hours as the monks are occupied elsewhere. There are signs with the word CLAUSTRUM all over the place, reminding them that they may not leave and me that I may not enter. To witness the scene I would have to vow to spend the rest of my days here, and that is asking too much.

There is a painting by Fouquet of Saint Bernard, one of the founding fathers of the Cistercian Order, preaching in just such a chapterhouse as the one I am standing in. Clear light enters the austere space through the Romanesque windows, Bernard stands before a simple lectern, the monks are seated on stone benches along the walls. What is extraordinary is not that these buildings still exist, but that a way of life that took a more or less definitive shape in the twelfth century should be intact today. And the origins go back further still. Even before the Christian era there were those, in the Near East, who lived alone, apart from the world: recluses, hermits, anchorites. They continued to do so until the early centuries of the first millennium. It is a faculty of the soul, an opportunity for people to divorce themselves from "the world", which existed and still exists in other cultures and times, too.

The monastic tradition in the West derives from Saint Anthony who, in the fourth century, led religious communities in the Egyptian desert, and from the Christian Platonists in Alexandria. At this point in the story (I am still in my cool Spanish chapterhouse) it is necessary to shut one's eyes for a moment and dismiss all thoughts of the Christian Democrat parties of today: in the days I am talking about Christians were a passionate, persecuted sect, a minority. It was the time of (often fervently desired) martyrdom, of ardent conversions, an era for which modern Christians occasionally yearn because everything was so much clearer and simpler then, or so it seems.

It was not until the fourth century that Christianity became the "official" religion. People of all races joined in; it became not only the fashion but also prudent to be a Christian. In due course corruption and laxity set in, and in reaction small, zealous communities were formed, in which the new faith could be lived as purely as possible. John

Cassian, born near the Black Sea and educated in Syria and Palestine, entered a monastery in Egypt – all these things are hard to picture if you lose sight of the surviving structure of the Roman Empire – and then he founded one of the first religious communities in Provence, at the very time that Germanic tribes were beginning to make incursions into the Empire from the north. The knowledge Cassian had gleaned in Syria and Egypt he now passed on to the West – his writings on the contemplative life were studied in every medieval monastery. Ideas which originated in the desolation of the desert found their way to other, more fertile regions, and something of the desert-like austerity has always remained – perhaps nowhere as intensely as in Spain, which has never really been part of Europe.

Basil, Jerome, Augustine of Hippo, they all have their place in the history of monastic life, but the man who laid down the rules for the centuries to come was Benedict of Nursia. The fire that burned in these lives is difficult for twentieth-century man to imagine, but the story tells itself. As a young man, Benedict (c. 480–c. 547) retired to the foothills of the Abruzzi, where, near the ruins of Nero's palace, he found a cave where he lived as a recluse for years. No one knew except for a monk in a nearby monastery, one Romanus, who provided him with food and monastic garb. When the secret eventually leaked out the monks begged him to become the abbot of their monastery, but his rule proved too strict for them and they attempted to poison him. He returned to his cave, but disciples flocked to him from all sides, and he created twelve monastic communities, each of twelve monks. His own abbey was that of Monte Cassino.

Benedict rejected the extreme asceticism that came from the Near East, he did not think it necessary to drive his monks beyond the limits of what is humanly feasible. What remained was severe enough: a community where the monk vowed lifelong residence and absolute obedience to the abbot, where he had to keep very early hours for sleeping and rising, and where he could be summoned at any time of day or night to partake in the *opus divinum*, the "Divine Office", the celebration of mass and the chanting of the canonical hours. The rest of the day was devoted to working and studying the scriptures. Fasting and abstinence were essential components of monastic life: the later Trappists never ate (and do not eat) fish or meat. Speaking was prohibited, too, except when necessary for the liturgy, preaching the Gospel or chapter meetings.

A rudimentary sign language sufficed for the conduct of day-to-day affairs. What Benedict founded was not a true Order – that was a later invention. In his day monasteries were autonomous communities over which the abbot maintained absolute power. Although the abbot would seek counsel of the senior monks concerning important decisions, he had the final say, his word was law, against which there was no appeal.

Benedict's ideas were decisive in shaping monastic life all over Europe, except in Ireland, where the tribal Celtic tradition gave rise to a tradition of its own under Columbanus. It was not until the year 910 that the Benedictines became a "true" Order – and even that was merely a loose federation of autonomous abbeys. This was a consequence of the foundation of Cluny, the abbey that was to have such a colossal political and cultural influence for centuries. In the mid-twelfth century there were more than 300 monasteries in all Europe – from Poland to Scotland – and each one stood directly or indirectly under the rule of Cluny, and owed allegiance to the abbot of Cluny. The liturgy was expanded, the singing of the office took up more time each day, simple manual work was dispensed with, and religious refinement increased, in their choral music as well as in their architecture and interior design.

This provoked a reaction from Bernard of Clairvaux. He and some thirty other young men had entered the impoverished Benedictine monastery of Cîteaux (which is where the name Cistercian comes from). His aim was to return to the original rule of Benedict of Nursia. The liturgy was simplified, all superfluous ornament discarded, and under his influence the Cistercian style evolved: rough, robust, austere, noble. The Trappist Order is a later, more severe variant of the Cistercian, and Trappist life is more rustic and harsh. The Benedictines are more aristocratic, intellectual, refined. Even my unaccustomed ear could pick out the single Benedictine visiting the Trappists: his voice sounded just that bit more ethereal, more exalted than those of the others. The Benedictine monk did not use his hands to work the land or in the brewery, but to embroider mitres. The oddest thing in this story, to my mind, is the aspect of time: that the history that I have retold in a hundred lines is still valid – that all those changes and variants which are so easily enumerated actually took centuries to have effect. The essence has remained untouched, so that now, as then and always, that sound of leather on stone approaches once more, the monk who comes to advise me that my time is up. He wears the same habit that his brothers in the Order wore nearly a thousand years ago: a white robe and black scapular. Time travel is indeed possible: protected against death and disaster, I have been lowered in a time capsule into the depths of the long-gone Middle Ages. Medieval society survives in this place; like a pure culture in a Petri dish this form of existence is perpetuated in modern times.

It is towards that medieval world that I am heading, a stranger driving a car through the land of Aragón.

II

A Journey across Names and Ages

An ETA assassination ~ Ferdinand and Isabella
Soria ~ San Pedro and Santo Domingo

THE DOOR OF THE MONASTERY at Veruela swings shut behind me. I hear the hollow sound reverberating through that age-old silence, I am back in the world of choices and decisions. Where shall I go? I have already made up my mind, I will go to Soria, but how shall I go, which route shall I take? At the end of the shady avenue the midday heat comes rolling over the landscape towards me like a ball. I have two maps, Michelin and Hallwag. They represent the same countryside and the same roads, but Hallwag's Spain seems to reflect more exactly the emptiness and silence around me. The skin of the landscape looks more weathered on the Hallwag than on the Michelin, the scalloped edges of the plain are indicated with grey shading, from dark to pale and still paler grey. The Michelin uses only plain white and green, the red of its main roads is more assertive, which is not how it feels in reality, because even main roads are deserted in these parts. On the Hallwag those same roads are yellow, which makes them more modest somehow, humbler even, as indeed they are. Better still, what is yellow on the Michelin is white on the Hallwag. White roads have a special appeal, I find, as if only they can get me clean away from the hubbub, as if the surrounding countryside had been sketched in almost by accident.

No one before me has visited those places with their strange names. I will be welcomed by villagers with bread and wine. Staring at the map, I trickle the Spanish names over my tongue . . . La Almunia de Doña Godina, Alhama de Aragón, Sistema Ibérico, Laguna Negra de Urbión. Like a necklace of spoken jewels those villages, mountain

passes, plains and streams converge on the dry, brief sound of Soria, each
name deliberately created at some point in time and now just a casual
utterance passed on from one person to the next: "I will go to Soria this
evening," "I come from Soria." It is impossible to fathom all that is
compounded in those names, how many thousands or millions of times
a word which now merely denotes a place has been spoken and
recorded, in what forms it lingers on in cadastres, loiters on letterheads
and ordnance survey maps, crops up in private correspondence and
diaries, title-deeds and invoices, flies up from the lips of children, nuns,
murderers: "I will go to Soria tonight," "I come from Soria." It has a
certain power, such a word: it will be repeated, later, in an inconceivably
distant future, by mouths that do not yet exist even in the imagination.
And make no mistake, you are never in a place that is nameless, in a
region without a name, on a mountain without a name, in a town
without a name – you always find yourself in some word invented by
others – others never seen, long forgotten – before it was recorded in
writing. We are always in words.

And not only in words, also in history – that of the present and that of
the past. I make a stop in Tarazona and see a two-day-old copy of *La
Vanguardia* lying in a café. In its relentless campaign to destroy Spanish
democracy GRAPO or ETA has once again assassinated a general. He is
the eightieth victim of terrorism this year. The idea behind the attacks is
that the army must be challenged and provoked into seizing power: then
the war can really get going. There are five photographs on the front
page. The first shows the assassinated general himself – Brigadier
General Don Enrique Briz Armengol, still alive when the camera caught
him at the moment of his investiture in some new function. He is standing on a small raised platform like a gallows, with pointed posts at the
corners; between the posts hang three knee-high chains. I cannot tell the
colour of his sash, but I know from experience that it must be purple.
His salute is accentuated by his white gloves, in fact he looks like an
actor playing the part of a general. A pale, mask-like face, gaping black
holes made by his sunglasses, not many medals on his chest, but his
shoes polished, and no reason whatever to kill him. In the empty courtyard where he appears to be reviewing a parade (not in the picture) there
is another figure, whose arm is likewise raised in salute and who,
because his features are blurred by the distance, appears to be a carbon
copy of the general. His two soldier-drivers have neither white gloves

nor medals. In portraits evidently extracted from a group photograph taken on some happy occasion they wear the good-natured, still carefree expression of Spanish youth. Their heads are marked with crosses. In the fourth picture only their berets are to be seen, lying amidst the splinters of a shattered windscreen on the black, uncomfortably shiny plastic of the front seat. The car doors are wide open, treacly daylight pours in. The photograph tastes of death. The last shows the president of the Generalitat – the more or less independent Catalan government – offering the widow his condolences. She is rather stout and wears a dress with a dazzling op-art pattern. The president clasps her capable hand in his and speaks to her. There is another woman in the picture, but I can't make out her expression – grief, rage, vengeance, shock: the faces that are always unseen in history books. The fourth figure is the dead man's superior, Lieutenant General Pascual Galmes. His face is that of an old Indian chief, he has taken his jacket off, and looks glum. No reason why it shouldn't be his turn next.

Poor Spain, you may sigh, and launch into a grave discourse about a nation that can never agree with itself because it never managed to become a unified whole. "If only we still had Franco," the right-wingers say. "Things weren't such a mess in the old days. Suárez has gone through more ministers than Franco did in all the years of his regime." "We are just the slaves of rich Spaniards," complain the Andalusians, "we are guest workers in our own country." "We have allowed tourism to ruin all our villages and landscapes and beaches," says the population of the Costa del Sol, "but where do all the profits go?" "We in Catalonia earn the money for the entire country, and we'd be better off on our own," say the Catalans (and Basques). And that isn't the end of all the divisions and rifts. Anyone who knows the history of Spain knows that it has always been like this, except when a great national movement, a great adventure, like the Reconquista – the reconquest of southern Spain from the Moors – or the quest for gold in the New World cast a spell over the whole of "Spain". But after such spirited flights of ambition the country always collapses all over again into its singular, idiosyncratic fragments. Celts, Iberians, Goths, Jews, Moors, Romans, they have all poured their blood into the great melting pot, and the strangest thing of all is that it was actually possible now and then to govern those multifarious chauvinistic nationalistic regions with their contrasting climates, landscapes, characters and interests, from that one point in the

middle of the vast, arid plain: Madrid. Poor and dry, it is cut off from
the rest of Europe by the Berlin Wall that is the Pyrenees and divided
within itself by the endless *meseta* in the centre. Connections are
difficult, characters disparate. The love of each man and woman for
the native soil, the affinity with the region, its language – all these things
far transcend the idea of nationhood. That's the way it is now, and that's
the way it was in the past.

One of the factors that contributed to the creation of some degree of
unity in the face of such diversity was the marriage of Ferdinand and
Isabella in 1469. Verdi should have written an opera about them, or
someone should have made a film in the widest-ever Cinemascope,
because the setting of this passionate yet calculated story has not
changed. Isabella was eighteen years old and her standing threatened by
her brother, Henry IV of Castile. Although heir to the Castilian throne,
she had a rival in her brother's apparently illegitimate daughter, Juana la
Beltraneja. Isabella was young but knew exactly what she wanted. She
had set her mind on marrying Ferdinand, future king of Aragón and
Sicily – poor, modest kingdoms compared with Castile, but the binding
of the two crowns would be a first step towards the binding of Spain.
The archbishop of Toledo – those were the days – was on her side and
came with a small company of horsemen to conduct her from her home
in Madrigal to Valladolid. Ferdinand had to overcome greater odds. He
departed Zaragoza with a few trusted friends and, disguised as a
merchant, journeyed through the region I am driving through now. In El
Burgo de Osma, a deserted town today with an oversized cathedral
stuffed with art treasures trying vainly to preserve the memory of past
glory, he was almost murdered, but he made it to Valladolid just four
days before the date of the wedding. The couple had never set eyes on
each other. Where is Verdi's aria, and the duet that would inevitably have
followed? Where is the camera slowly zooming in on the eighteen-year-
old Isabella, who stands at the top of the steps half hidden behind the
balustrade, turning her head to meet the gaze of the merchant from
Aragón? The bride and groom were so poor they had to borrow money
from all and sundry. Since they were somewhat too closely related by
blood, not a circumstance uncommon among royals, they produced a
papal decree of dispensation (which later proved to be false: a clever
forgery devised by Ferdinand himself, his father the king of Aragón, and
the archbishop of Toledo).

Just how the decision for this marriage came about is not clear – there were all sorts of groups involved and interests at stake, and not only in Spain. The son of the king of France was also interested in Isabella, and that union would have meant a Franco-Castilian alliance. The king of Portugal, even closer to hand and not quite as young, had similar plans, but against him there was a strong Aragonese faction at the court of Castile (splendid material for the choral scenes in the opera), while prominent Jewish families in both lands favoured Ferdinand in the hope that he, who had some Jewish blood thanks to his mother, would support them. Intrigues, bribery, jealousy and corruption were rife, but Isabella's mind was made up, and in the end Ferdinand was simply hired to serve the interests of Castile. He was obliged to live in Castile and to take second, not first place. In the wilderness of Spanish politics Ferdinand was a sensible choice. All sorts of democratic developments had long since taken place in Catalonia, Valencia, and even Aragón, giving rise to the mighty institutions that were already keeping a sharp eye on the power of the throne: the Justicia, the Cortes, the Diputación, and the Generalitat (then already!). The kings of Aragón had certain constitutional duties, there was some degree of collaboration between the bourgeoisie and the crown. Castile, however, was in a state of complete political chaos; there the power struggle was between the crown and the aristocracy, some of whose members were so rich (as some still are) that, like the celebrated Leonor de Albuquerque *la rica hembra*, the rich maid, they could travel across the whole of Castile, from Aragón to Portugal, without ever setting foot on someone else's land. Conflicts, names, episodes, and all of them perpetuated in the Spain of today. Institutions such as the Generalitat of Catalonia still exist, various regions are demanding their *autonomía*, noble families in the south still own half provinces. In Spain, history need not repeat itself, it can simply stay the same. Long before the Duke of Alba's efforts to suppress the rebellion in the Low Countries, there was a Duke of Alba in Spain, as there is today.

At times my memory is a collection of postcards. Should anyone ask me one day – in ten years' time, or in another country, or at night in a dream – "Tarazona, what was that?" I would have a vision of heat-drenched ochre and of sand-coloured bricks tormented by the sun. Thirst, empty streets, closed shutters behind which people doze, a futile quest along cafés for some mineral water, mule-drawn carts. The two postcards I have kept of the cathedral bring back the memory of an extraordinary edifice, its minaret-like spire rising high above the town. The style is known as Mudéjar – Arab elements embedded in Christian architecture, geometric figures piled on top of each other in myriad variations. Again, not the kind of place to delight purists: preposterous Corinthian columns on ridiculously tall bases grace a Romanesque portico, as if the combination were expressly designed to confound even the brightest student of art history. I want to enter the cathedral, but even God sleeps after his midday meal in Spain, so I linger in the cool fore-court, face to face with allegorical statues unwondering at my presence.

Grey, brown, purple landscapes, the whole paintbox of colours. I reach Soria towards evening. I have found a room in the parador on the hill-side overlooking the valley of the Duero which later, farther westwards, will be called Douro. The languid light of day is bluish, and the land-scape, half-erased already, still clings to the windowpanes, a gigantic moth in search of light. The last time I stayed in this parador was on the tenth anniversary (the tenth already!) of the first landing on the moon. I was in Spain then, too, in a café somewhere. There had been some fishermen playing cards; I had been the only one looking at the screen. Unforgettable images, but this time they were shown to the accom-paniment of baroque music, as if the Duke of Weimar had installed a chamber orchestra behind those two white figures taking their slow extraterrestrial dance steps. The astronauts danced, they were trans-parent, their voices muffled by space, they were reflected in each other's gleaming visors, they weren't supposed to be there at all and yet their swollen polar bear feet trod the granules, pores and diseases of the moon, which at that instant ceased to be a goddess. Now everyone was watching the Nescafé ads with the same concentration as Armstrong performing his slow-motion ballet in the lunar dust.

Oh to see the earth just once as a full moon, from a pavement café on the empty shores of the Sea of Tranquillity, a glass of plutonic champagne in front of me on my platinum table, dreaming of an impossible trip to Spain!

Anyone interested in what a Spanish town looked like in the early sixties should go to Soria. Tourism and prosperity have not yet made their mark, there has been no reason to destroy façades, to mutilate the scale of the town with offensive tower blocks, to replace wood by aluminium, doors by sheet-glass in which your reflection leers at you as on an under-exposed photograph. Marble café tables with curvy legs overlaid with innumerable coats of silvery grey paint, lamplight tawny with tobacco smoke instead of soul-destroying neon, tiny shops where you wade in darkness, proprietors without cash registers, wooden shelves stacked with mysterious things to eat, alleys full of surprises, gloomy bars with men in black suits and black hats sipping silently from glasses containing a dark liquid. The province is poor, the provincial capital is poor, and poverty does not shine, poverty is quiet, poverty does not discard the old in favour of the veneer of emblematic junk which, like a botched facelift, has messed up so much of what was old and authentic.

It is one o'clock, the hottest time of day. The entire population is resting in the shade of the big trees in the park. In the middle of the park is a centuries-old elm with a cast-iron bandstand erected around it, men read the *Heraldo de Aragón* or the *Voz de Soria*, I stroll along the carefully trimmed cypresses; everyone is sitting under elms and lime trees as they did a century ago: no one has moved since. I hear the crunch of my footsteps on the gravel amidst the inimitable sound of a Spanish multitude: the murmuring of old men and women and of lovers, the cellos of the adults, the higher-tuned instruments of the children, the splash of the fountain which in the hot dry south signifies something quite different from that of the grey north, where the water drops out of the sky of its own accord. At five, when the afternoon wearies of itself, the shops and stalls reopen. *Ultramarinos* – what we used to call colonial wares, *congrio seco*, a fish that is first dried and then splayed open to form a sort of outsize carpet beater dangling in doorways like a brownish labyrinth of food, coal-black sausages, fare from a different era and for a different population. At La Delicia, the cake shop owned by the widow of Epifanio Lis, pyramids of pastel-coloured meringues remind me of my great-grandmother. In the Café of the Sun one gentleman drinks a cup of black coffee with four ice cubes while his companion has a triple cognac. Out in the street it is still 40 °C.

In one of those bookshops with sallow-complexioned sales assistants where you can also buy note pads, pencils, and ledgers, I discover something to add to my collection of curious books. It will be given its rightful place beside the mimeographed Eskimo cookbook, the Kansas folk tales, and a treatise on Bolivia's since-abolished political system printed on wrapping paper. The book is aptly titled *Biografía curiosa de Soria* and the editor, Miguel Moreno, must suffer from the same affliction as I, for he has left no stone unturned. Nothing is more important to a Spaniard than his roots, his native region. Anyone hoping truly to understand Spain should read Gerald Brenan's *The Spanish Labyrinth*, in which the importance of those local sentiments is so lucidly expressed:

> Spain is the land of the *patria chica*. Every village, every town is the centre of an intense social and political life. As in classical times, a man's allegiance is first of all to his native place, or to his family or social group in it, and only secondly to his country and government. In what one may call its normal condition Spain is a collection of small, mutually hostile or indifferent republics held together in a loose federation. At certain great periods (the Caliphate, the Reconquista, the Siglo de Oro) these small centres have become infected by a common feeling or idea and have moved in unison: then when the impetus given by this idea declined, they have fallen apart and resumed their separate and egoistic existence. It is this that has given its spectacular character to Spanish history.

The curious biography of Soria is printed on that greyish poor man's paper, the kind that gives illustrations a mysteriously elusive quality. The photograph on p. 268 is an especially good example: it shows the embalmed body of the fourteenth-century Archbishop Don Rodrigo Ximénez de Rada, dressed in a new set of clothes for the first time in seven centuries. The photograph is printed in eighteen shades of grey, the shrivelled head is crowned with a half-exploded mitre and slumbers in a tangle of clerical textile. Grey is the colour of old Franco and of the new young king; grey are the local worthies; grey the beauty queens on the Day of the Province; all are veiled in greys that obscure the purpose of the image, which is to clarify. Verses, the origins of place names, the Sorian nobility past and present, pages full of knights and marquesses, it's all there. In 1453, Don Álvaro de Luna, grandmaster of the Military Order of Santiago and prime minister under King Juan II of Castile, received the title of Count of San Esteban de Gormaz. That title still exists – Spaniards don't like throwing things away, not corpses and not titles either – and is now borne by Señora Doña María del Rosario Cayetana Fitz-James Stuart y Silva, Falcó y Gurtubay, Duchess of Alba de Tormes. But also the biggest mushroom ever found in the region and the heaviest cabbage have been recorded for posterity, all the distances have been measured, the coats of arms illustrated, the documents copied, the etymologies of the names of hills and dales explained. There is in Soria (and this is exclusively for the connoisseur) one single *cuesta*, notably la Cuesta. And there are seven hills, *montes*, four *pinillas*, three *cubos*, five *peñas*, three *pozos*, four *cuevas* – peaks, springs, slopes, grottoes and other topographical peculiarities for the cadastre of eternity.

Génie du lieu is the phrase used by the French when a particular site emanates something very special and remarkable. There are no Knights Hospitallers of Saint John of Jerusalem in Soria today, but a vestige of the cloister they built in 1100 still stands, a sketch, a hint of what was once the arcade around the inner courtyard. It is early in the morning, wisps of mist float over the river, which is narrow here and courses swiftly and darkly along the banks lined with reeds and tall greenery. The pointed arches are interlaced and look like arabesques suspended in a void. It is a truly secluded courtyard, a tangle of roses against the walls of the little church, gladioli and man-high daisies sway under the poplar trees, but the square space between the four walls is unoccupied. That is what makes the courtyard so enigmatic: it is open to all sides, wind and air and voices blow through the apertures, it is free-standing, it is out of doors, and yet I am inside a Moorish courtyard. The shape of the ruins indicates what it must have been like, the walls of that long-vanished cloister still surround me. I enter the small church. I see several tombstones with Hebrew lettering, the arch over the apse is Arabic. There are two curious canopy-like structures, one domed, the other conical, next to and in front of the spot where the main altar must have stood; the carvings on the capitals surmounting the double pillars supporting the canopies are Christian, and so in this small deathly-quiet space the three worlds of Judaism, Christianity and Islam come together in a symbiosis that is unique in the world today.

Why are some places famous and not others? Why does everyone talk of Autun and Poitiers and you never hear a word about Soria, while it has one of the loveliest and most moving Romanesque portals of

medieval Christianity? Every true lover of Romanesque art should see
the façade of the Santo Domingo and the cloister of San Pedro. They are,
with the San Juan de Rabanera and the San Gil, treasuries with the most
wondrous details. Florid capitals crown pillars with plant motifs, to
which such subtle irregularities have been introduced as to make the
stone come alive, Arab influences, the artful manner of showing nudity
(by depicting vices), winged lions with birds' heads which remind me of
Persepolis – all those stories and admonitions and decorations that were
carved a thousand years ago by master craftsmen and that survive here
in the dry, harsh climate of Soria, they are truly worthy of pilgrimage.
You find yourself wishing you had an outsize magnifying glass through
which to study the carvings: a capital-scope. The decorations are often
miniatures in stone, and if you want to read what the images have to say,
you must come armed with a dictionary of Biblical and Christian icons
and symbols. I confess to a heartfelt irritation when I cannot interpret
precisely what the pictures are trying to tell me. What used to be
common knowledge is now the reserve of experts and scholars.

What, I wonder, is so attractive about all this? I am standing in
front of the Santo Domingo. Not famous, so there is no tourism, a
quiet corner in a quiet town. Is it the simplicity, if that word is at all
justifiable? The piety? The unshakeable totality of a world view? The
idea that it was made by people and for people to whom this was not
"art" but reality? That a story was being told in stone which everyone
already knew by heart but wanted to see and hear again and again – just
as Greeks (and Japanese) still flock to see their ancient tragedies? I don't
know. What I do know is that this low, almost squat façade, in which the
tympanum takes up relatively little space, exudes great force and
emotion. The idea that this was ever new. New! Just finished, hewn out
of those almost golden blocks of hard stone! How proud the makers
were, how everyone in the province crowded to see the sight!

The figures in the tympanum are so small that you have to get up close
to see them. Even then you must crane your neck, because the four rows
into which they are crammed are straight up above you, not in front of
you. With the four ascending registers on the archivolt securely fixed in
your gaze, each made up of a variety of scenes, you find that they lack
that rigid and hieratic quality which, for the sake of convenience, we
tend to label "primitive". Indeed, they are both lavish and droll, with
their oversize, pious gnomes' heads protruding from richly pleated

garments. And everything happens the way it is described in the Good
Book and has been preserved in countless surviving images and no doubt
in countless others long since lost: the head of the Baptist is severed, God
fashions the body of Adam from clay, the Annunciation, the adoration
of the Magi, the same old stories, only this time not in paint, not in silver,
not by Rembrandt, not by Manzú or Rouault, but carved, unsigned, by
vanished hands in the hard stone of a barren Spanish province, where
serenely they await the end of time.

III

A World of Death and History

ZARAGOZA. APART FROM two nuns and an old lady, I am the only visitor in the Bellas Artes Museum, which has a section devoted to archaeology. The nuns overtake me at the rate of one century a minute and then I am truly alone in the prehistory of Spain. Stone arrowheads, clay pots, an exhumed grave containing a startled ancestor lying on his side, an anonymous skeleton of a member of some ancient tribe, whose peace was rudely disturbed after 3,000 years by someone who himself would never become the object of archaeological investigation, because everything we leave behind will be properly labelled.

What really appeals to me about the history from before history is the absence of a cutting edge. Names, dates, battles, disputes – all have been erased. It is as if the expulsion from paradise did not come until later, as if prehistoric man led a peaceful, rural life of hunting, pot-making, fishing, a protracted existence bathed in all-enveloping silence. Nameless creatures of my own species lived a life on earth that was not recorded on paper nor registered in any way, and later generations have had to dig deep to recover their traces.

Clay bowls. These are soberly displayed in the cabinets, the earliest specimens devoid of ornamentation, and then, with a twig, a human hand has made a tentative mark, this mark has been repeated, thereby creating a pattern, a structure, a geometric figure, art. Were they all capable of this or was this the work of just one craftsman in the settlement? They had no idea that they were living before the birth of Christ; they just kindled their fires, drank or ate from these bowls. Such bowls are to be found in all civilizations. Was this a shape that imposed itself, a natural complement to the human mouth? We can travel to the moon nowadays, but the basic shape of a bowl is unchanged. I remember similar specimens in Africa, but they were not three thousand years old. I make a supreme effort to sense how ancient these are and I succeed because I know it's true: three thousand years of violence, of profound upheaval have left this pottery intact, ready for use. I would gladly steal a piece from the cabinet and take it home, not to sell it on for some exorbitant price but to drink from it behind locked doors just in order to prove the continuity of my species, and to reflect a little on the unknown potter who fashioned it.

Paleolítico Inferior, Paleolítico Superior. With each step I spring along the centuries, with exasperating ease I advance from stone to bronze, from bronze to iron. I gaze at the decorated tombstones of early princelings which the Spanish so charmingly call *reyezuelos*, little kings, and I can see them in my mind's eye, no bigger than children, trolls with crowns on. Later my dictionary tells me that *reyezuelos* also denotes a type of wren, sometimes called the gold-crest kinglet, which seems appropriate to me: diminutive kings that have vanished into the long primeval winter.

Yet things are never as I expect them to be. The display cabinets are well lit and classified by origin and geographical location, above each item hovers an aura of patience and dedication recalling the finders who were once seekers themselves. Archaeologists, men who delve indefatigably into the distant past to see what they can turn up. Only the artefacts remain, the world which existed around them seems unreal, remote – and yet what is three thousand years? There is no denying that in three thousand years we will ourselves be altered beyond all recognition.

The earliest coins. Hannibal, Hasdrubal, Hamilcar. I am reaching more familiar ground: my grammar school ancient history classes. They have long since become embedded in my memory, and yet the other element, the fictitious, the imaginary is more powerful. How many people have held these coins in their hands? Money, provided it is made of metal, looks surprisingly durable. Was it held in thousands of hands or just hundreds? What did it pay for? Wages, women, wine? Burial rites, togas, weapons, horses, bread? But money never stirs the emotions, perhaps because it gives rise, even materially, to speculation. No, what takes my breath away is something else that originated at the same time: the intriguing strokes, crossed, straight, angular, strange flourishes, *script*, sharp and spidery, language abstracted into symbols, the long relentless progression from the signs carved in stone to the letters on my typewriter keys. The incised stone lies behind Perspex, depriving me of the pleasure of running my fingertips over the surface, as if that would be enough to unravel the code hidden in the man-made grooves.

I linger in these silent galleries for hours and observe how history accrues, becoming more familiar and yet more distanced. A century cannot be contained in one room and yet it is done. By means of tombstones, coins, didrachmas from Naples and Syracuse, tetradrachmas from Athens, mosaics and potsherds, the well-trodden path is conjured up before me, the cliché of the past as it has been imparted to me. But that which is clarified is at the same time obfuscated by what is missing – the smells, the voices, the living. All we have, literally, are vestiges, and they make us aware of what is withheld. This accumulated evidence creates a momentary illusion that it is possible to possess the past, to appropriate it, but the present, being the order of the day, is selective in what it takes from the past and interprets history accordingly. One day we too will become part of this singular abstraction: the notion we have of ourselves will be revised as we are sifted through future generations. Then, like a film being rewound at great speed – with everything becoming a blur – I retrace my steps and drop out of prehistory into the street, a primeval man.

Almost 500 years ago Zaragoza was visited by another Dutchman, Pope Adrian VI, the last non-Italian pope before Karol Wojtyla. Adrian of Utrecht, as he is known, was bishop of the Spanish town of Tortosa and, on the death of Pope Leo X, was elected to succeed him on 2 January 1522. People in those days were not short of time. Ships were waiting in Barcelona to convey the new pope to Rome, but before embarking on the voyage he wanted to venerate the relics of Saint Lambert at Zaragoza. He set out on 29 March and remained in Zaragoza till 11 June. He lodged in the Aljafería, the old Moorish palace that was restored by the Catholic Kings after the Moors were hounded across the river. He rode through the city on a white mule in the company of Archbishop Juan of Aragón with an escort of Aragonese knights and noblemen. We even know what he was wearing: *bonete de terciopelo carmesí con armiños y un capelo de la misma tela con cordones de oro y seda roja* – a carmine velvet skullcap trimmed with ermine and a cardinal's hat made of the same material with gold and red silk braids. Not only did people have plenty of time in those days, they also had plenty of manpower. The mule was tied up at the Puerta del Portillo, where Adrian transferred to a palanquin specially constructed for the occasion, lined in red velvet and bearing the papal coat of arms on the back rest, and proceeded to the cathedral borne by a relay of twenty-four Aragonese knights. On 9 April, the pope visited the crypt of the "innumerable martyrs". At that very moment one of the twelve lamps of the *azófar* broke and oil spilled on to the papal robes, "which was considered by all to be an ill omen". Not without reason, as it turned out, for he was to be pope for a very short time and incurred the bitter hatred of the people of Rome. After celebrating mass the pope "opened the tomb of Saint Lambert, lifted the head of the martyr out of the coffin and held it aloft". At that time the saint had already been dead for 1,219 years, but the head started to bleed and the pope's robes, soiled already by the oil from the lamp, were stained once more. Monks collected the blood as it fell and, Spain being what it is, the drops have been preserved to this day.

South of the River Ebro the landscape changes. From hills like the backs of docile, grazing cattle to a barren planet, yellowish, stony, pitiless. In some of the fields the corn has been cut. Straw bales like cubist figures stand guard on the horizon. An army of automata. Then the world is lifted up in an invisible embrace and I drive out of the valley to the south, to Teruel. The road is empty, Spain is having lunch. For a while I follow the River Huerva. To my right a high mountain range shimmers in the hot afternoon sun. The river disappears from view. Cariñena, Daroca, Burbágena, Monreal del Campo. This landscape was once the scene of battles between Christians and Moors and then, in a much later war, of the fighting between Franco's troops and the Republican army. A bitter land, from time to time unfurling quite unexpectedly into a majestic panorama, then twisting into tortured mountain passes.

I arrive at Teruel at the dead hour. It's much smaller than I had imagined, in fact it is the smallest provincial capital in Spain. Here extreme temperatures are recorded. The winters are long and the summers have no mercy. During the winter of 1936–7 the temperature dropped to −18 °C. The town was alternately occupied by the Republicans and the Nationalists. In his book *Blood of Spain*, Ronald Fraser tells both sides of the story through eyewitness accounts and personal memories. Torture, summary executions, battles, betrayal, senseless destruction, desertion, the hopeless internal wrangling among the leftist groups, the acrimonious disputes between communists and anarchists, which in time grew more important than winning the war itself. At certain points in their history the Spanish have been prepared to slaughter each other for almost any reason and therefore by implication to die for almost any reason. Under the supposedly smooth surface of the new democracy the bruises of the Civil War still ache. Each day and each place evoke memories for those who care to see.

Blood of Spain is more than six hundred pages long. I have brought it with me on this trip. The index of place names is interminable and I only have to use it to discover which horrors were perpetrated in this or that, to outward appearances, peaceful town or village. It's a book about Everyman, it tells the story of the common folk, of the forgotten soldiers and civilians on the good side and the bad, of the lives that write history. But does history look like history *while it is in the making*? Isn't it true that the common names are always expunged? For surely history is about ideas, vested interests and celebrated names (later to become street names), the names listed in indexes and encyclopedias? Because no matter how much oral history is set down, the victims of world-shattering events are doomed to disappear. Their interchangeable names appear on monuments and memorials that hardly anyone notices any more, not only their bodies but also their identities are relegated to oblivion.

Not in *Blood of Spain*. There you will find the history of the teachers, bakers, fascists, communists, civil servants, anarchists, the women, the children. To seek out all those witnesses and to record their descriptions of executions, humiliations, hunger marches, must have been a Herculean task, but the result is that you come face to face with the blood and faeces of that war. Every trace of shining heroism wiped out. You stare into the foul, bloody pit of man's inhumanity to man.

One particular incident that took place at the Teruel front offers a Brechtian view of the confusion, although Brecht himself would no doubt be less inclined to use this example for political reasons.

It was snowing hard. On arrival, García Vivancos remained with the men in the uncovered lorries while Carod went in to report. Around a stove he found a group of men who offered him coffee. They began to talk. "It wasn't long before the eternal theme of unity between the communist party and the CNT was brought up." He said this was a matter to be dealt with directly between the leadership of the two organizations. As a disciplined member of the CNT he would obey whatever decision the national committee reached. But one of the men present insisted, saying that as a well-known militant he could put pressure on the CNT to agree.

"In their attempt to persuade me they argued that the future of Spain lay in the unity of the communist party and the CNT, that the war would be won by the two organizations. They proposed that the communist party should form the political organization of the CNT, and the CNT the trade union of the party . . ."

He replied again that this was not the moment to discuss the matter. His men were freezing outside, he needed arms and especially the arms that the brigade had been instructed were waiting for them. The tone of his voice was rising in anger when one of the men put his hand in his pocket and brought out a communist party membership card.

"'Take this, or none of the arms you see there will be given to the 25th Division.' I looked: in a shed at the back there were arms enough to re-equip the men. They included Maxim machine-guns which we had never had. 'I'll get the men off the lorries and we'll pick up the arms.' 'You'll do that only when you accept the membership card.' I presume it must already have been filled out, for I don't suppose they expected me to sit down and do so myself at that moment. I gave them a piece of my mind. One of them put his arm round my shoulder and said, 'Calm down, Carod, there's no need to get upset. The comrades have not posed this matter correctly. You Spaniards are all the same. Don't worry, everything will be sorted out.' I recognized the man: Ercoli. It was only later that I learnt his real name: Togliatti, the Italian communist leader . . ."

Unplacated, Carod stormed out. He ordered his men to make for another army corps HQ on the same front. From there he spoke by telephone with the general commanding the army of the Levante. The latter sounded angry and ordered the brigade to remain where it was. But this did not solve the problem of arms. The lieutenant-colonel in command of the army corps assured him that there was a dump nearby sufficient to re-equip the entire division. He had not even finished speaking when a signal arrived from the front. Pounding on the table, the colonel exclaimed: 'The entire dump has just been captured by the enemy.'*

Finally, and not least due to this sort of sectarian quarrelling, so undermining in wartime, Franco's army was victorious in Teruel and this served as a springboard to push through to the Mediterranean. The Republican army was divided in two.

You Spaniards are all the same . . . the conviction of always being in the right carried to the extreme, fanned by an indifference towards death which seems a legacy from their Islamic past. "Long live death" was the battle-cry of the Spanish Foreign Legion in that self-same Civil War, and that is what it appears to resemble most closely, a fatalistic desire to reach a point which is then called the moment of truth. Gerald Brenan's *The Spanish Labyrinth* opens with two quotations which give this streak of absurdness its full dimension. The first is from Práxedes Mateo Sagasta, a liberal writing in the last century: "I do not know where we are going, but I do know this – that wherever it is we shall lose our way." The second is from Sebastiano Foscarini, Venetian ambassador to the Spanish court from 1682 to 1686, who expresses the same astonishment (though more elegantly) as his compatriot Togliatti a few centuries later. "Finally I would say that though the Spaniards have wit, industry and means sufficient for the restoration of their kingdom, they will not restore it: and though entirely capable of saving the State, they will not save it – *because they do not want to*." (My emphasis.)

How can one relate to such a country? One can cherish it or hate it, and because I fancy I have a similarly absurd and chaotic streak in my own character, I have opted for the former, and that is why I am standing here, at the wrong time of day, in the wrong season, cursing because the cathedral doors will remain closed for several hours yet. Spanish hours suit Spanish people but are the bane of the traveller. If you think you might as well visit Teruel on your way from Zaragoza to Albarracín,

* Ronald Fraser, *Blood of Spain*, Allen Lane, 1979.

then think again: everything worth visiting is remorselessly locked away between the hours of noon and four o'clock, or one and five. All you can do is wander around in the heat or indulge in a far too heavy Spanish lunch, after which you will feel like doing the same as everyone else, which is to seek out a bed and lie on it and wait for the blazing midday hours to pass and for the museums and churches to reopen. For the passing traveller, however, there are no beds, so I stroll around under the shady arches where old men sit and doze, and then, high up on a column, I notice a grotesque little bull and read the inscription: "the bull and the star have been the emblems of Teruel since 1171 when Alfonso II el Casto (the chaste, the virtuous, the pure) wrested the city from the Moors." I peer into the Casa Juderías, a shop full of guns and hardware. Silence, patios with palm trees, cool shade and geraniums, shops full of smoked hams and surreal cakes, old women in black, a clock tugs at the hours of an afternoon in provincial Spain. The rest of the world is a long way away.

It'll have to be the restaurant, then. Low-ceilinged, dimly lit, joints of ham, black sausages stuffed with rice, flitches of bacon, rabbits, thick dark wine in earthenware jugs, large loaves from a different age. The next table is occupied by an extended Spanish family more like an army. The children are all wearing glasses and gaze respectfully at the mighty paterfamilias at the head of the table. What is to become of the Latin world when man-the-father is annihilated, after the northern example? Further along, a classic scene of two Spanish gentlemen having lunch. One of them is a Charles Aznavour type with eyelashes so long a child could sit on them, the other is more of a Visigoth (here all races and pedigrees have been preserved through the ages), upright, stern and silent, surrounded by the trappings of everyday Spanish life, their huge jug of wine, their joint of mutton, their black cigarettes with which they smoke the meat, and eventually their black, harsh coffees and large balloon glasses of syrupy anís, voluminous enough for a fair-sized goldfish. One of them talks and gesticulates, the other listens, the children cry *Papá*! – accentuating the last syllable so as not to confuse him with the pope – and I can see all of us sitting here in the infinite expanse of the Spanish continent.

Depending on your mood, Teruel can be the colour of gold or of dried mud. The cathedral – still closed – and the watchtowers are made of brick, thin slabs of baked earth from nearby, more the colours of camouflage. It looks as though the landscape has suddenly erupted into a building, as though the building were an excrescence of the soil itself. The angle of the sun throws the geometric Arabic patterns of the Mudéjar tower into relief. If you stare long enough at the façade it begins to seethe. It is scarcely possible to describe this whirlwind of decoration with its absence of the human form, a carpet of stone and tiles which it is difficult to imagine being solid and hard. Blind, interlaced arches, columns topped with stylized flowers, stars, corbels, cantilevers, green and white glazed tiles, an entire Islamic civilization has left its soul behind. The eye wanders to and fro between the ochre hills on the horizon and the paler earth-colour of the architecture, made of the same earth that, once you are outside the walls of the town, stretches away into the distance for hundreds of kilometres without interruption.

After the recapture of Teruel from the Moors by Alfonso II, the Moors were granted permission to stay in the town until the fifteenth century, where they developed their Mudéjar style into the loveliest in Spain. As a consequence one still has the feeling of being in Arab surroundings, although Teruel is different from Granada or Córdoba, different from the Aljafería at Zaragoza. Here the Gothic and Romanesque styles of architecture blend with that other tradition, preserved in fragile-seeming brickwork – for while Spain may have a destructive streak, the Spaniards are fiercely protective of their heritage in a way unique to them. Their mania for preservation extends not only to papal bulls, charters, battlements and cloisters, but also to the desiccated Grand Guignol spectacle of holy knees, heads and hands displayed in golden caskets.

Some people come here because they have seen Malraux's film about the Civil War, others come to admire the ochre Arab-influenced buildings, but most Spaniards are drawn here by the Lovers of Teruel. At some time in the sixteenth century two bodies were discovered lying in the same grave. They were the bodies of Isabella de Segura and Diego de Marcilla, who were born at the end of the twelfth century. Don't ask how anyone in the sixteenth century was able to tell that these remains dated from the thirteenth, because legends do not allow for awkward questions, legends are invariably true. Diego's lineage was nobler than Isabella's, but her family was wealthier. They fell in love and wanted to marry. Out of the question, said Isabella's father, and Diego went off to war in search of honour and fortune. He set out in the spring of

1212 and it was five years before he returned, but the very day he set foot again in his home town, Isabella, on her father's orders, was to be married to a man she detested. Driven mad by sorrow and rage, Diego collapsed and died within sight of his beloved, and Isabella succumbed the following day at his funeral. An iron logic is followed. Love is instantaneous, fathers are pitiless, lovers have youth and beauty, the homecoming is always on the fateful day, never a week too soon, and the ensuing misfortune ends in death. Legends serve to palliate our aversion to our own insignificance, the stuff of legends is absolute.

The news of the tragedy reached the farthest corners of Spain, it was whispered and recounted in umpteen hovels and grand houses. Tirso de Molina used it as the subject for a play and I have in my possession a book by Jaime Caruana Gómez de Barreda who, seven hundred years after the event, cites countless documents and arguments to authenticate the story – and anyone who does not believe it is either a buffoon or wicked or both.

The lovers lie in the burial chapel next door to the church of San Pedro. IF CLOSED, RING AT NO. 6 FOR THE KEY. I ring, but nothing happens. The door of the chapel is securely locked. I ring again, and again. At long last a distrustful little old woman opens the door and sells me a ticket, muttering to herself all the while. I see them at once, two recumbent alabaster statues on carved catafalques bearing the coats of arms of their respective families. His left hand rests in her right, thus bridging the distance between them. They date from this century and have the spooky hyperrealism of kitsch. The pillows are truly dented, the features set in noble sleep, the woman's breasts, which her husband will never set eyes on again, high and firm, his sensual mouth on the point of opening to allow his tongue to moisten his lips.

I am ready to leave when the little old woman points imperiously to the open tombs under the statues. I crouch down and peer in. Indeed, there they are, two carbonized mummies, each in its own fretwork casket. Three wisps of hair still rise from her bald black skull, the grey leather of her rib-cage is still slightly convex, his jaws agape in deathly uproarious laughter, his absent mouth wide open, the taut skin outlines the bony fingers with which they once caressed each other. By comparison the lascivious effigies resting above become real people caught in an alabaster silence and compelled to repose on a punishment they did not deserve. Still dazed from what I have just seen and the heady lunchtime wine, I drive out of the town into the blistering heat, the closely cropped, undulating, oscillating, wheeling landscape between Aragón and Castile. Beyond a line of poplars etched against the sky rises a church tower with a nest in the top: a stork alights with stiff, jerky movements, a snake in its bill. Somewhere in my mind the image seems to echo what I have just seen, but just where the parallel lies I cannot tell.

IV

A Land of Hidden Treasures

Transition from Moors to Christians
War past and present ~ Albarracín
The quiet cathedral of Sigüenza

DRIVING ACROSS A LANDSCAPE populated by spirits, I listen to the news on the car radio: "Picasso's *Guernica* is back in Spain!" A dramatic description ensues: the secret landing at Madrid airport, the heavily armed Guardia Civil escort, the special guard mounted over the painting that purports to remind a nation of one of its own war crimes, even if it was perpetrated by German aircraft. The Irony of History . . . I had the same feeling once before, when I saw in Berlin a painting of a porcine officer by George Grosz watched by two identical armed men in uniform. Grosz would have laughed, as Picasso is probably doing at this moment: a Guardia Civil escort to protect his indictment of the very system in which the Guardia Civil was instrumental. What could be more beautiful.

But perhaps Spaniards do not think in the same way. *El País* recently published a number of articles about Eugenio d'Ors, novelist, philosopher, journalist and so on. A great writer, comparable with Unamuno and Ortega y Gasset, but he sided openly with the new regime after 1939. That he did so is mentioned as an aside in the articles, without resentment, indulgently almost, as if to say "That's just the way he was, no need to go on about it." Very odd, and unthinkable by Dutch standards, but then we never had any really good right-wing writers. Or perhaps Spaniards are able to distinguish between artistic merit and errors of judgement even if the writer himself cannot.

How infinitely patient the land (earth, soil, terra) is. It suffers its surface to be scratched by the human race. Generations cultivate, irrigate, pull out weeds, build forts and villages, construct roads, but the mass of the land remains unperturbed, lies there patiently, pushes trees and wheat skyward, submits to fishing, hunting and the waging of wars, consents to be called kingdom, province, country, see, caliphate, free state, allows itself to be divided by those arbitrary, rarely geographical, man-made and hence illusory yet existing boundaries that are frontiers, giving in to a succession of name changes while remaining true to itself.

The road I am travelling was once a rough track over which Moorish and Christian armies marched, the empty air has absorbed the voices and odours of knights and foot soldiers, bacon and cabbage, curses and prayers, songs now long forgotten. The road is indicated on my map, but it has not been allotted a number. Just north of Teruel it turns left into the foothills to Castilla la Nueva, to Albarracín.

"Spain" is what the map and I call this land, but a thousand years ago things were different. The landscape I am driving through was at that time known as the *Taifa* of as-Sahla, with Albarracín as its capital. *Taifa*: little kingdom. The mighty caliphate of Córdoba, which once held sway as far as the north coast of "Spain", had disintegrated, and to anyone familiar with today's map of the Iberian peninsula the old one of 1050 looks curious indeed. In the north-west lay the Christian kingdom of León (now a province). That kingdom stretched from Porto and Zamora at one end, encompassed what are now Galicia and Asturias, and reached as far as the kingdom of Navarre, which dipped down to the Tagus in the south. To the east Navarre narrowed to a sliver of land. Zaragoza was a Moorish town, the frontier of the Christian world lay just south of Barcelona. Perpignan and the other southern towns of the Roussillon (now in France) were controlled by the dukedom of Ampurias. Twenty years later that map would change radically, and again thirty years later. History as a cartoon strip.

Those black contours on the historical map meant more than just borders, they were guarded by sentries. Whatever the names of all those large and little kingdoms, they had a common need for political organisation. Anyone who finds present-day politics complicated can comfort himself with a descent into history. Politics have always been complicated, and nearly always threatening, but the news did not spread so quickly. The media today are the emissaries of old. The whole world has become our Balkans, everyone's quarrels concern us because, so we are told, they threaten us – each remote but televised event, everywhere, every day. If we had less information things would be more complicated in a more essential way. But for the moment I am in the essential confusion of the year 1031, not in that of my own time.

Essential confusion begins when only two things get mixed up: the conflicting parties. In the eleventh century those parties were Muslim and Christian. Most of Spain was controlled by the *taifa* kingdoms. Each of them belonged to a party, a clan, a family – Hispanic-Arab, Slav, Berber. Now that all those factions were no longer held together by Córdoba they started operating independently, they became separate entities: Zaragoza, Toledo, Badajoz, Seville, Granada, Almería, Denia. Toledo took up the entire central area of Spain, most of the others were smaller. The *taifa*s were rich, but militarily weak. Their much "cruder" Christian and Visigothic neighbours to the north took due advantage of this. They offered protection to the southern Moorish states in exchange for gold. That made the north of Spain into one of the richest areas of Europe, second only to Flanders and northern Italy. At last Christian Spain also had the freedom to concern itself with the rest of Europe, and as a result the pilgrim's way to Santiago de Compostela became safer, and thus grew steadily in importance.

A thousand years have gone by since then and I have been travelling for some time already from Barcelona to Santiago. Call it a pilgrimage or a meditation if you wish, for with all the diversions and musings my progress is slow. I am making two journeys, one in my rented car and another through the past as evoked by fortresses, castles, monasteries and by the documents and legends I find there.

By the end of the eleventh century the Christian kingdom of Castile was in the ascendant. Alfonso VI (1073–1109) proclaimed the first "domestic" pilgrimages. His subjects were Christians, but a large proportion of them followed the Visigothic rites until this was prohibited by Rome. This ban caused Spain to lose touch with the Old Testament, because the Visigothic act of worship consisted largely of Bible reading. The same king now flung the doors of "his" Spain wide open for the monks of Cluny, who established the monasteries of Sahagún and San Juan de la Peña along the pilgrim's way to Santiago. Even today the face of Romanesque Spain is moulded by the architecture of that period. Villages sprang up around those monasteries, Frenchmen and Italians came to Spain. French merchants settled along the pilgrim's way, new bridges and roads were built and old ones

Detail of a capital showing Joseph's dream, San Juan de la Peña

improved, the north of Spain became increasingly entwined with its Christian neighbours.

In the Muslim south the situation was rather different. Both the standard of living and the trappings of civilization were more highly developed in al-Andalus than in North Africa. Islam was always a purist religion, but in Spain the rectitude had lost its edge. The Moors of al-Andalus were tolerant towards Jews and Christians, women were freer. Art and literature, especially poetry, blossomed and the economy was so well organized that the *taifa*s were able to pay huge tributes in gold to the Christian north. There was bitter rivalry among the various princes, poets were so highly esteemed that they were fought over; architecture, silver and goldsmithing, music, astronomy, philosophy, gave the Arab courts prestige in Spain and the notoriety of decadence in the Muslim regions overseas. All these things, compounded by political weakness, contributed to making the *taifa* of Toledo the first target of Christian expansion.

The town itself was divided: those who were in favour of Alfonso and those who were against him. Alfonso acted as great powers always do: he responded to a "call for help" from Toledo's Mozarabic community,

Christians who lived under Muslim rule. He occupied the town in 1085, but he did so in style. He endorsed self-government for the Muslim and Christian communities, a transitional period in which the Visigothic Christians were permitted to retain their own rites. He called himself Emperor of the Two Faiths. The other Muslim rulers in Spain were apprehensive. They had a choice – either to bow to Alfonso, or to call in the assistance of the militarily powerful, "austere" North African Berber dynasty known as the Almoravids. The Muslim theologians and spiritual leaders of those days had lost much of their influence under the decadent, secular rule of the *taifa* princes, and were in favour of summoning the help of the Almoravid chief Yousuf. That was done, but Yousuf was in no hurry. He was contemptuous of the compromised semi-apostate princes, moreover he knew that they in turn despised him for being an illiterate barbarian. But eventually he came. In 1086 he launched a lightning campaign and forced Alfonso to lift the siege of Zaragoza (look at the map and see how far north that is!). At the battle of Badajoz the Almoravid cavalry routed Alfonso's army. The king escaped with his life.

Words, like images, become upholstered in time, and thus obfuscated. When we say or read the word war we cannot dissociate it from tanks, intelligence networks, trenches, bomber aircraft. No one imagines that Alfonso and Yousuf engaged in modern warfare, but still it is very difficult to picture what their battles were really like. In that sense you could say that the past does not exist. There are images, to be sure, but they do not speak our visual language. They have become works of art, or prized possessions, but seldom have they come to represent the horror, the chaos, the stench and death of such a Red Cross-free battle. Italo Calvino has made an ironic attempt to describe one of Charlemagne's battles: knights like living, helpless tanks being hoisted into their suits of armour, their armour-plated and consequently untractable mounts, the clumsy brandishing of long lances to tumble adversaries out of the saddle, the un-horsed human tank immobilized like a beetle turned on its back; and finally the deserted battlefield with looters demolishing the carapaces and leaving the denuded corpses to the mercy of ever-watchful vultures. Skirmishes at dusk and dawn, but no searchlights. No walkie-talkie sets, but giant banners and pennants. All those coats of arms, incomprehensible to us today, literally labelled the knights in armour:

thanks to those heraldic symbols everyone could tell at a glance who was riding the charger, sallying forth, who the fallen figure was, begging for succour, dying.

Prolonged troop movements, no war correspondents, news that is slow to spread. How long did it take for the pope and the king of France to hear of this defeat, and how did they know it was time to make the next move in their chess game? Alfonso took the first step: he sought the help of el Cid (*sayyid*, *al-sajjid*, *Sidi*, Arabic for Lord), the outstanding condottiere of all time, who sold his services to Christians and Arabs alike. Yousuf was less pressed for time. He went back to Africa, and let Alfonso make a blunder of the first order. Urged on by the pope, Alfonso stepped up the harassment of the *taifa* princes, who found themselves having to choose between the devil and the deep blue sea: either submitting to the Christian world, or surrendering their refined, literary culture to a much harsher Muslim master. The latter option won, and the liberal brilliance of al-Andalus was lost. Islamic Spain, with poets like ar-Rusafi and philosophers like Ibn Rushd (Averroes), to preserve the Aristotelian heritage for the Christianity of Thomas Aquinas, had been tolerant towards both Christians and Jews, creating a model that had survived in Toledo. But decline set in, and it fell first into the hands of the Almoravids and then, when they too had been touched by the culture they had usurped, into the hands of a fanatical, orthodox clan from the Atlas mountains, the Almohads. These were early examples of an Islamic identity that we know today: an often disheartening spectacle of religious intolerance which, abetted by the riches of this century, constitutes an underestimated danger for the rest of the world.

I drive up the steep road to the citadel of Albarracín. No sentries, no foot-soldiers with boiling pitch on the ramparts of the castle, only two nuns in a 2CV. White-faced as bakers who never see the sun, dusted with the flour of God.

The old houses huddle together at the foot of the citadel, seeking protection: they look like a jumble of loose teeth in the awesome stone jaws of the rock-face. A car is no use to you here. I leave it by what was once the city gate, and set out to roam the narrow streets on foot. Silence, geraniums on window-sills, a clock, and high above me the unassailable walls that now enclose an empty space through which the wind whistles. The bare landscape lies far below me. I drink a glass of black wine in a dark cellar. Inside the church it is cool: in the small museum annexe a diminutive priest with sad eye-glasses sits reading the progressive daily newspaper. A grey knitted cardigan hangs over the back of his chair, it can get quite cold in Albarracín. We look at each other, have nothing to say, I stroll along the treasures, a chalice, a book, faded and mended tapestries from Brussels, and I can tell from the shoulders of the bowed reader that few visitors come here. I buy the little book with pen-and-ink sketches of the cathedral (once so mighty), the castle and the tall Castilian houses teetering on the edge of the ravine, and watch him counting my pesetas as they drop into the wooden coin-box. It's the same here as everywhere else: those high villages were once protected by their location, now that same geography is the cause of their isolation. A reckless thought: if you took hold of Spain by the edges and dragged it with giant's strength over the Pyrenees to lay it on top of France, much of what now remains hidden from most people would be suddenly part of the treasure house that is the European cultural heritage. The curse of Spain (or the blessing, if you prefer) is that inexhaustible sun-drenched coastline upon which all attention is focused. If Albarracín had been situated on the Côte d'Azur it would be swamped by tourism by now, like Saint-Paul-de-Vence, so I suppose I should be grateful, but on the other hand I find it infuriating that, just four hundred and forty kilometres from Barcelona, there should be a completely unknown world which millions of sun-worshippers race past – or fly over – each year.

Ever heard of Sigüenza, San Baudelio, El Burgo de Osma, Albarracín, Santa María de la Huerta? It doesn't reek of sun-tan lotion there, but of wild rosemary. The food is simple and the wine cheap, an excellent hunting-ground for the individual traveller, and now and then you do come across such adventurous loners: elderly couples weighed down by guidebooks or an almost extinct kind of young person armed with a sketchpad. People always go on about peace and quiet and that there isn't enough of it. Well, there's plenty of it, megatons of emptiness, aeons of rest, hectolitres of silence, and a past that is respected as if the locals were subsidized by an International Commission to leave everything as it is, as indeed it was a thousand years ago. The traveller in Spain should rid himself of the sense of time as anecdotal, he should be unconcerned by planned itineraries and times of arrival, he should be willing to lodge at modest village inns and to expose himself fearlessly to different concepts of temporality. Climate, obstinacy, the mercy of fate, even sheer lack of interest have caused some parts of Spain to be left well alone, making it possible for you to believe for a moment in the illusion that the world is not so chaotic after all, not as savage and transitory as the news-papers and television images would have us believe, that there are given constants which, even though they are made up of individual lives, tran-scend the vicissitudes of fate. This land is ancient, it has known many wars and catastrophes, historic movements, cruelty, bitter conflict, most recently in this century. All those dramatic events brought men to ruin, men who thought everything would be ruined with them, and yet the traveller of today encounters landscapes, monuments, attitudes that are unchanged. Change is always exaggerated by contemporaries, and their exaggerated views are reiterated by the news media which, in order to safeguard their very existence, are obliged to affirm the change because constancy has no appeal. There are other media for that: museums, books, cathedrals.

Seen from the air the citadel of Sigüenza looks quite human: a parallelogram in the random swirl of nature. If people had been able to fly in those days the stronghold would have been so vulnerable that there would have been no point in building it. The Spanish state has now converted it into a parador, I sleep among crenellations, empty suits of armour stand at the corners of rough-hewn stone passages, the weak, blue light of a television set shimmers in a vast hall. The programme that is being shown is one in a series: the history of the *corrida*. Footage of a bullfight in Mexico, 1916. Flickering black and white images, little men moving too rapidly, an absurdly prancing miniature bull, no sound, clouds scudding frivolously across the sky, how can I take all this seriously? I have to make an effort to convert that speeded-up version to a more natural pace so as not to burst out laughing. Nonetheless, to the bullfighter the fight was truly dangerous, he was truly wounded, and the black juice squirting just a little too rapidly from his embroidered costume is real blood. The same thing happens when you watch news-reels showing battle scenes from bygone wars. All those grotesque little figures clambering up out of those muddy trenches, moving jerkily like toys that have been too tightly wound up, lurching forward and then suddenly being hurled into the air before they drop down, dead. The idiocy of the accelerated images robs them of the reality of their death, and no doubt something similar will happen to us – if the speed is right then something is sure to go wrong with the colour or the smell. Real-life drama must necessarily be brought to a standstill, it must be evoked in silence, otherwise it eludes us. An evocation may move, but that which has moved must be evoked by arrested motion. An untenable statement, I am only making it to say that the picture of a siege in the Romanesque Bible of San Isidoro in León, in all its primitive immobility, impresses me more than the battle of Verdun on old newsreels, because, I must confess, they always make me think of Chaplin and Keaton. Here, however, thirteen brilliantly coloured, static figures have been selected to represent the entire siege. Those who are dead are supine: an outstretched hand emerges from the emblematic crimson of the flames. The swords are drawn, a shield is raised aloft on the ramparts. Now I can fill in all the dying, battling, and destruction.

Early in the morning I open the casement window of my room, but it is not a window, it is a peep-hole. Through the small rectangular embrasure I see the deserted world, not an enemy in sight. I hear the bells of the cathedral, a fortress in its own right, which I have observed looming like a dark shadow in the night.

An initial surprise: upon entering the cathedral through the south portal I have no choice but to go down a flight of steps. The building is half sunk into the ground, so it is much higher than the exterior suggests. Peaceful and spacious. I join a small group of Spaniards following the guide, a pale man who tells a good story. I am struck by the concentration of the others. I think they must be what used to be called artisans, they run their hands over the wood, caress the stones, ask questions about historical periods, admire the craftsmanship, agree that the polychrome wooden altar piece of Covarrubias needs dusting, and they are right. Upon reaching the famous statue of the Doncel they fall silent, as I do.

The Doncel was one of Isabella the Catholic's pages; he died during the siege of Granada in 1486. The queen commissioned this statue to be carved, and so there he is, Don Martín Vázquez de Arce, reading a stone book, unconcerned by his own death, quiet and lost to the world. His statue is lifelike and mysterious. He is reclining on the tomb, his upper body raised, leaning on his right elbow, the left armour-clad knee slightly bent, his dagger has slipped to one side. A kneeling figure at his feet. His parents lie next to each other on their backs close by, their hands folded on their chests, their feet resting against the hunting dogs who watch

Sigüenza Cathedral

over them. In the wall, on his side, the grandfather. Medieval chivalry, the intimacy of kinship, all the voices have been lowered now, so as not to disturb the peace. We trail after the guide from one end of the eleventh-century Cistercian floorplan to the other, past Romanesque windows under the delicate high Gothic arches in this otherwise so robust building. Medieval tombs, Plateresque murals, incised as if chased in silver rather than chiselled out of hard, weather-defying stone – all those styles are held together by the quiet sanctity of the building, one of the loveliest churches I know.

The bells start clattering, the sound is deafening. The guide, who doubles as sacristan, interrupts his tour. A few believers come in, commas on an empty page, and I go to sit by them. Canons sweep up the aisles in long black robes, red capes around the shoulders. Their body language says that all this is theirs. Some of them wear vacant expressions, others cast a disdainful eye over the mostly empty pews like divas dissatisfied with the extent of their audience. The reverberating singing betrays the wear and tear of routine. A strident Spanish voice utters the words of the God of Israel. I catch snippets of instruction concerning slaughter, the sacrifice of animals and the consumption thereof, the fetters of orthodoxy: this part of the animal yes, that part no, thou shalt do this and that, and thus I command you, I, the Lord, from generation upon generation. Phrases that have been preserved for thousands of years, since they were composed in the desert. I shudder at the memory of the hateful boarding school of my boyhood, I rise from my pew and wander into the sacristy without the guide. Gregorian chanting fills the space like sounds from a cave, I stand transfixed: hundreds of carved heads look down at me from the barrel-vaulted ceiling, an orgy of faces, earnest, mocking, wreathed in roses: heads of scholars, church fathers, saints, bearded heads, held high or askance, blind, reflecting, sleeping, singing, speaking. It feels very strange now, to be all alone in this sacristy where I have no business. The tinkle of bells and ancient incantations coming in from the adjoining space, a cloud of faces overhead. Dizzy from craning my neck I look into the eyes of warriors, noblemen, priests, until the Gregorian chant in the distance begins to sound like merriment emanating from the mass of those heads: an insane, slow-motion peal of laughter. Hours later, as I drive through the shorn wheat-fields again, the sound is ringing still in my ears.

V

Not Yet in Santiago

On pilgrimage ~ The Mozarabic chapel of San Baudelio
The mappa mundi ~ Santo Domingo de Silos
Santo Domingo de la Calzada ~ The holy hen
The golden gloom of Burgos Cathedral

MY JOURNEY HAS BECOME a detour made up of composite detours, and I allow myself to be diverted even from them. Things were more straightforward for the medieval pilgrim, at least in this respect. If he came from the north he would cross the Pyrenees at the Col du Pourtalet or at Roncesvalles. The map of the pilgrim's ways in those times resembles a river delta, streams of pilgrims from all directions converged at Puente la Reina to join that single Great Way of Saint James, the Camino de Santiago, which ran from the north of Spain across the dry plain and the barren mountains of Castile over the Cebrero pass to the ultimate, so ardently desired destination.

Road sign in Roncesvalles

Puente la Reina, the bridge that a million feet have crossed

Memories in language and stone still exist; like a chain set with gems the churches, inns and place names commemorate a pious zeal that is unimaginable today, a piety that drove Christians to that distant corner of windswept Galicia for hundreds of years. It takes a while for the full scope of that ardour to sink in. People simply set aside their lives to walk halfway across Europe in dangerous times. Following in the footsteps of a legend, the pilgrims became a legend in their own right. The only conceivable parallel, it seems to me, is the pilgrimage to Mecca, the no less longed-for goal of devout Muslims, but they now travel in ships, planes and coaches. For them, too, the longer they live the less time they have.

To understand the essence of the pilgrimage to Santiago it is necessary to separate medieval man from the comfortable romantic image we have formed of him (if we have one at all). He was a truly different human being, with different preoccupations. His society was spiritual unity; the importance that he attached to the relics of saints and martyrs is beyond modern comprehension. Seeking out and venerating those sacred reliquaries, devout Christians tramped from country to country, from shrine to shrine, an inspired multitude of prayerful, lifelong travellers. In the petty jargon of our present century, we call such things social, political or religious phenomena. Political because this movement drew non-Islamic Spain closer to Christian Europe in a prelude to that other development which consolidated European Christendom, the Crusades; social because of the international contact and what the pilgrims brought with them and in their wake, in the spheres of trade as well as art; religious because for those who joined the movement the importance of spirituality surpassed that of material existence. The historian Labande defines the medieval pilgrim as "a Christian who at some point in his life makes the decision to travel to a particular place and who surrenders his entire existence to achieving that goal". No small matter.

What of me? I still have a long way to go. I have roamed the country-side of Catalonia and Aragón, stopping at churches and castles, and am now entering Castile. I am driving from Sigüenza to El Burgo de Osma: the red road on the map has given way to a yellow one, the yellow road to a white one. I stop the car on one of those unnumbered white roads, in the midst of a silence punctuated only by the wind, and my attention is caught by a rust-coloured sandy track winding away from this minor road. Where does it lead? The last place I drove through was called Barcones. Dwellings with side walls not taller than one metre, huddled against the hillside. Mud walls, thatched roofs, pigs in the mire. There is no one to be seen save an urchin who runs up to the car shouting "*hijo de puta*", son of a whore, before scurrying off as fast as he can. What next? I drive some way along the track. The ground becomes rock hard, rigid channels have been scored in the soil, some crop may have been cultivated here once, but now there are sharp, stiff plants with prickles, greyish blue, low on the ground and hostile. Iron spikes, hooks, instruments of torture, for what can these plants exist?

The seemingly random track falls away into a sudden hollow, the surface is deeply rutted; I am afraid my wheels may get stuck, so I get out of the car. Now that even the sound of the engine has died I can hear the silence that I could only see a moment ago. It is an eery quiet, not like anywhere else. No sounds of animals, not even the flight of a bird, only the wind hauling the hot air across the plain and on its way brushing against the blades of those parched plants. But that sound is silence, too. The ground dips slightly in the distance and the track disappears from view. I am determined to see where it goes, and like an agent on a mission, alone with myself, I set off into the distance. The next panorama unfolds before me, but it is the same as the one I have already seen. I am obstinate, or mad, and I press on. It must lead somewhere. Then the slope steepens. The track bends, I recognize goat droppings. And there: two huts made of turf. In front of them two troughs roughly hewn from a block of wood. I call out, but there is no answer. A cloud of big black flies rises from the gnawed remains of a rabbit, making a horrible buzzing, like a bow drawn once across a malevolent cello. Then they settle on the cadaver again and resume their labour: it is their duty.

I approach the huts gingerly. I keep thinking there must be someone there, but inside I find no one. No animal either. A bloodstained sheepskin, lately flayed, hangs across a beam. Traces of a fire. It's dark between the earthen walls. The ceiling is so low that I have to keep my head bent. It must be a shelter for a shepherd and his flock. The floor of dried mud is stamped with thousands of shiny, smooth little hoof-prints. I hurry outside again, as if I might be caught. The thatched roof is propped up with a few tree trunks. The place could date from any time, from five hundred years ago, a thousand, or even longer. The blue plants clamp their serrated spurs on my ankles as I make my way back to the car.

There's no point in repeating over and over how empty these Spanish landscapes are, however true it may be. Perhaps I am more susceptible because I come from a country suffering from overpopulation, but it never ceases to amaze me – to strike me, like a blow, or a shot. Not all day long, but at particular moments. BANG, and there it is again, the complete absence of artefacts, the absence of movement, as if the vastness of the landscape can only express itself by something equally immeasurable: time. This is getting rather too close to the "everlasting silence of infinite space", but it can't be helped: this land evokes feelings of eternity. To sojourn here is to have lived a long time, to have to pursue one's direction for ever.

All that is left of the hermitage of San Baudelio de Berlanga is a small, Mozarabic chapel in the vicinity of Berlanga de Duero. I have been here before and I can remember that the custodian at the time said he recognized me from a previous visit. He makes the same comment now, and this time he is right. It is the same old man, spare and solitary. The hermitage is situated far from the main road, his home is in a village ten kilometres away. Standing together on the crest of the hill, we gaze over the landscape. "There somewhere," he says, waving in a direction where there is nothing to be seen. The hermits of long ago had their retreats in these parts, but these, too, have vanished. He arrives in the morning and leaves in the evening, and spends the day waiting for the rare visitor. It's very quiet here, he must be able to hear a car coming from a long way off.

The interior of the chapel is white and cool. A central column with ribs fanning out like the fronds of a petrified palm supports the vaulted ceiling. Vestiges of murals, shadows of animals, human faces with almond eyes, wide open and with a tiny circle in the centre to indicate the pupil, fix me with their Byzantine stare. "There used to be much more," he says, "but one day, sixty years ago it is already, an American gentleman arrived here. He asked to see the church. Perhaps he had heard about the frescoes. He offered to buy them and the local farmers agreed to sell." I leaf through the brochure he hands me. New York, Boston, Indianapolis. Black-and-white photographs of the *Entry into Jerusalem*, of the *Last Supper*, painted in the remote past by nameless artists on the walls of their chapel in this desolate plain, excised now from the context of their time, their significance, their environment, and displayed in museums in the USA. Collector's items, art objects. There is a sadness there, as if they were orphans. What little was left is now in the Prado. "It would have been stolen anyway, otherwise," he says. "We can't guard the place day and night."

It is a refrain that I will hear many times. There are paintings, statues, retables, altarpieces, from small, forsaken churches scattered all over the provincial and diocesan museums in Spain. How can something that was originally in a sense utilitarian turn into a work of art? Utilitarian: an image that served to instruct people about their faith. The frescoes recounted the Bible to the faithful who came to the church and who could not read, the statues were there to be adored, to be invoked in prayer. So now they have been put on display in art galleries, side by side with comparable specimens. The content of the story told by the paintings has evaporated for most visitors, only the form counts now. Few people, except students of art history, can still distinguish the symbols of the evangelists, still know about the Old Men of the Apocalypse, are still familiar with the attributes of the martyrs. Religion is transmuted into art, because stories become images that signify only themselves. The twentieth-century viewer observes a narrative that he can no longer interpret, to which he has grown blind.

I linger in the little church a while longer, trying to picture the hermits at worship in the empty space. Then I go outside again through the Arab horseshoe archway and drive slowly down the hill.

I can see the old man in my rear-view mirror, watching as I drive off. On some future occasion I will stand in the Prado or in Indianapolis and what I see there will remind me of those white walls and I will have a vision of a low, weathered building on a gently sloping hillside and an old man watching a car until it is out of sight. I have never heard the voice of Louis Couperus.* He was dead long before I had ears and I do not know if his voice was ever phonographically recorded. He is said to have had a high-pitched voice and an affected manner of speaking. Familiar as I am with his many travel stories, I think I know how he would have sounded when he said: "Reader, you have accompanied me on a long journey. Together we have marvelled at treasures, churches and cathedrals, landscapes and museums . . . I could describe at length all the emotions that came over me . . . but that would take too long . . . too much have I seen . . ." It is no longer the fashion for a writer to address his reader, but for once I'd like to borrow his reedy voice to make a similar statement. For every story I could tell ten more about all of the things I saw on my way to Santiago de Compostela. The date of my journey would have gathered dust by the time I had finished, the newspapers would be yellowed, the summer superseded by winter and winter by summer again, and still I would not have reached the end: the undiscovered treasure-house of Spain is inexhaustible.

My journey took me to El Burgo de Osma, which has a cathedral and a museum. A bad-tempered priest leads me around the exhibition, garbles his stock information, hurries me along. In a glass showcase lies one of the most beautiful books on earth. It is opened at a page showing the map of the world: *mappa mundi*. I wish I could turn the page, read the book, but the cabinet is locked. So this is what the world looked like in the year 1086. A decorated circle on parchment, then a wavy zone of water with fishes, then similarly wavy, unwieldy shapes in a paler shade, again traversed by streams, inscribed with Visigothic lettering, scattered with drawings of heads, turrets, a strange bisected square bordered in red, a red sphere, serrated peaks that may be mountains. The booklet I have bought in the church waxes pedantic and directs my untutored

*Louis Couperus (1863–1923), the well-known Dutch poet and novelist.

gaze to the convolutions of the eleventh century: this *Codex Beato* is *Carolingian* in its colouristic treatment and ornamentation, *Arabic* in the application of yellow and ivory and geometric patterns, *Lombardian* in the interlaced arabesques and animal motifs, *Irish* in the spiralled braiding, *Islamic* in the predominance of red and black, while eastern influences manifest themselves in the Mozarabic stylization. Am I not permitted to turn even one page? No.

Oblivious to all the other exhibits I linger before that map. How strange that a map which in no way represents the geographic, physical reality of the world should be able to tell me so much about the spiritual reality of old. What I mean is this: the continents then were already where we now know them to be. The artist-cartographer was not even aware that three of them existed. But we know how profound the pollinating influence in those days was, that the world was already a world, that people communicated and saw each other's art, that artists and craftsmen travelled and inspired one another.

In the region I am driving through, the names sound like a poem. Hontoria del Pinar, Huerta del Rey, Palacios de la Sierra, Cuevas de San Clemente, Salas de los Infantes, Castrillo de la Reina . . . palace on the mount, garden of the king, Saint Clement's grottoes, halls of princelings, the queen's encampment. For the hundredth time the landscape changes, the road curves this way and that following the course of an invisible stream, craggy rocks like the petrified skulls of old men rise above indeterminate green foliage, an Italianate romanticism.

I saw a photograph of the cloister at the monastery of Santo Domingo de Silos many years ago, in a book about Romanesque architecture. There was something about the secluded garden, the pure regularity, the holy square, that struck me. Something odd. The columns bearing the Romanesque arches with their carved capitals succeeded one another not in single or double rows as in a sacred forest, but somewhere that order was disturbed, a dent had been made in the world, there was something wrong. It was perhaps only one second before I saw what it was, but that one second of puzzlement on my part had been anticipated by a stonemason six centuries earlier. Three of the small columns were buckled, subsiding around each other in an upright embrace, they were on the point of collapse, only just holding each other in balance. But the presence of that one ensemble is enough to subvert the superior

The cloister of Santo Domingo de Silos

Detail of a relief showing bird women, Santo Domingo de Silos

order of the edifice in its entirety, like an ironic aside. I found it infinitely intriguing, how the world could be de-regulated by such a simple gesture.

I drive in the direction of Silos, filled with a sense of expectation. It was after all only a photograph. How would it be in reality? In the same book I had seen illustrations and descriptions of capitals and reliefs, there was a lot more to be seen in Silos than those three genuflecting columns. I arrive just in time for the guided tour. A student with a grave expression describes capital after capital, Persian bird patterns, Arab interlaced motifs, I see it all and am properly impressed, but I keep looking around for my little columns. To do so in this plethora of exuberant capitals, dozens of them, is almost frivolous, but I attribute that to the Spaniard in me; there has to be an element of the absurd, of the incongruous. And then I catch sight of what I have come to see and find myself thinking: so it is really true. A building can be persuaded to contradict itself, the serenity can be emended, the balance disturbed, doubt can be cast on perfection. For an instant the entire universe teeters, and the resulting sensation is one of relief.

A similar effect is achieved by a fresco. It is a painting of a later date, on a ceiling. A wolf kills an ass, two wolves bury the dead animal, and the last scene shows the murderer-wolf reciting mass at the ass's graveside. The primitive wolf on its hind legs at the altar, an outsize wafer in its paws, the jaws open wide to receive communion – there is a hint of mockery and sacrilege there. How Spanish this mockery is I don't know – I'm told there is a similar depiction in the cathedral of Strasbourg – but the spectacle, first heard and then seen, that I come upon that evening in Santo Domingo de la Calzada eighty kilometres away I cannot imagine existing outside Spain.

I have veered a little to the east to rejoin the pilgrim's way. The old pilgrims' hospice at Santo Domingo has been converted into a hotel. It's almost dark when I get there. So this is where they halted, in greater or lesser states of dishevelment, the scallop of Saint James a proud emblem on their wide cloaks, staff in hand. Whether they were still going or on their way home, when they stopped here they still had months of walking ahead of them. I think of their songs, their footsteps, their voices, their untranslatable piety. A suit of armour stands sentry in the large hall of the refurbished hospice, and when no one is looking I raise the visor to check that there really is no one inside, but that's because I have just read that book by Italo Calvino about a non-existent knight, whose empty suit of armour is manned exclusively by the will to live.

Capital showing paired harpies, Santo Domingo de Silos

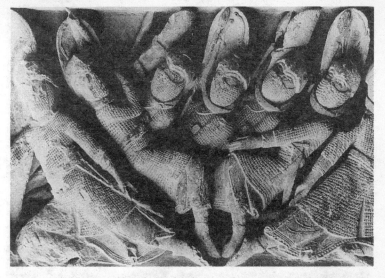

Relief showing soldiers sleeping by Christ's tomb, Santo Domingo de Silos

Capital with fabulous monsters, Santo Domingo de Silos

Relief showing Christ and the two disciples at Emaus, Santo Domingo de Silos

The armour fights bravely on the battlefield, sups at Charlemagne's table, is desired by ladies. It is only much later, when the non-existent occupant's will to live slackens, that the suit of armour is found in a forest, abandoned, a lifeless object. A peculiar story, and it feels just as peculiar peering inside that metal puppet today. Even the hands are steel, I can move the fingers slightly, but no, there's no one inside. A row of swords hangs from a rack on the rough stone wall, I run my fingers along the blunted cutting edge of the blades.

The bells of the cathedral start pealing. It is not quite what we would call ringing, but it is not striking either, rather a mixture of the two, as if the bells want to speak about other things than time itself. One bell sounds shrill, purposeful and rousing, the other muffled and fleeting, pointing, between those pressing summonses, to the place where time is now. I listen, and make my way across the little square. It gets dark early at this time of year. The sounds come from a lone tower, the moon sweeps across the fleece clinging to the nocturnal vault, the church looms massively in the dark. I go inside and find another, complicated heaven in another high vault, stone configurations unfolding into extraordinary patterns advancing and receding, whose function seems more decorative than supportive. A restorer is at work in a distant corner. He sits on a trestle-table in a pool of the starkest light, surrounded by dozens of little paint pots. Tiny squares are already lighting up in his painting, the rest

Detail of Christ and the two disciples

The cathedral of Santo Domingo de la Calzada

is an obscure field of half-erased figures. I can't make out what the scene represents, but it is strange suddenly to discern in that morass of vanished images an eye, a hand, a green cap.

Old women shuffle by, a handbell announces that mass is about to start. A male voice intones a prayer, to which the women respond in unison, old girlish voices. Even without looking I can follow the enactment of the ritual. I think of how often I have heard and seen the same thing in the half-century of my existence, and then suddenly, like a warning, high and strident, the wanton crowing of a cock, once, twice, three times. The restorer does not look up from his work, the priest empties his chalice, the old women mouth their arcane syllables. Am I the only one to hear that sound? Again that primeval ululation of masculine triumph rings across the huge vault. I walk in the direction of the sound, and sure enough there, on a ledge set against one of the interior walls of the church, is a gilded and decorated cage, surmounted by a semicircular arch with rosettes and Gothic pinnacles. In the soft, yellowish light behind the grille I see them, the holy hen and the holy

The world's most beautiful chicken coop

cock, giant specimens in the world's most beautiful chicken-coop. I hear the story behind it later.

Many centuries ago three pilgrims travelled here from Germany. Father, mother and son. They stopped for food at a wayside inn, where one of the serving girls fell in love with the son. He did not return her affections, so she reported him to the magistrate, not for unrequited love, but for stealing. The young man was seized and sentenced to death. On learning of their son's arrest the parents hurried to the magistrate, who happened to be dining on roast chicken. Protesting the boy's innocence they begged him to spare their son's life. The magistrate wiped his lips and said: "First: he is hanged already, and second: he is as innocent as this chicken on my plate is alive." Whereupon the plump, plucked fowl miraculously regained its white plumage and stepped off the plate, clucking. The whole town now flocked to the gallows and sure enough, the hanging youth was still alive. Ever since that day a live hen and cock have been kept in the cathedral of Santo Domingo de la Calzada. There are those who believe it is still the same hen, and I dare say they are right.

Landscapes, churches, churches, landscapes. And that one word time and again: Camino. Camino de Santiago, Redecilla del Camino, the traffic signs register the kilometres, the figure beside the word Santiago becomes ever smaller, more and more frequently now I see the Saint

Milestone to Santiago

James scallops adorning village pumps and park benches, I am nearing my destination and yet I remain distant.

A shadowy memory of a previous visit to the cathedral at Burgos flits across my mind as I enter the cathedral again: the initial feeling of repugnance. You stand in the middle of that vast massed space and you can see nothing, a gloomy cavern inlaid with gold, movements of people around you, audible whispers, no height, although everything is high enough. First I stroll aimlessly, not knowing where to start (as if there were a proper place to start) and turning down the offers of obtrusive guides. More objects, statues gradually emerging from the gloom, now and then a guide switches on a light over a golden altar for the benefit of his flock: I cross the nave to take a look and the light goes off again. The whole space is a sprawling, dark launching pad, prepared for a departure that has been postponed for centuries.

Outside the cathedral two towering, chiselled rockets stand in attendance, set with stone after stone "like a precious ring" as Théophile Gautier saw it, and he was right. Not until the final, uppermost stone had been placed did they point forever more in the direction of the intended voyage into the heavens. But the launch never takes place, regardless of how busy things become inside. It is close on five, bells tinkle here and there, ancient canons pop out of niches and secret doors, they totter across their shadowy terrain like lame bats, one of them pauses by the little stairway until a colleague arrives to help him up, and they disappear together into the decorated choir, they hide in their chairs, I can only just see it all behind the grille, I hear the mumbling, the rustling of large sheets of paper.

A new guide touches my arm. This one has a truly waxen complexion, his marble hand gestures in some vague direction, I surrender and follow him. He may be the first reincarnation of Peter Sellers. A hundred tics and mannerisms, he shuffles his feet, clears his throat, slaps his hand on his back, raises his eyes to the ceiling and pours his lisping, thick French marinated in Spanish oil all over me. We pass through, walk down passages, past altars, treasuries, there is no end to this church. I look around eagerly, but he is relentless, he turns away and proceeds to the next item. Pausing in front of some delicate stone tracery he says "like lace", and so it is – like old lace, a frenzy of stolen gold. I trail after him like a child through this orgy of Spanish ornamentation. It is staggering in its exuberance, also because of the silent, majestic presence of the curled, modelled, chased, beaten gold of the Incas in the sombre gloom: he switches on a light and it begins to glow, he switches it off and the gold remains, invisible, powerful; it belongs to the frayed voices in the distance, and worse still, to the landscape surrounding the town, dry and bare, the colour of sand and also of gold, land on which nothing can grow and which has yielded this gorgeous, inedible harvest.

I go outside and buy two long strips of postcards out of sheer impotence, so as to be able to see *something* at last, but the scale is gone. Semi-visibility will have to do. I return to the tomb of the two *condestables*, marble like soft white clay glazily preserving the memory of those two round-cheeked noblemen, preserving the pleats in their robes, preserving the faithful, curly-coated dogs at their feet, preserving all the pearls in their crowns. At night they rise and perform a little dance, run up and down the golden royal staircase or pay a visit to all those other masked dead of gold and stone, they rummage around in the Cid's coffers, eat a snippet of gold brocade, fly like great white herons across the eternal twilight, only to doze off again at first light, imprisoned in the folds of their marble garments.

Following idly in the wake of yet another guide I find myself in a windowless room containing a painting by Memling, *The Virgin and Child*. It is the reddest painting I have ever seen, she wears a dress of lasting fire. But behind her and beside her there is another colour, which is even rarer in these parts: the colour of a lush meadow in Flanders, and it is with a jolt of nostalgia that I contrast that full, lush green landscape (a field with curly trees, sea-green hills in the distance, a hunter with leaping hounds in a green meadow, a clear blue lake with swans, a farmhouse with an open gate, a fruit tree, a path, a slope, two tall trees) with the barrenness of the golden treasure which seduced colonial Spain, and with which Spain sought to seduce God himself. And this was Spain's undoing, because the land they had to live off was neglected for the sake of gold. Now that I know what I am not looking for, I go outside, where the light is. I am not yet in Santiago.

VI

A Queen Does Not Laugh:
Diego Velásquez in the Prado

The king's friend and confidant
A dynasty breeds itself to extinction ~ Mariana revealed
Court painter ~ The secret to "Las Meninas" ~ Shades of Zurbarán

LEAVING THE PRADO, I did not encounter the usual queue winding itself like a human ball of twine around the austere building. It was a Monday and I had enjoyed the privilege of visiting the exhibition virtually alone, in the uncanny silence of deserted galleries. No mean achievement. Great art envelops the viewer in riddles, and it's up to him to hunt for the clues.

It was spring. Madrid without the crushing heat of the months to come was light and airy, a city on a high plateau. I had seen some paintings I had known for years and others that were quite new to me, seventy-nine in total: still lifes, history paintings and portraits that accompanied the reign of a king, scenes mythological and religious, horsemen, dwarfs, drinkers, half-wits, and repeatedly the eyes and mouth of the Habsburg king, Philip IV. But most of all I had seen Velásquez, and I did not know who this courtier was who had penetrated so deeply into the web of power that he was on domestic, intimate terms with the central characters he was assigned to portray. He is shrouded in mystery, just as Rembrandt and Vermeer are mysterious, not only in that most enigmatic of paintings, "*Las Meninas*", but also in the series of portraits of the king which span the period of both his and the artist's adult lives.

More than thirty years separate the first portrait and the last, and this shared life – Velásquez lived at court, the king frequently visited his studio and took him with him on his travels – undoubtedly added an element of self-portraiture to the likenesses of the king, which was perhaps discernible only to them. The one a courtier rising to ever higher positions of Byzantine complexity at a court where the king could neither eat in the presence of his wife nor attend the baptism of his children, the other a king who wrote clandestine letters to an Aragonese nun describing his uncontrollable sexual desires, his adultery, his promiscuity and subsequent punishment by God, the defeat at the hands of the French at Rocroi and the Portuguese rebellion; the decline of the Habsburg and the ineluctable rise of the hidalgo-artist, it is all there in the final likeness of the king, which is actually a double portrait. Both must have been painted somewhere between 1655 and 1660. The artist

Philip IV (c. 1655–60), by Velásquez, in the Prado

died in 1660 and the king, who was five years younger, survived him
by only a couple of years.

Two paintings, a single king, a disillusioned middle-aged man, unable
to stem the gradual dissipation of his vast, inherited empire, a weak
man, racked by Habsburg self-doubt, a ruler who recognized his own
weakness, and who left the business of government to the wrong advisers, such as the Count Duke of Olivares. Looking at those northern
features it is hard to imagine that mouth ever speaking Spanish, but
this is academic, since paintings do not talk, and anyway the king who,

Philip IV (c. 1655–60), by Velásquez, in the National Gallery

as legend has it, smiled only three times in his life, is frozen to silence in his portraits. Indeed, there was no need for words. He had eyes, and he had an artist to paint him. The sumptuous lace collar having been banned as immodest, he wore a *golilla* instead, an almost saucer-shaped starched white collar which, if you look long and hard enough, appears to divide the head from the body, a sort of displaced exterior midriff on which the royal head rests as on a serving dish. It hardly matters that the portrait, on loan from the National Gallery in London, bears the insignia of the Golden Fleece, nor that his doublet is of much plainer fabric than in the Prado portrait – it is the face that draws all attention, and it is not the face of despairing letters but that of kingship, which is what it must indicate to others. Fish-eyes, they have been called, but then surely those of an unimaginable, primeval species that lurks at the bottom of the ocean and has never been seen by man. The face is reserved, secretive, but at the same time, and this is what makes it all so mysterious, it discloses its secret to the artist and thus splits in two, bares itself in aloofness, creates an unbridgeable distance and yet is near at hand. As remote as a sovereign and as close as a man having his portrait painted by a friend.

What the friend must have seen was the end of a dynasty. There was to be only one more Habsburg on the Spanish throne: Charles the Hexed. Seven of his ancestors were descended from Joanna the Mad, mother of Charles V. These Habsburgs not only passed down the grotesque jaw-bone (Charles was unable to close his mouth properly) but all manner of other deficiencies from the incestuous melting pot, so that the physical collapse of the last in the line of the Spanish Habsburgs coincided with the beginning of the demise of his empire. Indecision, fatal vacilla-tion, profligacy, economic maladministration, religious zeal, fanatical imperialism: the ills and misdeeds of six successive generations had been given plenty of time to simmer together in varying proportions, along with gout, epilepsy, speech defects, obsessive sexual urges, extreme nervousness, religious melancholia.

In 1647 Philip IV married his niece Mariana of Austria. The bride was thirteen years old. Of her fifty-six forebears she had forty-eight in common with her uncle whom she was to marry and whose son she would have married had he not prematurely died. To keep the French Bourbons at a safe distance it was imperative that there should be a Spanish Habsburg heir. The menstrual cycle of the child-queen became a factor in the struggle for power in Europe, and all the while at court, where political rumour took on a life of its own, the artist portrayed the pawns in the game as well as the chess players.

When Velásquez painted the queen in 1653 she was barely nineteen and far from happy. There is no convention dictating that kings and queens should be portrayed happy, but if there is such a thing as the antithesis of a smile then that is what you see in the skin around the small red mouth which glistens alluringly thanks to a raffish fleck of white heightening. Velásquez is a past master of this technique, time and again he makes you forget that it is mere artifice, a flick of the brush, a touch of paint. In the portrait of Philip IV, the late one, you can see the scattering of brief, delicate strokes indicating the curl of fair hair rising from his forehead before it falls back, you know exactly how fine it was and what it was like to touch. Indeed you have then actually touched the hair, although the man has been dead for centuries, even as you can sense the disdain in the taut skin round his wife's mouth, her lips set forever in an expression of cold rage. The illusion is not due to the consummate artist's hyper-realism, to the imitation of nature, but to the creation of an image, an illusion, nonchalant deception which intensifies the realism, *sprezzatura*, the gesture of the courtier, the perfect angle of his sweeping bow, the indivisible and unrepeatable fraction of a second that the artist needed and a cold mouth glistens for eternity. Is that rage just my interpretation? I think not. It is apparent to me because it was apparent to the artist.

Royal children were collateral, on their mortal bodies depended territorial expansions, alliances, vast stretches of land; their adolescent bodies were expected to produce heirs to the throne and to confirm dynastic ties. They were pedigree cattle at the service of the state. All this is to be seen in Mariana's mouth: the news that you will not marry your cousin after all because he is dead, but that you are to marry his father, who is alive, instead. He may be your uncle, though he does not speak your language. The entourage at his court, which has become yours, consists of madmen, dwarfs and fools, but you are forbidden to laugh at them because a queen does not laugh. And that is not all: from now on you must suffer that large royal body to lie upon yours because an heir must be produced, the fate of continents depends upon it.

Just as Japanese emperors must spend the night before their investiture communing with the sun goddess in some lonely spot, so the

Spanish Habsburgs would be introduced to their future wives in the most god-forsaken places, conspicuously lacking in luxury and even in food or drink. In the case of Philip and Mariana it was Navalcarnero, a desolate hamlet in a desolate, rock-strewn plain. She was kept ignorant of his presence so that he could spy on her unawares. After all, he had never seen her before. The marriage would be a disaster, but on that particular evening she pleased him. We will never know what she looked like when she smiled, but she may well have laughed on that occasion, because a little comedy was performed to amuse them.

Was the artist present? There is no way of knowing that either. His king had conferred ever higher ranks on him since 1623, from *pintor de cámara*, court painter, he had risen to *ujier de cámara*, keeper of the bed-chamber, followed by his appointment as *alguacil de casa y corte*, high chamberlain of the royal family and court, and then *ayuda de guardarropa*, a title so daft in translation I prefer to leave it as it stands. He was to rise much higher in later years, but the bizarre designations reflected social reality, the offices were real enough and time-consuming, which probably explains why Velásquez did not leave a more extensive oeuvre. Be that as it may, the sheer proximity of his future model enabled him to study her at length, and soon enough she in turn felt no need to hide her persona from this man whose presence was so familiar, and there she stands: a body within a construction.

It can happen that, with overexposure, a painting's particularities cease to amaze you. The article of clothing worn by the queen is called a *guardainfante*, after the cushion-like extensions arching from either side of her waist, the farthingale. She looks like a ship in full sail, one has difficulty imagining the body underneath as that of a tall, long-legged northern woman. Because of the *guardainfante* and the twiggy scaffolding holding it all in place the skirt has become so wide that there is gross distortion and denial of the physical body beneath. The skirt is wider than her body is tall, and so she becomes a sort of dress-woman, a dress-mermaid, whose lower part consists of a hemisphere of black velvet richly embroidered with silver thread, which must have felt hard to the touch.

There is no doubt about it, the bottom half of this woman is an object, upon which she rests the hint of a small, glossy, pink-white hand with the large handkerchief (the same hand that later, when she is a widow and has adopted a nun's habit, will be depicted by other artists

Mariana of Austria, by Velásquez

as a naked chicken-claw) as though this velvet expanse projecting from her body has nothing to do with her. A similarly alienating effect is created around her head, where a semicircular nimbus of club-cut hair, which does not seem to have depth, stands out on either side of her face, forming once again an object surrounding the body, constricting and intensifying at the same time. The result is a sense of majesty which, once established, permits the psyche of the majestic subject to be revealed. Scarcely 5 per cent of the total picture surface is taken up by skin – hands, throat, face – and that is all the space available to either artist or royal personage for expressing the soul of this dress-woman, and this is the part they paint together, although it was his genius, to be sure, which seduced her into the collusion.

It can be very hard to detach oneself from a painting when the face-to-face encounter is so compelling. Having managed to put the artist for a moment out of my mind I am left alone with the woman (now that there is no one else here with me). The immediacy of what is taking place on the canvas leaves one feeling she is real. She breathes, she might move, notwithstanding the stillness of her pose. There is a certain erotic connotation here which I cannot ignore, even though she is dead and I am not yet among the living, and hence invisible. The social barriers have been removed only to be replaced by physical ones, and they come within the realm of melancholy. But just as I am about to indulge in sentimental reverie something extraordinary happens. A television crew has taken advantage of the peace of a Monday afternoon to do some filming, and sets the space which she and I find ourselves in ablaze with such light as was perfectly unknown in her time. Magic! Before I am asked to leave (this confrontation is never to be repeated) I see, in a flash, the magnitude of the deception, the *manchas distantes*, the distant smudges mentioned by Quevedo and which to many art historians prefigure Impressionism. As if, in the declining, arid Spain of the seventeenth century, this high chamberlain and friend of kings had lured, Pied Piper fashion, the Manets and Cézannes into the domain of colour and immediacy.

In the abrupt glare of twentieth-century arc-lights she loses none of the composure that is synonymous with her position. True, the over-bright red in her cheeks is set on fire, but the steely glint in her eyes is equally intensified. Indeed, the intensification is all-pervading and suffuses her whole being. The red in the circular stains on her cheeks is

echoed in the ribbons tied in the screen of hair. Then I realize they
are mere brushstrokes and that the shimmer of silk in that red is just a
splash of colour – I had been deceived with my eyes open, I knew and yet
I was taken in – and that the immediacy, that willingness to remove her
hand from the back of the chair (upon which only those of royal blood
were authorized to rest their hands, just as only courtiers above a certain
rank were allowed to hold the hands of royal children) consists in paint
exclusively. Exclusively? Of course not. It is the artist's concept,
expressed in matter, in pigment. This is common knowledge, and yet . . .
The harsh light and my unseemly proximity shatter the woman into
a thousand pieces. Not until I step back do they reassemble into the
vision of the painter. Then she is transformed once more from real into
ideal and the tug-of-war between truth and semblance can start all over
again. A century later Anton Raphael Mengs would say: "Velásquez
paints the truth not as it is but as it appears to be."

Truth, reality, lies, illusion, the thing itself or its name, are all will-
o'-the-wisps seeking to relegate the confusing tangos of meaning to the
ballroom of postmodernism or of metafiction, just to be rid of them for
a while, like a hornet that you chase away either because you are afraid
or because you find it annoying. But the hornet has always been there,
from the time when Plato took exception to deliberate illusion in sculpture up to and including the academic pussyfooting around realism and
nominalism, and thence to Berkeley and the rigged game Borges plays
with all these elements. The same hornet buzzes invisibly around the
mirror polemics of Van Eyck's *Giovanni Arnolfini and His Bride*, and
those of Velásquez's "*Las Meninas*", which in turn confounds Foucault,
but that doesn't happen until later. In the portrait of Queen Mariana it is
the deception of the method, or the method of deception that intrigues
me, not or not yet the metaphysical duplicity with which the painter of
"*Las Meninas*" fixes us in a mirror above the abyss.

According to Gombrich (in *Art and Illusion*), Rembrandt is supposed
to have said: "Don't stick your nose too far into my pictures or you will
be poisoned by the smell of paint." What he meant was that you would
literally see the light (as you would with Velásquez): luminous streaks,
swathes, sparkles, touches, creating the illusion of light and movement
and hence of veracity. Plato disapproved of such methods: this was a
way to create not the genuine article but a fake. That is why he was
also opposed to sculptors deliberately distorting the proportions of

"Las Hilanderas", by Velásquez

their statues so that, seen in a temple or from afar, they would appear natural, real. Velásquez went a step further. He falsified the fake, and employed paintbrushes with such long handles that distance became inherent. Look at the stroboscopic effect of the spinning wheel in *"Las Hilanderas"* (it really does turn), also the poppy-coloured splashes in the fan around the queen's head, the wild chase of red and white flecks in that animal brush of hair which elevates her mannered coiffure to a crown.

How did he do it? With great speed, say his contemporaries. But what about his slowness, his phlegmatism, which is also mentioned? When the artist lingers too long in Italy, the king misses him and instructs the Duke del Infantado that he must return forthwith for, as he writes in his own hand, *"ya conocéis su flema"*, you know how phlegmatic he can be. And yet he paints *alla prima*, without preliminary sketches (there are very few of his drawings in existence) and his earliest paintings already show prodigious technical skill, as though he had nothing further to learn. Expediency, dilatoriness and the unity of opposites. Ortega y Gasset knew how to deal with that: there are people whose only response to existential urgency is one of absolute calm, and such a man was Velásquez: "*Yo veo en Velásquez uno de los hombres que más ejemplarmente han sabido . . . no existir.*" Who knew in the most exemplary fashion how not to exist. The highly formalized life at court was regulated by a thousand clocks, and the artist had many time-consuming duties to perform that had no bearing on his art, and only someone who had dispensed with time for himself could find the time to create objects which cheat or deny the very existence of time.

He was twelve years old in 1611 when he was apprenticed to the academy of Francisco Pacheco in his birthplace, Seville. It was a meeting-place for the highly cultivated and erudite, and it was there that he first met the Count Duke of Olivares, who was later to introduce him to the court. By 1618 he had completed his studies, and the following year he married his mentor's daughter (she would survive him by one week). He painted his first portrait of the king in 1623, and thereafter his life revolved around the court. For Spain it was a period of decline, poverty, crippling taxation, and ill-fated wars, whereas at court it was a time of frenzied entertainment, factionalism and intrigue. Velásquez' thoughts on these things are not known. During a campaign in Aragón he paints two portraits in a few days. One is of the king in full battle dress and the other of the king's dwarf, Don Diego de Acedo, *El Primo*. The former was imprisoned in his kingship, the latter in his diminutive stature. Naturally, the artist accords each his proper rank, but from the depths of each portrait radiates the spirit, the soul, that which tells you that Velásquez recognized the intrinsic qualities of each, because he knew their truth.

There remains "*Las Meninas*". It is unlikely that I shall ever again have the opportunity to be so alone with that painting, but I have not made much progress. It is still a riddle, a cunning trick, and I'm not the only one to have fallen for it. Foucault thrashed this out in *Les mots et les choses*, Luca Giordano proposed that "this is the theology of painting", and Théophile Gautier complained: "but where is the painting?" The question is a reasonable one, because what I see is an artist painting a picture I cannot see. What I can see, however, is a painting which shows the artist painting a picture I cannot see, while his gaze is directed at me, whom he cannot see. I will be the first to admit that he's not actually looking at me (because that's impossible), but when he painted the picture he must have known that each Nooteboom, Foucault or Gautier standing in front of it would imagine the artist was looking at *him*. The artist takes a step back from the canvas he is working on (which we shall never see, *unless* it is the canvas we are looking at), he has dipped his fine long-handled brush in some light-coloured pigment (not a colour I happen to be wearing that day), takes another quick look (at whom?) and will presently continue to paint. I know all this because he has depicted himself in the painting I can see. But is he also in the painting I cannot see? Artists paint self-portraits with the aid of a mirror. Is there, in the spot where I am standing now (that is, one minute and three centuries later), a mirror in which he is painting himself? But is he really painting the picture I see? Surely the picture I am looking at shows him painting a *different* picture? But then who is in the other picture? Who are they all – apart from the painter himself there are others: three, maybe five, seven if you include the two onlookers in the mirror – looking at, if not at me? It is not me they see, of course, and yet they are looking in my direction. Are they looking at the king and queen who can see themselves reflected in the background? But if the artist is painting the portrait of the king and queen on the canvas I cannot see, how can he have painted them behind him in the mirror of the picture I *can* see?

Three, maybe five. The face of the man behind the hydrocephalic female dwarf is partly shaded, so I can't be sure about which way he is looking. The same goes for the man standing in the doorway like a gate-keeper to the world outside (thereby suggesting at least the possibility of escape from the labyrinth). But the radiant little princess, the sun around which the two planetary ladies-in-waiting (*las meninas*) gravitate, looks out at me (who is not there) or at her father and mother (who are there, according to the mirror). What Velásquez is painting here, towards the end of his life, is the sigh of a child, a wisp of down waiting to be blown away. He could not know, and yet he did. At sixteen she will be empress of Austria, at twenty-two she will be dead. But now (!) she looks at me still, as does the artist, as does the mighty hydrocephalus, and even when I turn and walk away, I come back again to find them still looking and there is something about their gaze that reminds me of something else and if I think about it long enough I may remember what it is.

Once, in Bangkok, a friend took me to see "something I hadn't seen before". Too true. Behind a gate there was a passage with a large shop

"Las Meninas", by Velásquez

window, for that is what it was, containing around thirty women wearing numbers pinned to their chests. They sat knitting, chatting, or staring into space. Sometimes they looked straight at you, but there was something unsettling about their blank eyes, as if they were looking through you, not seeing you at all, though they continued to look at you and you at them. Some of the men on my side of the glass picked a number and went in. Then you would see one of the women get up, her number had presumably been called, although we couldn't hear. That was the secret: we couldn't hear and they couldn't see. The glass in front of us was a two-way mirror. What they saw was themselves, not us.

"You mustn't forget that the *Meninas* picture is a construct," Rudi Fuchs, director of the Stedelijke Museum in Amsterdam, tells me when

I bump into him at Barcelona airport. "You must leave that painting alone," is the painter Jeroen Henneman's advice a few days later. But what if it is in fact a mirror they are all looking at, not just the artist but the rest too, dwarf, princess, courtier, *menina*? But not the dog, dogs don't look in mirrors. And what about the king and queen, how can they be seen as reflections in the picture if they are not standing in front of the mirror? Could they be standing next to the mirror reflecting the whole scene complete with them? I have tried to sketch the scene from above, a diagram with dotted lines indicating angles of vision and reflection, but I never succeeded. This conundrum was set up to exclude me, and by doing so has lured me inside. A construct indeed. Better to leave well alone. But even when you have crossed the painted space to exit into the world – José Nieto Velásquez, no relation, *jefe de la tapicería de la reina*, having courteously held aside the curtain before the lighted doorway – you can still feel the tough strands of an invisible spider's web, spun by a man three hundred years ago, tugging you back.

I leave Madrid and drive by way of Sigüenza to Alcañiz in Aragón. Table mountains, wilderness, now and then a few almond trees in blossom. The landscape exchanges the shades of Velásquez for those of Zurbarán,

The road from Sigüenza to Alcañiz

the colour of soil, drought, monks' habits. The king travelled here with his entourage in 1644, a year after the humiliating defeat of his 20,000 strong army at Rocroi.

It was the beginning of the end of this world-spanning empire, the watershed. The king and his company drew a halt at Fraga on the Catalonian border. In a tumbledown house the artist paints the king and his dwarf. The king was no longer welcome in the territory they had just crossed and yet he posed for three days while his portrait was painted. Fresh straw was brought in each day for him to stand on, to shield him from the cold that rose from the flagstones. Red, silver, black, full plumage, a dying species of bird. King, painter, dwarf, decked out in full court dress in these grim surroundings, must have thought they were dreaming.

VII

Whispers of Gold and Brown and Grey

The author's love of Zurbarán
The New York and Paris exhibitions ~ The artist's likeness
His origins, Fuente de Cantos ~ His biography
Studies of material ~ Painter of the imagination

OVER THE YEARS YOU BUILD UP relationships with the artists you love and admire, until in the end you're not sure when or why exactly it all started. My relationship with Zurbarán has been going on for years, as I can see from old travel diaries and the notes I made in the National Museum of Sculpture in Valladolid, in the Prado, in the monastery at Guadalupe, and in Seville. Only one of his paintings hangs in Valladolid, but it is certainly one of the strangest. On re-reading my notes – so far as I can decipher them now – one thing always comes to the fore: the matter, the fabric, what in Dutch we call *de stof*. In the days when people wore a lot of fabric on or about their person, artists depicted quantities of material, but no one did it in quite the same way as Zurbarán. With him the material ceases to be an attribute, it is a subject in its own right. Take away the head and the hands of the martyred Serapius and what remains is an upright monument of cloth, a construction which, regardless of where on that painting you begin the task of looking, rises before you as an adversary of equal merit, fencing you off with riddles as it sheers away. But more of that later.

Perhaps I was predestined to love the work of Zurbarán: perhaps I love it for the wrong reasons, though that seems hardly possible. First there's Spain. When Louis-Philippe opened his Spanish Gallery in Paris in 1837, Circourt referred to it as the "Iberian charnel house". By this he meant the Spain of the Inquisition, religious fanaticism, fascination with death, the Spain whose isolation from the rest of Europe made it the antithesis of the Enlightenment. The irony is that it was thanks to the spread of the Enlightenment that he was able to see the paintings at all. The liberals in power had closed the Spanish monasteries and declared their possessions forfeit. The result was an unimaginable clearance sale of whole collections of art.

Secondly, there were the monks. Zurbarán painted more of them than any other artist: monks in white, grey, brown, black habits. Some Orders have in the meantime died out, others live on, and their habits are the same as in those paintings. Otherwise, in the history of painting, only the naked body has changed as little. Painting as the art of conservation.

I was educated by monks (Franciscans, Augustinians) and I still visit the occasional abbey when I am on my travels (Trappist, Benedictine, Carthusian). So they still exist, although they have become almost invisible nowadays and are rarely sighted in the wild. But when you do see one his appearance is the same as in the paintings of Zurbarán. You cannot make much of this, but neither can one really deny it. Gown, habit, hood, scapular, all are usually made of tough material: monasteries tend to be cold. As I write I can feel the coarse scratchiness of the cloth, I have not forgotten that sensation since my boarding school days. I can feel it whenever I look at a painting by Zurbarán. Synaesthesia.

What would they have to be, the wrong reasons for loving Zurbarán's work? Could they have something to do with a notion of Spain I have long since abandoned, but which still lurks at the back of my mind, because Spain is such a cauldron of contradictions? A pathetic Spain, in love with death, prepared to turn itself away from Europe, a country that, once the Habsburgs' dreams have turned sour, rots away in isolation behind the Pyrenees, a country both bigoted and absolutist. The nineteenth century cherishes that vision:

> Moines de Zurbarán, blancs Chartreux
> qui, dans l'ombre
> glissent silencieux sur les dalles des
> morts,
> murmurant des Paters et des Avés sans
> nombre . . .*

So writes Théophile Gautier, and that obscurantist pastiche lingers on, finding ample confirmation, for anyone who cares to see, in the images

---

* Zurbarán's monks, white Carthusian habits / Who, in the shadows / Glide silently over the stones of the / Dead / Murmuring Our Fathers and Avé Marias without / End . . .

supplied by our present century: people crawling on their knees to shrines, bullfights that hark back to an unconscionable prehistoric time, processions of terrifying hooded and masked figures, and above all – when death really gets involved – the horrors perpetrated by both sides in the Civil War.

But he who has eyes only for the atrocities forgets that modernity was precisely what the Civil War was about, and that it was won by those who seemed to have lost. It felt as though Franco would rule for ever, but in the meantime the other Spain was quietly preparing itself, and now it is as if someone has pushed aside the barrier of the Pyrenees, as if the country has just now recovered from the bankruptcy of Philip II and, having digested the loss of colonies and international influence, can at last join in with all the pent-up energy of someone who has slept for four centuries. In Spain they refer to this moment in history as *Transición*, and one has to remember what the country was like under Franco to appreciate the frenetic vitality with which the changes are occurring, not least in the art world. You could say that Spain is *celebrating* change, mounting huge exhibitions to underscore its new presence, its special position between Europe and Latin America, its emotional and historical ties with the countries of North Africa.

But why Zurbarán? Why this singular obsession with saints, martyrs, monks, and crucifixion? Who is still interested in that earlier Spain which looks to be drifting rapidly away from us, which seems closer to the world of Dante than to our own? The answer must be a very simple one: that the subjects, the age, are of no importance. Zurbarán was doomed by circumstance and by the century of his birth to paint pictures of monks. Monks were his patrons and masters, they instructed him, to the smallest particular, on the subjects he might portray.

I remember some time ago in Florence having a conversation with a Dutch painter who declared himself to be "sick to death" of all the crucifixions and annunciations, of the interminable series of adorations of the Magi, of Jesus being scourged. He spoke from the privileged position of someone who selects his own subjects, who despises working to commission, who would probably prefer death to a lifetime of painting monks. But the point is that Zurbarán did not actually paint monks. He painted habits. He painted material. Hokusai painted a lion every day in the hope of one day achieving the perfect lion.

I know I am doing many aspects of Zurbarán's mastery an injustice, but it can't be helped. Fabric, material, *stuff*. What Zurbarán studied in painting after painting was matter, the plasticity of matter, the primary colours. He must have painted untold lengths of black and white cloth, sometimes several square metres in a single painting. All the riddles of light and shade, the shifting shadows made by folds and pleats in the material – he painted them all. And if I make bold enough to separate the commissioned subject-matter that Zurbarán the craftsman was expected to deliver from what he actually painted, the outcome is this: an essay on the relation between light, colour and material such as would not be seen again before Cézanne. He was concerned with something that lay far beyond the borders of human psychology or the anecdotal, a passion of such intensity as to justify calling it mystical. And there you have the paradox: that the idea of mysticism is not evoked by the representation, even if the subject is a mystical experience, but that two square metres of white or black, over which the anecdotal eye slides so casually (just a portion of the tunic in the lower right hand corner, say) do actually produce that effect.

Reproductions reveal none of this. The paintings must be studied in the original, and that is indeed what I did. I visited them in the places to which they had travelled or where they are at home (Guadalupe, Seville). Paintings, too, can be at home, albeit in exile. My last two encounters were in New York and Paris. The same exhibitions and yet not quite the same. Paintings missing in New York (*La Santa Faz*, "*Veronica's Cloth*" from Valladolid) could be seen in Paris, and paintings sorely missed in Paris (*Bodegón*, the hair-raising still life from the Museo de Arte de Cataluña in Barcelona) were there in New York.

This is perhaps the right place for me to confess to an inconsistency. After seeing the exhibition in New York I wanted to buy the catalogue, but only the hardback version was available, weighing a couple of kilos. I still had some travelling to do and didn't want to be lumbered with it, especially as I knew I would see the exhibition again in Paris. There the catalogue was sold out the second day. Again this was no great disappointment – over the years I have built up quite a substantial Zurbarán library. Later on I happened to see copies of both the American and the French catalogues in Amsterdam. According to the American edition I am in the wrong: the "*Veronica*" was in New York after all, indeed in two versions. One from Valladolid and one from the museum in Stockholm. Yet I am prepared to swear that the one from Valladolid was not to be seen in New York and that the one from Stockholm (much less fine and considerably less interesting) was absent from both New York and Paris. The Paris catalogue also lists the famous *Bodegón* from the Catalan art museum, whereas I know for certain it was not on view in Paris. Do such things matter? Only in as much as they demonstrate the fetish-value of the "genuine article". You are familiar with the paintings, you have seen them in their natural habitat (there where they have always been) and you want to see them again. A few days before the opening in Paris I saw two pantechnicons with Spanish licence plates rolling down the Champs Elysées under police escort, and I knew they contained the Zurbaráns. Maybe I was just being sentimental, but so be it. Paintings you first saw in a far-off Spanish monastery, and which you see again in New York, and then again in Paris, become like people. They can travel, just as you can; each time you meet is a reunion, and reunions are with people, not with things.

But who was this artist who disappeared behind his canvases? In *The Polish Rider* the twentieth-century Dutch novelist Simon Vestdijk presents a number of hypotheses about Rembrandt, to which he adds: "We will never know what Rembrandt's thoughts, emotions or intentions were. We are just as ignorant about his motives as we are about those of the makers of African sculptures, in which the modern admirer recognizes an array of cosmic horrors and barbaric demonism that no Negro could ever have dreamed of. Perhaps this is the ultimate confirmation of a work of art: that it transcends the artist's intentions, and that it is viewed differently and from new and surprising angles by each century and each observer." He goes on to say that this makes further speculation redundant, but I am inclined to take him more literally than he intended: that great art makes the artist redundant, his motives no longer count, he disappears into his paintings. The painter fuses with the painting and thereby with all those who look at it, and even with the thoughts it evokes in the viewer. Perhaps Zurbarán would dismiss my thoughts on his monochrome exercises as nonsense, but nevertheless he is the instigator of those thoughts. If some of this can be said to apply to Rembrandt, who after all left behind a series of self-portraits which preserve at least his vanished likeness, how much more true is it of Francisco de Zurbarán, whose biography is so fragmentary and obscure, and who left behind not a single self-portrait that is undisputed. There are theories, but they are based on two different portraits of two utterly dissimilar-looking men.

A remarkable book published in 1929 (Andrés Manuel Calzada, *Estampas de Zurbarán*) contains an illustration of one of these so-called portraits, a man with a curiously strained expression above a starched collar (from the Brunswick Museum). He points to a medallion, his hair is short and unevenly cut, the beard is strikingly geometric with one sharp point rising to the bottom lip. Experts have said that this intractable, somewhat unworldly figure is not Zurbarán and who am I to contradict them, although as far as I'm concerned this compact face does not contradict the unearthly silence in many of his paintings. But two men who do not look alike cancel each other out, leaving no face at all.

The "other" Zurbarán was on view at the Paris exhibition at the Petit Palais *From Greco to Picasso*, 1987. In this picture he supposedly portrayed himself as Saint Luke at the foot of the cross. The ages are the same, but that's about all. This man is bald, his face angular, his mouth set in an expression of meekness and forbearing which would be anathema to his alter ego. As a painting the latter is infinitely more beautiful, the dead or dying man on the cross and the living man with his palette below light up in the kind of gloom that gave its name to tenebrism, the wood of the cross is just a nuance against the nocturnal background, there is nothing but these two figures, the blackness of death and night itself, a monochrome plane which, when you draw near, sucks you in. Then, just as with the white, you discover the mysterious make of those primary colours; only *within themselves* do they tolerate nuances. If you put your face indecently close to the canvas you can see myriad events taking place within that black or that white: shifts, hairline cracks, markings, lispings of brown and gold and lead grey which dissolve as soon as you take a step back because an attendant is approaching or because you perceive that the other visitors take you for the village idiot.

Zurbarán. The name comes from the Basque and that is why some critics have tried to attribute his gloom to the northern heritage. Many of his paintings have a glow that, however subdued, has an ecstatic effect. In these paintings he breaks free from the meditations in black and white, but the expertise he gained therein enabled him to create a burst of flames, always within a fixed linear framework which, much later on in life, he would cast aside in favour of the delicate atmospheric effect of *sfumato*. The linearity gives rise to an extreme classical clarity from which the colour bursts forth, as in the cloak worn by the angel in the *Annunciation* in the Grenoble Museum. *Maniera, materia,* manner and material, here the material expresses the manner, the divine messenger's robe is on fire, the ochre mantle on his shoulders is the kind of yellow one sees in the red of a flame. Over her pink dress Mary wears a cloak of blue which darkens gradually, as so often with Zurbarán, until it is subsumed into the black. The "painterly" quality of the tender landscape which is visible in the background and which, briefly, recalls the Flemish Primitives, contributes to the sense of theatre, of performance. The woman's face is withdrawn, reclusive, this woman does not belong to the world, her eyes are truly hooded. At such moments one must be grateful to language for having preserved a word: these eyes are not closed, nor are they half-open, they are *hooded*, they signify absence, she no longer needs to see the angel, she herself has become the message.

There is no obligation to endorse the ideas of the period in which this painting originated, shared by the artist because he lived at that time. No one *needs* to, you can look at it just as an image. There is enough left.

Zurbarán lived in the south of Spain during the Counter-Reformation. Within that context, the woman he painted already existed for an eternity in the thoughts of God. In the monasteries he visits he hears the verses from Proverbs (8: 23, 24) that are spoken on the feast of her Immaculate Conception: "*Ab aeterno ordinata sum, et ex antiquis, antequam terra fieret* . . . I was set up from everlasting, from the beginning, or ever the earth was. When there were no depths, I was brought forth; when there were no fountains abounding with water . . ." This has nothing to do with reality and yet it *is* a kind of reality, the reality of the artist. It is inconceivable that none of this should be perceptible in the painting, and therefore it is perceptible, even to people who do not know or believe. Reality, unreality: the domain of art. In this painting heaven and earth are united in dogma; visible magic, for even when the dogma has faded the magic remains.

I am familiar with the region of Zurbarán's birth, and also with the places where he lived and worked. He was born in Fuente de Cantos, which sounds like Fountain of Songs, although Geanine Baticle (*Zurbarán, Aperçu de sa vie et son œuvre,* in the Paris exhibition catalogue) maintains that a better translation would be the so much more Spanish phrase Fountain of Stones. Stones aplenty in that sere, flat region between Mérida, Badajoz and Seville. The Romans left behind monuments, the landscape is stern, classic, sober, the villages are splashes of white that hurt your eyes. A person can be seen approaching from a great distance, outlined against the light that defines people as statues, the dimensions of the landscape lend every movement a certain solemnity. All these things penetrated deep into his eyes, his environment was his first teacher.

In that contemplative, ascetic landscape Seville is a great oasis, there flows the Guadalquivir, colours sparkle. Zurbarán sees the colours without ever forgetting their absence and solemn monotony in his native region. With the exception of a few years spent in the vicinity of the court in Madrid, this is where he lives for most of his life. Seville is mighty, the port of embarkation to the colonies, and only later in his life will this change.

His biography raises the same questions as his non-existent self-portraits, the books about him contradict and correct one another, his shadowy existence is sometimes truly mysterious, new documents are still coming to light. Death stalked his life, two of his wives died, not one of the many children borne by his last and very much younger wife was alive at the time of his death, and his son by his first wife, who painted wonderful, hushed *bodegones*, still lifes with fruit, pitchers, bowls, died before him of the plague. He was a contemporary of Velásquez, who was a friend but who towered above him at court. Another contemporary was Alonso Cano, who tried to subject him to a humiliating entrance exam to the painters' guild when he had already produced some of his finest works. Murillo was younger, and his Italianizing flair brought him more success. Some books claim that Zurbarán was jealous of the younger artist, but this is refuted by a recently discovered letter, and anyway jealousy is too unworthy a sentiment for the man who painted these canvases.

Let me get back to them now. They have something in common with their master, their fate is marked by vicissitudes that often defy explanation, sometimes there are sections missing, as in the enigmatic still life with quinces which was to be seen at the Petit Palais. It hangs in the Museo de Arte de Cataluña, but the provenance is unknown. Experts believe it is part of a larger canvas, but the four quinces do not mind, they lie there like a study for a Zen master, a riddle to be solved, *things*, powerful and self-assured. Some pictures have disappeared without trace, others, which once belonged in a group, have been forcibly separated and are scattered across the world. In Paris, for the first time, they are reunited, and later, when the exhibition closes, they must part again, maybe for ever or maybe for a few centuries. Then the angel with the fiery orange robe (originally from the Carthusian monastery of Nuestra Señora de la Defensión in Jerez de la Frontera) will return to Grenoble; the paintings on either side will go to New York and Cádiz.

As I write, I have on my desk a postcard of *La Santa Faz* ("*Veronica's Cloth*", *Verdadera efigie*, the true effigy). Pictures of that effigy are to be found in all the books I possess, but the postcard is dearest to me, because I bought it in Valladolid, in the museum where I first saw the painting. *La Santa Faz*, the holy face, painted by Francisco de Zurbarán, who called himself *pintor de ymaginaria*, in the old Spanish that still employed the *y* as *i*, the Y, *La Pythagorica letra*, the Pythagorean letter that points in two directions (Andrés Manuel Calzada, *Estampas de Zurbarán*). Painter of the imagination, indeed. Legend has it that Christ, on his way to Golgotha bearing the instrument that was to become the emblem of Christendom, pressed his face into the cloth held out to him by Veronica. The "real" cloth, which is kept in Turin, shows the features of a man in agony. Zurbarán's *ymaginaria* paints the face otherwise, not a frontal view this time but a three-quarter profile, the left ear nearest the observer. That's about all there is. This face is literally faceless. There are no eyes and only if you are adamant is there a mouth, simply because you know there has to be one. But the place where it should be is empty, the face is absent, a canvas-coloured smudge in the orange, rusty, ginger nimbus of hair and beard.

"Zelt, Kapelle, Kreuz," said a German voice as I stood before the painting, and indeed one can see it as such: the tent as chapel, the form as crucifix.

It is a late work, from 1658, and that "*Veronica*" epitomizes his textural mastery, the mastery of the interminable lengths of monastic white he depicted throughout his life. "Flesh he painted from memory but the habits he draped on a doll (*maniquí*)", noted a contemporary, and you try to imagine how he set about painting the cloth (why am I suddenly reminded of the man in the Brunswick portrait?). He takes the cloth, unfolds it, feels the material. He was a tactile painter, you can always *see* how a fabric felt to the touch. He lifts the cloth, observes how it hangs in folds, holds it out, each hand grasping the fabric at a point just below the top edge and equidistant from the middle, and then the surplus material bunched in each fist is tied with string by an invisible assistant. Within the white fabric looms the face that is faceless, and once the cloth is hanging it turns out that it is better to use a barely perceptible thread to secure a point right in the middle of the top edge to the deep red glow of the wall behind, in order to prevent the material from sagging over the forehead. The cloth hangs in the folds prescribed by the weight, thickness and texture of the material, the creases made by Veronica when she folded her cloth are still faintly visible, there is nothing accidental in the way it is draped; this cannot be proven and yet it is so.

Now the artist writes his name on a crumpled piece of paper, which he subsequently nails to the wall. The paper is slightly torn, a similar tear (though in a different place) can be seen in the scrap of paper next to the figure of the tormented Serapius, as if with these minute tears he wishes to indicate some kind of imperfection. It is obvious that this saint has been martyred, the left hand is lifeless, that of a dead man, it is only because the wrists are tied with ropes that the scaffolded tunic stays upright. The dead man is a puppet.

What the painter has concealed is the disembowelment, the missing entrails coiled on to a winch, which I saw once in another painting. Put your face up close to the robe again and the effect is mesmerizing.

And now for a childish trick, but what of it: cover a large part of the canvas and see what you have left. Cover just the hands and the head and you are left with a monument; sink further, past the waist, and you are left with an abstraction – the word says it all – in which the eye can lose itself. Now the infinitesimal transverse strokes become visible, pustules, cracks, flecks of red, of grey and darker shades, there where you look into the depths of what reveals itself as a fold once you step back again and the paintwork reassembles into a picture. How I wish I had a magnifying glass!

I saw the other painting of Serapius in Paris too, in 1981, and I would willingly have believed it to be by another artist. The exhibition I saw was an attempt to reconstruct the collection of Louis-Philippe, which was scattered far and wide. In that picture, or in the reproduction, could be seen the devolution from facture to factory. Zurbarán, like so many of

Saint Serapius, by Zurbarán

his contemporaries, also ran a little factory. He supplied angels, Caesars on horseback, Immaculate Conceptions by the dozen, to the colonies. There are bills of lading to Lima and Buenos Aires, and even in those days Argentinian debts were not honoured: eleven years after sending the invoice he was still waiting for his money. The extent of his contribution to this mass production cannot always be ascertained, but the "other" Serapius certainly looked more repulsive, pathetic even, with his disembowelled belly jutting out and his entrails wound on to a reel.

But that Serapius is not included in this show, other martyrs, women, have taken his place: and the contrast could not be greater.

Their martyrdom is not portrayed, it is emblematically represented as metaphor, the death they died has vanished miraculously, they are ladies in full regalia, they are going places, off to the theatre, on the move, they always turn to look at the viewer, they are *mujeres que andan*. All they have is the emblem of their death, and suddenly those elements that are intended to inspire horror take on a culinary slant: the eyes of Saint Lucy lie on the pewter dish like a couple of poached eggs, the holy Agatha's breasts are two perfectly turned-out little puddings. Rather than suffering, the mood of these women is pensive. Their bodies are hidden under billowing, flowing robes of fabulous luxury. Not for them the mortification of the hair shirt, but rather the voluptuousness of velvet, silk and satin. There is a passionate, controlled sensuality in this clothing, the other side of the Spanish soul, flamboyant yet restrained. Nowhere is this more evident than when lust and excess (*lujuria*, luxury) go hand in hand with death.

Something similar happens at the entombment of Saint Catherine: the sword, the deadly wheel studded with curved knives, next to the open tomb into which she is lifted by angels. Some angels! I remember how, in a Viennese palace garden once, I realized for the first time what a strange creature the sphinx is, simply because I asked myself at which point the woman's flesh ended and the lion's began, and how the eagle's wings were anchored in the woman's flesh. Suddenly I saw her through the eyes of a forensic pathologist, and was amazed that I had never thought of it that way.

Something similar happens to me here. I see three extremely handsome male angels as *possible* beings, I see how carefully they have to manoeuvre the silk-shrouded body so as not to impede each other with their huge upright wings, I imagine them flapping, and the sound that makes, and I want to know what sort of feathers they have, and then I want wings of my own, and then the moment passes.

For a fleeting instant I had wings, at an exhibition of Francisco de Zurbarán, in Paris, in 1988.

VIII

In the Footsteps of Don Quixote –
the Roads of La Mancha *

Fact and fiction ~ Cervantes eclipsed by the Don ~ Cervantes' home
in Madrid ~ A meal in Chinchón ~ Quixote's windmills
Dulcinea's house ~ The cave where Quixote was born
Cervantes triumphs

MIGUEL DE CERVANTES IS SEATED at his writing desk. He is penning for the first time the name of his hero. Some characters who have never existed are so firmly anchored in history that one cannot imagine a world without them. One such is Don Quixote de La Mancha. Cervantes is nearly fifty years old when he creates his hero, invents a name for him, and gives him the same age. "Our gentleman was verging on fifty, of tough constitution, lean-bodied, thin-faced, a great early riser and a lover of hunting." Perhaps the author couldn't quite decide on a name for his hero at first, indeed there is a suspicion of prevarication in: "They say that his surname was Quixada or Quesada – for there is some difference of opinion amongst authors on this point."

Thus is the reader drawn into that shadowy realm halfway between reality and fantasy by which, if he is a good reader, he will be captivated. Plainly there were no authors at all, and hence no conflicting views. Cervantes simply hasn't yet made up his mind. He tries using the name Quexana, but leaves the ultimate decision to his non-existent protagonist: "Finally he resolved to call himself Don Quixote." The only thing that was clear from the start was where he came from, although the writer himself was reluctant to divulge the secret of which he was the sole keeper: "In a certain village in La Mancha, which I do not wish to name . . ." So we do not know the exact location, only the general area. And that brings us face to face with one of the fantastic ambiguities of

*Quotations in this chapter from Cervantes, *Don Quixote*, translated by J. M. Cohen, Penguin Books, 1950.

La Mancha that will preoccupy the traveller throughout his tour. The region is real enough, the hero is not. The author who was named Cervantes was real, too, but from that blessed moment when he decided that his non-existent hero was a man of La Mancha he endowed that curious region of Spain with an added value that the towns, villages and landscapes of La Mancha would never give up.

And that is why the traveller four centuries later has the greatest difficulty in separating fact from fiction in the same regions where Miguel de Cervantes set his Don Quixote to roam. The author has become more shadowy than his hero. Everyone knows what Don Quixote looked like, for all that he never existed, but there is no trustworthy depiction of his creator. Cervantes did provide a description of his appearance, but his likeness was not drawn or painted during his lifetime. That explains why the statues of him resemble each other only in apparel. It may be said that he did not make things easy for his would-be portraitists:

> The man you see before you, with his sharp profile, chestnut brown hair, smooth and high forehead, cheerful eyes and curved nose, although it is of good size; with his silver beard, which was golden twenty years ago; with heavy moustaches, a small mouth, teeth which one can describe as neither large nor small, for he has but six and those are poorly cared for and even more poorly placed, as there are gaps between them all; with his stature between two extremes, for he is not tall, but neither is he short; with his lively complexion, which tends towards the pale rather than the swarthy; with his somewhat bent back, and not too quick-footed; this man, I repeat, is the author of *La Galatea* and of *Don Quixote of La Mancha*.

The problem with Cervantes is that because, unlike his Don, he was a real person, apparently no one felt they could indulge their fantasies of him. Ever since Daumier's and Gustave Doré's illustrations of Don Quixote and Sancho Panza their appearance has been established. Shut your eyes and this is how you see them. In this contest between the imaginary and the real the former emerges the winner. The author is the one who is imagined, his characters are real; nor do you doubt this for a moment when you see the many statues of the Knight and his Squire in all those still surviving towns where their imaginary adventures took place.

I began my journey to La Mancha in Madrid. In a book of 1871 entitled *Castilian Days* and written by John Hay, I had read about the house where Cervantes lived in Madrid, and I wanted to see it. It is to be found, no surprise, in the Calle de Cervantes, the same street where Lope de Vega lived, although it was named differently in those days. Now there are two ancient, narrow streets close together, named after these two great men of Spanish letters who, as is usual in literary circles, had many unpleasant things to say about each other.

Lope de Vega, the man who wrote two thousand plays and "one-and-twenty million verses", was a very successful author in his day, while Cervantes led a life of adventure. He fought at sea, was wounded in battle, was captured by Barbary corsairs and spent five years with his brother as a slave in North Africa until he was ransomed by a monk. But even then fortune did not come his way. He served in a humble capacity in Seville, and was imprisoned for debt. He applied unsuccessfully for an appointment in the colonies. He hoped to accompany his benefactor, the Count of Lemos (to whom the Quixote is dedicated), to the court of Naples in his old age – but none of these hopes materialized. Even the immediate popularity of his *Don Quixote* did not make him a rich man, and it was nine years before he eventually completed the second part. It was published one year before his death.

The last letter to his benefactor shows that he remained true to his idiosyncratic self until the end: "The foot poised in the stirrup, the pallor of death already on the cheeks, I write to you, illustrious lord, these lines. Yesterday I received the last rites, today I write you this letter; the time-span is brief, the breathlessness increases, hope diminishes, and yet the will to live keeps me upright: Would that I could keep that will long enough to salute Your Excellency and kiss your feet." Four days later he died and was buried in a convent nearby, in the street that is now named after Lope de Vega.

It is early Monday morning when I stroll down these two streets bearing writers' names. It is raining in Madrid this month of May. I look around for the commemorative plaque referred to in my book of 1871, but because the author does not give the house number it takes some time to find. It's at number 20. While my friend Eddy Posthuma de Boer does his best in the rain to photograph the plaque I take shelter in the doorway. A little old woman in black is sprinkling sawdust on the doorstep; her tiny shop has an extremely narrow doorway and a small display in the window of buttons, lengths of material and reels of thread. She does not approve of my being there. She is ancient, she belongs to the Madrid of Cervantes, not to the Madrid of the economic boom.

Across from the great author's house there is now a launderette, but that is just about the only sign of modernity in all the street. A few doors down I see a *despacho de carbones*, a dimly lit cavern piled high with charcoal, and a *churrería*, a small wall-tiled bakery where *churros*, loops of dough fried in oil, are baked in a wood-burning oven. I observe the old charcoal vendor, black as a miner, and the iron-banded wheels of his handcart. I do not need to hear the wheels to know how they will sound on the big cobblestones. Round the corner I find the convent where Cervantes is supposed to have been buried. An inscription on the façade identifies the building as a convent of the Holy Trinity; the writer was buried there at his own request in gratitude for his rescue from slavery by a member of the Trinitarian Order.

I fumble with the doorknob and let myself into a gloomy hallway off which a second door stands ajar. Then I find myself before something that is clearly the entrance to the church, but it is closed. Another door is pushed open gently and two nuns peer around it. "Is this where Cervantes is buried?" I enquire, and the answer they give me is highly Spanish: "Yes, but he is not here." I say I'd like to take a look in the church anyway, but am told that this is impossible. The mass has already been celebrated, and the church is always locked afterwards.

"Is there a tomb?"

"No, there isn't really a tomb."

The author has done what he can to erase his tracks, but it isn't quite so easy to escape posterity. Near the parliament building, the Cortes, there is a small triangular park with a statue. The ground is muddy from the incessant downpour and perhaps that is why the statue looks a bit dazed, a writer-soldier who has wandered into the wrong century, the sharp profile protruding from the stone ruff like that of some exotic bird. The reliefs on the pedestal show scenes from his novel, the Knight and his Squire whom I will encounter in so many guises during the next few days, and an Empire-style female figure floating in the air holding a lily – his muse, to be sure. There we stand, face to face, in the rain, somewhat sheepish, he of stone and I of rather less durable matter. It's almost as if he is mocking me, nor do I blame him. Writers are not alive in their statues but in their books, and if I want something from him I had better

Cervantes, Madrid

go out into the landscapes which are the setting for the adventures he relates.

A few hours later, after we have driven out of Madrid, the land is open and vast, imposing cloud-ships sail across the mighty sky, but the rain has stopped. This is still Castile, the land which, seen from an aeroplane, is an arid plateau, red, brown, sandy: the *meseta*. Now it has rained so much, it is not as stark as in summer, the verges are dotted with the bright flowers of late spring, poppies, nettles, daisies, dandelions, orgies of gold and red and blue and purple, the horizon sways ahead of us, and once we have turned off the main road everything is empty around us, with the feeling of liberation that goes with it.

We have decided to stop in Chinchón, where the best *anís* in Spain is produced. In the centre of the village is the Plaza Mayor, that most Spanish of all inventions, the heart and core of every town in Castile, from Madrid to the remotest backwater. But there is something unorthodox about this square. It is not rectangular, but elliptical. It reminds me of an arena or theatre. The ground is sandy, the houses surrounding it have terraces which double as theatre boxes and which are now being used as restaurants.

Eating is still an earthy pleasure here, great tureens of soup with garlic, bread and egg, *sopas de ajo*, roast lamb and sucking pig, peasant dishes like *duelos y quebrantos*, eggs with a big wedge of red sausage, salads of tomato and onion, litre-sized pitchers of heavy red wine. From the terrace I have a grandstand view of the performance of the single actor on the stage, the village policeman keeping an eye on us all from below. I can hear the sound of fountains, of birds, the church bell that tells us that yet another piece of time has expired. From the different side streets off the plaza, the same old man seems to emerge time and again as if in some surrealist play: leaning on a stick, he takes a very long time to cross the expanse of sand where the bulls are let loose once a year. The paving in front of the town hall is being swept, swallows dive low over the ground. Now and then the sun comes out, in the bakery, the *fábrica de pan*, the lovely Señora Vidal teaches me the names of all the different cakes and rolls and loaves, and I wish I could sit there for ever on the Plaza Mayor in the protective embrace of the *galerías*, with a paper bag full of *mantecados de anís* beside me. But this is not yet La Mancha. The dark tiled walls of the bar of the Mesón de la Vireyna are hung with photographs of dancing girls in Castilian costume and of fearsome bulls chasing men around the arena of the plaza. We have an appointment with those other, far more fearsome adversaries, Don Quixote's windmills.

The first one we see, standing in battle formation that afternoon on a long range of hills near Consuegra, offers firm proof that the Knight of the Sad Countenance was right. If you can't see that, you are crazy yourself. The light is false, a leaden grey streaked with brass like the backdrop of a tragic opera. And of course they are not windmills but men wildly flailing their arms, dangerous warriors, high-born knights. Nabokov, who devoted an exhaustive study to the Don, says succinctly: "Notice how alive the windmills are in Cervantes' description." And alive is what they are:

> "Look over there, friend Sancho Panza, where more than thirty monstrous giants appear. I intend to do battle with them and take all their lives . . ."
>
> "What giants?" asked Sancho Panza.
>
> "Those you see there," replied his master, "with their long arms. Some giants have them about six miles long."
>
> "Take care, your worship," said Sancho; "those things over there are not giants but windmills, and what seem to be their arms are the sails, which are whirled round in the wind and make the millstone turn."
>
> "It is quite clear," replied Don Quixote, "that you are not experienced in this matter of adventures. They are giants, and if you are afraid, go away and say your prayers, whilst I advance and engage them in fierce and unequal battle."
>
> As he spoke, he dug his spurs into his steed Rocinante, paying no attention to his squire's shouted warning that beyond all doubt they were windmills . . . At that moment a slight wind arose, and the great sails began to move . . . then, covering himself with his shield and putting his lance in the rest, he urged Rocinante forward at a full gallop and attacked the nearest windmill, thrusting his lance into the sail. But the wind turned it with such violence that it shivered his weapon in pieces, dragging the horse and his rider with it, and sent the knight rolling badly injured across the plain.

What you see as you approach Consuegra is the author's flash of inspiration. In a certain light, a certain configuration of clouds, the shimmering heat suspended over the plateau gives everything a spectral, unreal quality. It was Cervantes himself who recognized giants in these windmills before his Knight set eyes on them, and now that I am standing by the ruins of the castle, I cannot quite rid myself of that fantasy. They are mills, to be sure, but with that one dead eye marking the pivot of the four revolving sails they are also living creatures in a menacing battle formation. I linger among the slate-coloured rocky outcrops, gaze over the plateau stretching limitlessly westwards, past the crumbling crenellated walls, and each time I turn I see the ever-watchful windmills silhouetted against the darkening, doom-laden sky. No, up there on the crest you are not in the ordinary world, but in the world of the imagination. Below lies La Mancha of the earth: the fields, the pigs, the hams and cheeses, a material world of tangible things. But from up here that same material world acquires a dream-like, unconscionable quality, where nothing is as it seems. The world of Cervantes and his hero, of whom Nabokov said: "We no longer laugh at him, his escutcheon is compassion, his banner is beauty. He stands for everything that is gentle, lost, pure, altruistic, and gallant."

Surveying the sweeping landscape from this eminence it is as if the way ahead has been laid out on display for my benefit. The roads straggle across the southern *meseta*, a scorched plateau in summer, cold and inhospitable in winter. Bounded by the Tagus in the north and the Guadiana in the south, the land of the Campo de Calatrava stretches before me with its knight's fortresses and palaces, La Mancha with its cornfields and vineyards without end. Those are the roads travelled by knights, whores, couriers, soldiers, beggars, monks, bankers, Moors, Jews, Christians, the fabric of history.

That evening we reach Almagro, one of those Spanish wonders the sun-seekers of Benidorm have never heard of: white, still, enigmatic, a memory of lost greatness. The Plaza Mayor is rectangular here, a large living room with glassed-in verandas like walls. This is where the Fuggers, Charles V's Swabian bankers, who had trade relations in all corners of the Spanish empire, constructed their Renaissance palace. We sleep in the convent of Santa Catalina, now a parador, built around an old cloister. Here there is nothing for the imagination to do, one is drawn into ancient times without resistance. This was the headquarters of the Order of Calatrava, the oldest in Spain, founded by Cistercian monks in 1158 to drive out the Moors. Initially they wore monks' garb, later they took to wearing a white cloak with a cross of red lilies. In the twilight you think you can see them flitting about the narrow streets. Everywhere you look there are buildings emblazoned with the arms of extinct families: lions, crowns, quarterings, banners, hints of courtly loves and battles, power and transience.

When dusk has fallen, I take a stroll around the square, but I do not see it properly until the next day. In the torpor of the afternoon men doze on park benches, the flag above the town hall hangs limp, I read the poem on the statue of Diego de Almagro, captain general of the kingdom of Chile, who died in Cuzco without setting eyes on his birthplace in Almagro again. He does not resemble Don Quixote, this knight on his steed, he charged not at windmills but against Amerindians, and perhaps that is why the world – save for Almagro – has forgotten him.

I visit the churches and the wonderful little playhouse with its roof of open sky, and wonder what it was like to observe the stage from one of the boxes with a flickering oil lamp by your side, and to hear the words of Lope de Vega and Calderón de la Barca under the moon and the stars.

The literary pilgrim – let us call him – following in the footsteps of the Knight and his Squire, need not search very far. On the edge of each town along the Ruta de Don Quijote helpful souls have fixed a metal sculpture of the two heroes to a wall, the same each time, so you can't get it out of your mind: you see the two of them, cut out like a black, iron daguerreotype, travelling the same road as you, the tall frayed Knight on horseback, his lance at the ready, flanked by his short stout companion riding a donkey. The sculptors have busied themselves in the town centres, too, all the way from Ciudad Real up to and including El Toboso. Sometimes there are quotations from the book on street corners, so that after a while it is hard to tell whether you are travelling in a book or in the real world.

So what can I say about visiting Dulcinea's home? It is in El Toboso, a silent town, the kind of silence that kindles the imagination. In the centre of the village stands the church of Saint James, which in Don Quixote's imagination was the palace of his beloved. I follow the signs on the walls and after the final one I find myself in a narrow cul-de-sac, *en una callejuela sin salida*, in front of the house where Dulcinea lived. There it is, you can reach out and touch it, you can even go inside. For someone to whom writing is his lifeblood this is an extraordinary moment.

To enter a house that once belonged to someone who never existed is no small matter. Milan Kundera has called *Don Quixote* the first true novel, and if one of the main characteristics of the novel is the supremacy of the imagination over reality, with all the attendant possibilities of escaping from the restrictions of that so-called reality, then the genius of Cervantes has demonstrated the power of the imagination once and for all, if only because I am standing here now almost four centuries later staring at the house, the hearth, the bed, the kitchen utensils of someone who is but an invention. Only once before have I experienced the same excitement, and that was when I was gazing up at Romeo and Juliet's balcony in Verona, jostled by a hundred Japanese with cameras.

I inspect the garden, the courtyard, the olive tree, the wine press, and listen to the babble of the nun-like guide doing her very best to explain whom Dulcinea is modelled upon. But I don't want to hear any of that, I don't want the fantasy to be contaminated by random speculations about historical reality, I want to leave this place at once and go to that other town, not 50 kilometres from here, where Dulcinea is supposed to have been invented, Argamasilla de Alba, and whether that story is true or not is immaterial to me. But first I must go to the town hall, where a diligent mayor has assembled a collection of Quixotes (I mean the paper ones this time, the books).

The awful thing about masterpieces is that they belong to the common weal, and thus as well to people you hate and despise. It goes for Hamlet, as for the Don. An old man leads us through a classroom full of openmouthed schoolchildren to a side room where the books are displayed, open for all to see. Who has not read *Don Quixote*? All the rich and famous appear to have donated their personal copies – Mitterrand, Prince Bernhard of the Netherlands, Margaret Thatcher, Adolf Hitler, Hindenburg, Mussolini, King Juan Carlos of Spain, Alec Guinness, Juan Perón, Ronald Reagan, a collection of saints and sinners, from which Stalin is absent only because the copy he sent with a dedication on the flyleaf has been lost.

There are two kinds of light in the world, the light of humans and the light of photographers, and the latter dictates that we postpone our departure until tomorrow. We spend the night in a hotel on the main road from Madrid to Valencia, in Mota del Cuervo. Unsurprisingly, it is named Hostal Don Quijote. My room is small and dark, and my soporific is the patter of rain and the rumble of articulated lorries. But before retiring, writer and photographer have a conversation about the appearance of the Knight and his Squire. "I see a lot of Sanchos in the street," the photographer says, "and not very many Don Quixotes. Still, they must be somewhere." He has a point, but *I* think the squires will become as scarce as their masters. One is struck by Sancho through the comparison with his master. So, who really endowed Don Quixote with his physical appearance? Who *coined* him? Cervantes, of course, but still we wonder whether he would have recognized his hero in the engravings of Gustave Doré, for all that it is clear that Doré based his illustrations on the author's description. But even in Picasso's *Don Quixote* the Doré prototype shines through, so who in the end can be said to be the creator of the flesh-and-blood Don we see before us when we read the book? How much stronger is an image conjured up by words than the words themselves, when that image is capable of transcending its own verbal origins? The question remains unsettled. Meals in La Mancha are a tour de force, as if the Middle Ages still hold sway here. The partridges that fly up from the bushes during the day lie on the table in earthenware dishes by nightfall, and the Zagarrón, bottled next door, is a wine that can take on a whole battalion of game.

The next day the rain plays cat and mouse with us. It is dry at the enormous castle of Belmonte, which lies like a stranded ark in the rippling landscape, but it is raining again when we drive into Argamasilla in search of Cervantes' prison. We follow the directions of a shepherd and walk through the narrow streets of the village to a big green door. I knock, and after a long pause I hear an old, shrill voice calling out *Sí!* Nothing else. I let fall the big iron knocker once more, and then appears an old woman, bent almost double. Her hair is white and she has a beautiful face. The cave is somewhere else, she says, and we follow her through the rain, two giants suddenly, with a dwarf, invented by the writer. She unlocks a door with a key bigger than her hands and points to a descending flight of steps. This is where the writer was gaoled, and where he is said to have written the first chapters. I believe it all, for there is a small wooden table with an inkwell and two quills. Never take a writer into the study of a fellow writer because it will either make him miserable, or he will be sorely tempted to take a seat at the table himself. I am of the second persuasion, and I try to see what

Cervantes saw when he wrote those opening words. But then I have also to think away the electricity, the memorial plaques on the walls, the photographer and his camera. That leaves me with the stone vaulted ceiling, the sound of the rain from above, footfalls in the street, the wind, the scratching of a pen. For the rest silence, the silence in which those opening sentences of the prologue were composed: "Idle reader, you can believe without any oath of mine that I would wish this book, as the child of my brain, to be the most beautiful, the liveliest and the cleverest imaginable. But I have been unable to transgress the order of nature, by which like gives birth to like. And so, what could my sterile and ill-cultivated genius beget but the story of a lean, shrivelled, whimsical child, full of varied fancies that no one else has ever imagined." These strange thoughts have preoccupied mankind ever since, they have been lost and found their way into sayings and pictures, have been translated into every language – this cellar would have to be a hundred times bigger to hold them all. And yet it is as empty as it was when the writer first entered it. Riddles. Words, and images, plucked from the empty air.

The old woman stands at the top of the steps, waiting. She points outside, to a bust of the writer under an apricot tree, but that doesn't help solve the riddles.

The following day we travel through La Mancha under changing skies. We visit the inn in Puerto Lápice where the innkeeper made Don Quixote a knight, sleep in the high castle of Alarcón with an embrasure offering a view over the entire region, and drive past the Lagunas de Ruidera to the wild Sierra de Alcaraz. We see churches, castles, the hanging houses and the marvellous museum of abstract art in Cuenca, and the Roman ruins in the deserted land of Segóbriga. The sun comes out again and bathes the cornfields in light. I write down the names of dishes, cheeses, wines, inns, villages; an old needlewoman explains to me that all the different embroidery stitches are named after insects and reptiles, but in spite of all those distractions the Knight of the Sad Countenance and his author still hold me captive.

I remember reading in John Hay's book that the author intended to visit the font where Cervantes was baptized in the church of Santa María la Mayor in Alcalá de Henares. It is Sunday when we arrive. There is already the faint smell of the city here, Madrid is close by, this spin has almost come full circle. We see the splendid façade of the old university with its Plateresque main entrance and its Manueline stonework knots, the umpteenth statue of the author, this time holding a goose quill up to the blue sky as if he wants to fill that too with his script, the strolling crowds in the colonnade of the Calle Mayor, the house he lived in if he ever lived there, and finally the church. The church was closed when Hay visited it a hundred and more years ago, and it is closed now, but we go in through a side entrance and find ourselves on the stairs leading to the choir. Two men come to say that we are not allowed in here, but I explain to them that we are looking for Cervantes' baptismal font.

They are no match for such nonsense and leave us alone in the semi-darkness. Everything is closed below, they say, so if you want to stay here it's at own risk. The church seems to have fallen into disuse, but when my eyes have grown accustomed to the gloom I suddenly catch sight of it after all: the marble, faintly luminous contours of the font. Filled with the elation of a mission completed, we go outside again, into the harsh light of the Spanish afternoon.

IX

A Little History

I SEE THE PHOTOGRAPH IN *El País* 5 March 1983. On the left, his face turned away from me and from all Spaniards, sits *el jefe del Estado Mayor del Aire*, Emilio García Conde. He is the chief of staff of the Air Force, but why does his title sound in Spanish as if he is in command of the very air? He is wearing large suede shoes. On his left is the Minister of Defence, slouched in an armchair. The proud sweep of its arm-rest reaches that of *el jefe del Estado Mayor de la Armada*, the Navy. The minister is bearded and corpulent; the admiral is lean and the only one in uniform. Next is Felipe González, young, smiling, *el Presidente del Gobierno*, and then a figure with hooded eyes and a faintly cynical expression, smoking, a man with the face of my father in his last photograph, from 1944. He is the chief of staff of the JUJEM, the *Junta de Jefes del Estado Mayor*. Columns and vases in the background, a glass-topped table with ornate brass studs in the centre. Ashtrays, glasses, a flower arrangement. Nothing special. It's only a picture of the elected prime minister in the company of the military high command. But I cannot resist holding the photograph up to the past: the fears, the prophecies of a year before, when this scene had yet to become reality. González still had an election to win, the military had to refrain from seizing power, only then would it all come true.

With which past am I contrasting the photograph? Is it just the past of one year earlier, when I was travelling in Spain and had taken a room in the parador at Segovia?

The parador is a few kilometres away, and is designed so that all the rooms have views across the valley to the city silhouetted high on a hill, which in Holland we would call a mountain. It is an oddly jagged skyline, it alters with the time of day, it looks as if it cannot belong to a real city, as if it must be a sculpture, a fantasy in stone, massive, dense, where no human may enter. The dome and the towers of the cathedral, the high walls and battlements of the Alcázar. I know the aqueduct is down below somewhere, although I cannot see it. It was built by the Romans, and the photograph I have of it includes several cars. They reach barely a third of the way up the huge blocks of granite that form the base of the structure. There it stands, impassive, tall and slender, the houses of the city shimmering behind it as if none of all this is real, merely a mirage conjured up by history as proof of its existence. Vespasian and Trajan were emperors when these 165 arches were built, 128 metres from the ground where the ground is lowest, 813 metres across. Until 1974 all the water for the city and the Alcázar took this route. There was no question of history repeating itself here, just that it had been going on for a very long time.

History, that which has happened. The sum of fragments so infinitesimal that they can never be measured. Only the stark, unwieldy facts remain, clinging to dates that schoolchildren can memorize. Or to buildings, monuments. Perhaps that is why we approach monuments so circumspectly, guidebook in hand, because in some way they are the cumulative evidence of the additions forming the sum of the past. But how should the sum be totted up? The slave who laboured on the aqueduct, the centurion homesick for Rome, the collapse of the Roman Empire and the repercussions this had on the lives of the nameless, long vanished populace? All those private fates, condensed into a single line in the book of events, piled up in the invisible labyrinth of time, ostensibly solid, like the photograph of González with his warlords, but doomed to be engulfed by a spring tide of added-up facts and incidents which will change the nature of each individual event again and again.

It is 1939. Another man rules the country: Franco, who came to power by overthrowing the Republic (like knocking over a chair). A voice resounds in the cathedral of Segovia, the same one I can see from my balcony, sharply defined against the sky. "The Fatherland must be renewed, all evil uprooted, all bad seed extirpated. This is not the time for scruples." It is the beginning of a reign of terror against everything left-wing. There are two currents of opinion in the city: one is legalistic and holds that people ought to be arrested and brought before the court, the other endorses some degree of terror by means of summary executions. The Falange of Valladolid is in control of the province of Segovia, countless men and women are arrested and imprisoned in the tram depots of Valladolid. An eyewitness account taken from *Blood of Spain*:

> One morning we were ordered to form a cordon; the spectators were pressing too close to the firing squads carrying out public executions in the Campo. We had to keep them at least 200 metres away, and were given strict orders to prevent children joining the spectators.
>
> The prisoners were brought from the tram depots. Among the dozen the first day I did duty there were some I recognized from a village near mine. Imagine my feelings! Like several others, the woman raised her hand in a clenched-fist salute and cried: "*Viva la República!*" as the shots rang out.
>
> For the rest of the week, while I continued on duty, a dozen people were shot every dawn. They included three more women. Two of them, as the firing squad took aim, lifted their skirts over their faces, revealing themselves completely. Gesture of defiance? Of despair? I don't know: it was for scenes like this that people went to watch. And then, when we returned to the city, the streets were completely deserted; all the spectators had disappeared into their homes, their beds. The city was silent . . .

The labyrinth of time . . . it's only a metaphor, an interpretation. Think of how, in a real labyrinth (they exist), you find yourself going backwards even as you are looking for the exit; in the same way history sometimes seems to take a certain direction, which is considered by contemporaries to be progress, say, or "the inevitable course of history". If that "progress" is obstructed people talk of "a step backwards". And retracing one's steps, or having to retreat before advancing, is a labyrinthine movement: many a course of events would, if represented graphically, follow such a pattern. But to contemporaries nothing is ever represented graphically. They either think of themselves as active instruments of fate, or experience the succession of events as chaos, as an invasion of their private lives, as fear. Sometimes, too, as we have seen, the events signify his death, her death. That's when history comes to a halt for that one particular individual, but in the eyes of others he or she has now become part of it. There are, of course, two ways of participating in history: the active and the passive. A bomb victim finds his way into the book as a fraction of an overall figure; the woman who shouts "Long live the Republic!" in the face of a firing squad has in a sense determined her own fate by deciding in favour of one thing and against another. The same applies to those doing the shooting, as to those looking on. All that suffering, endured and inflicted, the reports and testimonies, all those emotions echoing in the testimonies of survivors, it is all part of the abstraction we call history.

When *The Sorrow of Belgium* by the Flemish author Hugo Claus was published, he was interviewed in the Dutch newspaper *de Volkskrant*. "But in the book itself historiography and its purpose are explicitly formulated," the interviewer observed, and Claus retorted:

> "Of course I have tried to show how things happened by describing the lives of ordinary men and women, who do not have an overview, indeed who *cannot* see how history interferes with their own personal lives. I do not believe it is enough to present the historical facts side by side with the effects they had on people's lives. The historical element must be mixed into the molten material under the crust of life, into what people say, do, feel, think, how they react. Once you take this approach you can't help bumping into the question: how could a form of fascism, of nationalism, take root among people who think it has nothing to do with them? Or who are not interested, even though it affects their own thought processes, their reactions, vis à vis the Germans, the English?"

People who think it has nothing to do with them. That's what is so mysterious – that even those who believe they have nothing to do with it are involved. History, to me, is just as abstract an element as space, or time. I am not even certain whether history is a component of time, although history without people is unthinkable, and yet time is. Now that the Spanish Civil War is well in the past it is possible to indicate the broad outlines of history, the interests of the different European countries, the active roles played by Hitler, Mussolini, Stalin, the perfidious attitude of Great Britain (which had huge financial interests in Spain), the individual heroism of many members of the International Brigades, the fratricide among anarchists and communists.

Does progress exist? Do things *have* to develop in a certain way? Could things have been different? The last question bothers me particularly: once events have happened in such and such a way, does that mean they couldn't have happened differently? In the mind, yes; in practice, never.

Perhaps it is the benefit of hindsight that makes history so *cold*, that makes it *seem* as if individual decisions do not or did not make the slightest bit of difference. Did those who gave their lives for the Republic die in vain? I think not, but it is an appalling sacrifice. What is it like to be the *loser*, to face the barrel of a gun and to devote your last breath to shouting "Long live the Republic!", to lift your skirts over your head and expose your sex to the executioner, and then to die? May I, years on, trace a line connecting that moment to the picture in *El País* of the young socialist leader who holds a position of authority in a monarchy, with the military high command? I think I am entitled to make that connection, but I know it is only one of the thousands, millions of links that can be established between this photograph or that fateful moment and other moments in time. The paradox is perhaps that history has no purpose, but that we, simply because we exist, always think we do have a purpose and thereby we make history.

My philosopher friend reminds me of the Hegelian view: that there is a purpose to history, and that I must never equate history with time. I have no doubt he is right as regards the latter. History makes the passage of time visible, I mumble in a faint attempt to have the last word, but that means nothing, because a clock does the same. The hours of the clock are the years of the century, and how does that help? Allow me to repeat just once more: history is the sum of all our conflicting, contradictory and rival intentions. But that still doesn't give history a purpose.

Cross purposes, more like. Almost five hundred years ago Segovia saw the outbreak of the *comuneros* rebellion led by Juan Bravo. Since history insists on referring to itself we must, in order to understand that uprising, go back further in time, into the Middle Ages. The common folk had lived in virtual serfdom until the recovery of large areas from the Moors, and after the Reconquista people were encouraged to settle in the newly claimed lands by the granting of *fueros*, privileges, which had hitherto been the preserve of the nobility and clergy. And so the people in various Spanish kingdoms established their own Cortes. These parliamentary institutions, while not comparable to the parliaments of today, certainly reflected a democratic consciousness visible in Spain earlier than anywhere else in Europe. León already had its Cortes in 1188, Aragón in 1163, Catalonia in 1228, Castile in 1250. It is clear that in due course the kings came to see the growing self-esteem of the parliaments (consisting of nobility, *nobilarios*, clergymen, *eclesiásticos*, and deputies of the towns, *populares*) as a threat to their own power.

From being bodies convened only when the sovereign needed yet more money, the Cortes developed into articulate and self-willed institutions, and when the Habsburg Charles V (Carlos I), who was disliked by the Spaniards anyway because he spoke only Flemish and because he appointed foreigners to high offices, raised the already heavy taxes to cover the cost of his international policies, the people rebelled. "Mass movements," writes Gustav Faber in his book *Spaniens Mitte* (Middle Spain), "rise from grass-roots level, but nonetheless they require organizers to give shape to the movement." There we are again, that invisible, largely irretrievable element, the ideas, the anger, the grievances swelling like a great wave and setting the anonymous masses in motion.

A "Holy Junta" of people, nobility and clergy under Juan Bravo demanded lower taxation, the appointment of native governors, and legal reforms. The authority of the Crown itself was not at issue, it was those who were appointed by Charles to represent him. The citizenry of Toledo established people's communes, a term one associates rather with the (French) nineteenth century than the sixteenth. Spain was in turmoil, and despite the vast distances between the cities the spirit of rebellion spread. Segovia and Toledo were succeeded by Guadalajara, Avila, Madrid, Alcalá de Henares, and the rebellious cities issued a joint declaration whereby Charles' regent, Adrian of Utrecht, was deposed. Adrian marched on Segovia with an army of mercenaries, but his attempts to recapture the arsenal at Medina del Campo caused an explosion which demolished the entire town, thereby provoking a fresh wave of fury and bitterness. More cities joined in, two deputies in Segovia were charged with treason and were hanged by the feet.

Then came another of those dramatic incidents that are the stuff of classical tragedy and opera (but Spain has no Verdi). Charles V's grandparents Ferdinand and Isabella, the Catholic King and Queen,* had

---

* Only the Spanish gave their royal couple the plural title *Reyes Católicos* and still do so today – whenever Juan Carlos and Sophia have an official engagement the Spanish media say that *The Kings* today visit . . . , as if they were two men.

already married off their daughters to European royalty. Juana, known as *la Loca*, Joanna the Mad, was paired with Philip the Fair, son of the Austrian emperor, and thus did the Habsburgs "acquire" Spain – as part of the dowry. Philip's sudden death of a fever in Burgos in 1506 left Joanna inconsolable. She had shown symptoms of manic depression earlier and, to put it bluntly, she went mad. She refused to have her husband's coffin sealed, and insisted on seeing the corpse every day. The cortège travelled across Spain making macabre progress, spreading the stench of pestilence, and every evening the lid of the coffin was raised for the queen. Not much later Joanna was locked up in Tordesillas at the behest of her young son the emperor.

Let us dwell on her fate for a moment. The emperor is in Flanders, the rebel *comuneros* turn to her for support, but so does Charles' royal party. She cannot understand why the very people who have imprisoned her now so desperately need her, and she refuses to make up her mind. Then the Holy Junta with Juan Bravo at its head offers her the crowns of the Spanish kingdoms, which were indeed her rightful inheritance. The court was transferred to her convent prison in Tordesillas (which may still be visited, and where her disintegrating spinet bears eloquent witness to her misery); the Cortes swore allegiance to her. Was she really mad? Did she have flashes of insight into what was going on, or did she know all along? If she said yes, all power would be restored to her, and her captivity would be over. But if she said no she would be denying her absent "Flemish" son.

Let's transpose this to the opera: the Aria of Indecision. On the one hand we have the crown and liberty offered by the *comuneros*, on the other, outside the city walls, the royal party of the son who put her in prison. Then the leaders of the *comuneros* make a fatal error. They engage a priest to exorcise the confused woman, whose distrust has been fanned by her father confessor (a baritone, I can hear the duet), to cast out the devil in her. But it all takes too long; the king's party recapture the city, and thanks to a cunning manoeuvre on the part of Charles, the nobility, who were militarily the stronger party, withdrew from the Junta.

The popular uprising was finally snuffed out at the battle of Villalar in 1521. The bishop of Zamora was garrotted, Juan Bravo was beheaded along with seventy-three other *comuneros* in Segovia, and the Cortes were stripped of all power.

Rebels turn into street names, blood into addresses. I walk along the shops in the Calle Juan Bravo, I cross the street of Isabella the Catholic, and arrive at the cathedral. The same far-off dreamy vision that I have observed from my balcony undergoing the transformation from a gloomy, forbidding shadow into a radiant, blazing emblem depending on the hour, takes on an almost sinister quality close up. There is no god of loving kindness. On the contrary, the god of the desert roaming the parched wilderness with his ark of the covenant has here done well. True, he must suffer the presence of idols beside him, but he is still the same god of Abraham and Isaac, and he is still a cruel and jealous god, even though his element is no longer the heat, but the cold. Gone is the gentleness of the Romanesque churches, this is a citadel, exuding power and oppression. I wander in that petrified triumphalism. Mass is being said at one of the altars, but the human voice is overwhelmed in this place, is not permitted to be itself. It dwindles into distant and obsequious whispering that drifts away in the dank high vault which seems more remote than heaven itself.

In that gigantic station-like building full of white sanctity, the high enclosure of the choir stands aloof and isolated in the expanse of stone. The side chapels are hidden in the half-light. Emaciated, tortured saints suffer, hardly visible, behind their grilles. Only the high, distant windows let in a little sunlight. Four men standing on each other's shoulders would still not reach the summit of the great portal, and I step through a small door cut out of one of the huge doors; the fresh air of the world comes as a relief and I pause in a square with tough and ungodly weeds growing between the large paving stones. The wind of the plain barrels across the square. In the distance I can see the snowy peaks of the Sierra de Guadarrama.

Segovia is a curiously compact city. Once you have entered through one of the many arches of the aqueduct it is as if the narrow streets shut themselves behind you. You walk up steep alleys, past restaurants with naked sucking pigs resting their cheeks chastely on their front trotters, past old-fashioned stores selling haberdashery and *ultramarinos*, to come upon a lovely Romanesque church at almost every turn (there are twenty of them); then you catch a glimpse of the Eresma winding its way through the greenery in the valley below and you find yourself at the foot of the Alcázar. If you didn't know it was real, you'd suppose it was a film set. A bunch of children leaning over the ramparts of the castle keep yelling: "*Viva Asturias!*" Their shouts hang in the air for a moment and then a gust of wind disperses them over the deep ravine.

Irreducible, that is how it looks, so high up on the rocks. Slender towers, windowless walls, the keep with its curious circular watchtowers like a candelabra for giant candles that could illuminate the entire Castilian *meseta* at night. The Spanish kings, who trekked from castle to castle like gypsies on the run, liked this one best of all. Philip II's fourth and final marriage ceremony was held here. As would his grandson, Philip IV, in years to come, he wanted to observe his bride before she set eyes on him. So, on the morning of his wedding he dressed himself in disguise before going down to mingle with his guests. As we have seen, history is not only made on the battlefield, but also in bed, and often very deliberately so. This sexual variant is no longer practised today, which is regrettable because it must have been quite a sensation, the coupling of kingdoms and bodies at one and the same time. Philip's new wife, who was to provide him with an heir, was also a Habsburg, and the genetic consequences did not fail to manifest themselves. The monastic Philip II begat Philip III, who in his turn also married a Habsburg princess and then sired Philip IV, the most lecherous sovereign of Europe, whose inevitably Habsburg spouse bore him eight children, six of whom died in infancy while sundry royal bastards survived. The end product was Charles II. The boy who would have become Philip V had died at the tender age of four. Nothing had helped. Our Lady of Solitude had been dragged from one place of pilgrimage to the next, Our Lady of Atocha had been moved from her shrine to the convent of the unshod Carmelite nuns, and as a last resort the body of Saint Isidore, which was always carried to the sickbeds of the mighty when they were in fear of death, but all was in vain, even the urn of Saint Diego de Alcalá.

Again Spain awaited the birth of a king. Without a king the great heritage with all its lands and populations would fall apart among rival heirs. This time, too, all the necessary precautions had been taken. When the queen felt the first birth pangs she hastened to the tower chamber. She had supped alone, because the cruel etiquette of the court forbade the king from eating in the company of his wife. In the tower everything was ready: three thorns from the crown of the Saviour, one of the nails with which he had been hung from the cross, a splinter of wood from the holy cross itself, a snippet of the Virgin Mary's cloak, the walking stick of the holy abbot of Silos and the girdle of Saint Juan de Ortega. It helped: the child born on 6 November 1661 lived. He would lead a life of misery and misfortune as Charles II (Carlos II, *el Hechizado*, Charles the Hexed), a sickly and faint-hearted pawn in the hands of rival factions.

There is no sign of all this yet in Carreño's portrait, even so it is not a cheerful picture. The long jutting chin is that of his forefather, Charles of Spain, Charles V. The mouth with the short upper lip expresses disdain, the eyes are full of suspicion. He would end his life childless, the protagonist in a tragicomedy of witchcraft and exorcism, under his pillow a sachet containing egg shells, toenails, hair and other magical ingredients. Shivering with icy cold during the hottest part of the day, unable to walk unassisted, he staggered from one intrigue to the next, caught in a web of father confessors, grand inquisitors, physicians, exorcists and courtiers. The whole of Europe was waiting for his death, and especially for his last will and testament.

Everyone was partisan: Emperor Leopold, Louis XIV, William of Orange. Confounding all expectations, his suffering dragged on one year after the next: a protracted misery for him as for Europe. It was obvious that nothing less than a world war would determine his legacy. Louis accepted an eleventh-hour proposal from William of Orange whereby Spain, the Spanish Netherlands and the colonies fell to Austria, while France would have to be content with Naples, Sicily and Milan. But the Austrian emperor refused the generous offer. He had received divine intelligence through his ambassador in Spain and the bishop of Vienna, telling him what the devil had said during the exorcism of certain possessed souls in the cathedral of Santa Sofía. So he knew for a fact that Charles was bewitched; all that had to be done now was to drive the devils out of the dying Charles and out of his queen, and then God would ensure that Naples, Sicily and Milan dropped into the Austrian emperor's lap as well. You see, I am right, history *is* a labyrinth, and it was constructed by no one.

It is October, Charles' days are numbered. The bodies of Saints Isidore and Diego are once more at the palace. The mood at court is sombre. October has always been a bad month for Spanish kings. The queen in person feeds him pearly milk, he loses his hearing, freshly slaughtered pigeons are laid upon his head to alleviate his vertigo, he loses his voice, his surgeons try to keep his temperature up by laying the still-warm, reeking intestines of slain animals on his belly. All to no avail: he perishes. His will contains the recipe for a disaster, and includes the recommendation to install Saint Teresa of Avila as the patron saint of Spain alongside the Holy Virgin. The war of the Spanish succession can begin.

In front of the Alcázar, where his great-grandfather Philip II entered into his last, ill-fated marriage, there is a monument. It has nothing – and yet everything, as usual – to do with Charles' story, for it commemorates another, later war. Time is personified by a male figure, History by a

Statue representing History, Segovia

female. She is carved out of white marble and her breasts are more generous than any you would find in the most atavistic girlie magazine. A large book on her lap bears her name: *Historia*. From her elevated position she surveys the bronze battle scene at her immense feet. Swords, bayonets, the corpse of a heroic officer is drooped over the barrel of a cannon. *A los capitanes de Artillería D. Luis Daoíz y D. Pedro Velarde*, 2 May 1808, with the gratitude of the Spanish Nation.

Later that day I sit out on my balcony at the parador and look towards the silhouette of Segovia, a great, magical ship bathed in the glow of the setting sun, with masts of spires and the towering Alcázar as bow, sailing stately into the blazing west. Way below, unmoved, vast like an ocean, lies the stage of harvests and catastrophes, mass migration and warfare, earth that knows no names and no dates, a land.

X

Kings and Dwarfs

La Granja de San Ildefonso ~ The Escorial ~ Philip II
Philip struggles with his empire ~ Johan Brouwer
Philip and the Dutch ~ Philip's dwarf

YOU HAVE GOT USED TO THE bleakness of all those vast, obdurate landscapes devoid of green, to the unassuming villages deserted in the midday sun, the heavy fortresses rising out of nowhere in the distance. And then suddenly you come upon La Granja de San Ildefonso, 10 kilometres from Segovia: the palace and pleasure gardens created by the first Bourbon king, who pined for Versailles. In the Spanish context of arid drought those wildly spurting fountains strike a frivolous note, the situation of the palace at the foot of the Sierra de Guadarrama provides northern freshness, and the architecture of the royal estate – baroque, rococo – clashes with the atavistic austerity of the Alcázar in Segovia and the awesome Escorial not far away.

I have no desire to go into the palace, I just want to walk in the gardens. It is very quiet, only the sound of water, leaves, birds. Nature was coerced here, by French gardeners, into adopting stiff, uncompromising, geometric patterns. Straight lines and curves of clipped privet hedges rise in symmetrical battle formation. Thus the spirit of the times finds expression in the rational application of garden shears. Only the fountains defy regimentation as the wind snatches the spray at its peak, flattening it into a screen of transparent, sparkling vapour. Lions and horses spout never-ending streams into the air, at the fountain of the frogs the jets are directed at each other, at the baths of Diana the water gushes forth from giant amphoras along wide marble bowls and becomes marble itself. Wherever you go, all around you, it gurgles, trickles, streams, drips, whispers, hits and hugs itself, it builds itself up into a column 35 metres high which then collapses. You hear it as a great, passionate downpour of rain. Rose bushes stand poised on the lawns like decadent shorn poodles, the rectilinear paths lead past marble urns and mythological figures. Strolling here unaccompanied gives you the feeling of being observed by the eye of a camera, and it is a relief when you reach the copse into which you can disappear unseen, like the game that was once stalked by Philip V, an impassioned hunter.

Philip V, grandson of Louis XIV. The house of Bourbon. Observe the dynasties as you would an underground map. Change trains at Habsburg and count backwards: Charles II, sickly, epileptic, feeble-minded; Philip IV, an obsessive womanizer, punished by God (so he thought) with defeat, injury and wilting offspring; Philip III, weak and fickle: Philip II, the man who inherited an empire which he was unable to keep in one piece. He died, ravaged by disease, in his small, dank chamber in the Escorial, the palace which he built for himself and which mirrors his troubled soul: a fortress and a monastery, a stern rectangle, modelled on a grid, the one on which Saint Laurence was roasted alive.

I remember clearly how I first stood there in that small room, many years ago. The red-flagged floor, the embroidered, brocaded canopy pushed to the sides of the narrow bed, the bedspread, which must once have been blood-red but now looked faded and purplish, the little shuttered aperture that enabled him to follow mass in the adjoining chapel while he lay sick. Bare walls only half tiled. This is where he lay, like a spider in his web. From here there were invisible threads linking him to the far corners of his world-spanning empire, here too was where he mulled over the fate of the Low Countries. A cruel sovereign, so we were taught at school, the ruler who dispatched the no less brutal Duke of Alba to oppress the Dutch people. It was somehow sinister, to stand there like that. The ceiling was low, the chairs in the next room looked like the chair on which Philip rests his hand in the portrait by Juan Pantoja de la Cruz. The king is holding a pair of gloves in that hand, and wearing tall black boots without heels. They look like leggings, the way they reach over the knees. He stands with his left leg slightly forward, and it catches some of the light that also casts a vague, yellowish glow on the rest of his stiff black dress. The small hands protrude from narrow lace-edged cuffs, the head is encased in an equally narrow tight ruff. Sober, monk-like, motionless. Immovable power. A single gold ornament on the black doublet. The chin juts forward, but less so than that of his father the emperor; the ears are small, the hair silky and fine like

Philip II, by Juan Pantoja de la Cruz

a badger's fur, the eyes under the straight, handsome eyebrows are watchful, the moustache drooping at the corners gives the mouth a certain air of condescension which is not, however, confirmed by the shape of the lips. The curious high-crowned hat has the same vertical markings as the classical column behind him.

From that first visit I also remember the Panteón Real, an octagonal vault of marble and gold where the bodies of the Spanish kings are laid to rest until such time as they break out of their baroque chocolate-box caskets of grey marble like a rare species of bird hatching noisily from their marble shells. I remember that I was alone down there, in an all-enveloping silence, and that I read the golden names on the boxes: the men to the left, the women to the right, in chronological order.

But the days of the lone tourist are over in places such as these. The straggler from one guided tour is swallowed by the next shoal of visitors. His glance lingers on a tapestry on the wall, a royal throne, a tomb, a tabernacle, all the things everyone else seems capable of taking in with a single, vacuum-cleaner-like glance to the drone of rudimentary explanations offered by those who have made this their business. What a dream to have, to be let into the Escorial at night by an accomplice and to roam those deathly silent, ghostly rooms on one's own, with only a candle and a ground plan for company. But one night would not be enough, for this is a world apart, a maze of passages haunted by the unquiet souls of kings. How strange it must be to set eyes again on the very objects you handled so heedlessly in life, how strange to observe paintings and statues you always took for granted, works of art now screened by a layer of centuries, the marble as hard as ever, the gold as bright, the religion unchanged, and how strange to imbibe the sheepish awe and admiration of the masses who still flock here, day in day out, to gape at your sovereign might. More miraculous than that which disappears perhaps, is that which remains, for when will it end, when will the generations upon generations stop thronging these rooms, staring at the El Grecos and the Van der Weydens, listening to the litany of dimensions and dates of the guide not yet born.

Time travel as in science fiction films – how I would love to step into the future, not for a glimpse of a futuristic civilization in which I would never feel at home anyway, but to have a vantage point from which to see the things I see now. All the Christian symbols that are still commonly understood today would have to be explained, and the explanations would sound as far-fetched as the Australian aboriginals' story of creation sounds to us. A god who created the world in seven days, original sin, the expulsion from paradise, the virgin who gave birth to the son of god, the son who died on the cross, and the depictions of all those fables in paint and stone, in wood and gold. And they will stay there, those more than life-size, bronze-gilt funerary monuments of Charles V and Philip II flanking the altar in the Capilla Real. The kneeling emperor wears a suit of armour and on his imperial mantle the two-headed eagle (a creature by then extinct, like having a dinosaur in your family arms) is to be seen carved out of the black marble of Mérida. To his right, Empress Isabella, mother to Philip II, behind him his daughter and his two sisters, queens of Hungary and France. The guide explains what all this means, a king, an emperor, prayer, going down on one's knees, a Doric column, the golden fleece, and it will sound like a story from a remote mythological past that will fill the tourists in this future life with awe at the glory of a time, long gone, when people were larger than life, when they went about dressed in gold and believed in gods. But I am stuck in the present, and now I walk past a painted forest of lances, a pitched battle covering a wall without end. It is the *Batalla de Higueruela*. The horses wear the colours of the opposing parties, cavalrymen with lances and crossbows launch an attack, behind them wait cordoned formations of foot soldiers, each with its own banner. The blood and the dust, the stench of death are absent, the clamour of rage, fear and pain is inaudible, the flag with the crescent moon is trampled underfoot, the brightly coloured shields catch the rays of the sun, of the future; I walk past as if I am inspecting a military parade and follow the crowd into the throne room, but when the others walk on I slip behind a partition and stand there on my own for a bit, staring at the throne, which is just a small chair. There Philip would sit and gaze out over the land without end and think of the distant provinces he had never visited and would never visit.

It is light in this room, light and deserted, as if that little chair with the red cushion was left just a moment ago by someone who will presently return. The walls are covered with maps of all his territories, of Flanders and of the Noblest Province of Brabant, but also of lands far beyond the equator. It is impossible to imagine the sheer size of that empire, or rather, the affiliations that were united in his person. In the foreword to the Dutch edition of Geoffrey Parker's biography of the king,

S. Groenveld makes it clear that his domain was not united, Spain no more than the other lands.

> Spain was an amalgamation of kingdoms of which Aragón (itself comprising three kingdoms and expanded with Italian territories during the Middle Ages) and Castile (with its growing colonial lands in the west) were the foremost. The situation was no different in the Low Countries, that ensemble of seventeen regions with their own rulers, which from the late Middle Ages had come into the hands of a single family – since 1482 the House of Habsburg. But that did not make these lands a unity. Each regarded Philip and his predecessors as their own sovereign, their "natural" lord; that this sovereign ruled over other territories was immaterial to them. Even though they called Philip "king" because that happened to be his highest rank, still he was, to the inhabitants of a particular region, merely their duke, or count, or lord.

Like a spider in its web. Reading Parker's book, I find I am not the first to use this simile. The man in the room, the room in the palace, the palace in the middle of Spain, and Spain at the centre of those distant lands acquired through inheritance or conquest, all the way from Chile to the Philippines. That, and the fact that one man wanted to keep everything under his personal control, that he managed to do so for more than forty years, so that eventually all the threads came together in the small room where he pored over innumerable documents, annotating many of them in his spidery hand – it all contributes to the somewhat lugubrious image from the animal kingdom, the spider in its web.

It is impossible not to be impressed. If you were born in Holland at any rate, you will have become familiar with the picture of dread which endures after so many centuries, and which was so intensified by the Protestant propaganda of contemporary historiography. To us Philip was a brutal tyrant, and that was that. The accusations against him ranged from incest to bloody yet calculating machinations. The first qualified assessment of his character I came across was written by Johan Brouwer in *De achtergrond der Spaanse mystiek* (The Background of Spanish Mysticism), from his Collected Works who said, "anyone wishing to take historical truth seriously will have to judge Philip within the framework of his time, his nature and his background, and not on the basis of assumptions formed by resentment or prejudice, nor on the basis of legends that have been around for centuries".

Such is the opinion of a sincere historian. But Brouwer had another, more romantic side too. He was in fact one of the oddest characters in the Dutch world of letters. Sentenced to prison for robbery with murder, he spent the years of his incarceration studying Spanish and became a great Hispanist, going on to write several books about Spain and Spanish history. As a Franco sympathizer he went to Spain during the Civil War. As soon as he arrived he was "converted" and promptly sided with the legal government, that is, with the Republicans. During the Second World War he joined the resistance in the Netherlands, taking part in the historic raid on the population registry in Amsterdam, during which he was caught. He received the death sentence and was executed by the Germans in 1943. A passionate, not-very-Dutch sort of life. After his return from the Spanish Civil War he wrote a bizarre novel about that cruel war. The book, entitled *De schatten van Medina-Sidonia* (The Treasures of Medina-Sidonia), is fascinating in spite of the dotty occultism, and was written under the pseudonym of Maarten van de Moer. It was banned during the German occupation of Holland, and after the war the book was re-issued in Brouwer's own name and with a new title: *In de schaduw van de dood* (In the Shadow of Death). A less dispassionate, more admiring view of Philip II is put forward in the novel. The protagonist, a student from Utrecht and a member of the International Brigades, comes into contact with a German "who belonged to the Prussian nobility", but who calls himself Lenz. They meet in the neighbourhood of the Escorial, and Lenz, who came out of the First World War disillusioned, proceeds to explain to the young Dutchman how he "found himself again when he came to Spain".

> "See that rocky outcrop up there to your right? Half way up you can see a sort of hollow, a sort of cubby-hole. 'The seat of Philip II', they call it in these parts. They say that Philip sat there to survey the construction of this colossus. I climbed up there myself one day towards evening. The setting sun bathed the whole edifice in a russet glow, transforming it into a radiant yet elusive mirage within this barren wilderness. Then I understood both Philip and myself . . . When I was up there, in Philip's seat, I became a new man. Philip simply saw the pettiness of life and the majesty of God. We must discover the majesty of Mankind, too. We bear responsibility for all the life around us."

The exalted tone of this conversation should not be attributed solely
to the time in which Brouwer wrote, nor to his romantic nature. There is
something about the Escorial, about the Sierra de Guadarrama (the very
soul of Spain according to Ortega y Gasset in his *Meditaciones sobre
Don Quijote*), and indeed about Philip II himself, that fires the imagination, and it is only from the king's stone seat that you can see why. From
there he watched his creation take shape little by little, until the palace
looked the way it does now, a forbidding rectangle enclosing an array of
domes and lofty towers. In the sunlight the walls seem to be on fire, at
such times the edifice becomes a blazing vision in the wide, rippling
green plain. Fire and ice, for the compressed, severe form of that petrified
idea exudes an icy discipline, and once you have seen the inside, you
cannot get enough of it. There lived the dwarfs and imbeciles whose
company the king found pleasing and about whom he wrote such
amusing letters to his daughter Isabella. And there, too, the king received
the news from all his territories, dire messages that left him angry and
depressed. In the same period that he was waging his war in the Low
Countries, he must also have been worrying about the rise of Turkey's
naval power, and to pay for all those wars the taxes had to be raised
repeatedly. In April 1574 Juan de Ovando, his chief financial adviser,
calculated that the king was in debt for seventy-four million ducats. No
wonder Philip complained: "I have never been able to get this business of
loans and interests into my head. I have never managed to understand
it." The problems sound very modern: a bankrupt state, the government's short-term debt at high interest being converted automatically
into long-term debt at low interest – where have we heard that before?
The stream of gold and silver from the colonies trickled away in all directions, and the image of the spider in its web is mitigated somewhat when
you read of Philip's distress:

> To be frank, I do not understand a word of this document. I do not
> know what I should do. Should I send it to someone else for
> comment, and if so, who? Time is slipping away: tell me what you
> advise. If I see the author of the memorandum I do not believe I
> shall understand him, although perhaps if I had the papers in front
> of me it might not be too bad.

Documents are of course the best means of bringing about the kind of
reversal of fortune without which history ceases to be history. When I

read the king's message to his secretary: "I spend all my time thinking about Flanders", then it is difficult for me to imagine that it is *my* history he is referring to, the history of my native country, of the Duke of Alba and his spectacles, the Council of Troubles, the counts of Egmond and Hoorne, the Sea Beggars, the *Wilhelmus* (the Dutch national anthem). Deep down inside me I can still hear the voice that imbued me and my classmates at primary school with the notion of a cruel enemy, certainly not of someone who thought about the Netherlands day and night "because everything else depends upon it. We have taken so long to provide money and the situation is so desperate that even if we succeed in making funds available I doubt if we can save the Low Countries." "Save", he said – naturally, I had never thought of it like that. The point was that the king was prepared to grant a general pardon and would even agree to give back a considerable portion of the confiscated proper- ties, but he would not hear of any alteration to the nature of his sovereignty, let alone of religious freedom. In a letter to his captain- general in the Netherlands, Don Luis de Requesens (I can smell my school desk – I can see red-haired Miss de Vos, I can hear our childish mouths echoing those strange sounds: Re-kway-zens), dated October 1574, he wrote: "Even if we had all the time and money in the world, it would not be enough to force the twenty-four rebel towns to surrender if we are to spend as long in reducing each one of them as we have taken over similar ones so far." And it takes the modern brain some effort to realize how slow communications were at the time. Sometimes I try to imagine what the effect must have been on the human psyche. You sent off a letter, or an army, or a governor – then you heard nothing for many months, then that nothing was doubled by the distance back to you before you heard the outcome: the synchronicity we are so used to today simply did not exist. Astronauts in space can converse with the White House or the Kremlin, but when Philip sent a letter to Chile it took a year for him to receive a reply, if indeed such a reply ever came. The king dispatched an army to fight a battle: had he taken the time factor into account, so that he could stop worrying for a while, or did this mark the start of weeks of tormenting uncertainty?

Messengers, orders, decrees, horsemen. The king is given respite one last time: on 14 April 1574 the army which has assembled in Germany to come to the assistance of the Dutch rebels suffers a crippling defeat. Somewhere in the Escorial there is a picture of this event – the opposing parties are shown poised for battle. Film, photographs, television would eventually replace that motionless picture, but for Philip and his contemporaries this static report was the only visible actuality. I have some difficulty decoding the inscriptions – as if I am a spy in a hostile era:

> 4. EL CAMPO.DEL,RE,DE FRAN
> 5. EL.PR.DE PARME
> 6. EL. DU DE MEME
>   LA, VILLE, DE,
> 4. NIMEGEN
> 2. MOQER, HEYDEN
> 3. DO. CRISTOFFEL, PALS, MORT.
> 5. EL, CO, HERI, DE, NASSAU, MORT.

I take them to mean: the encampment of the king of France, the prince of Parma, the duke "of the same", i.e. of Parma. The town of Nijmegen, the Moker Heath, a dead count palatine and a dead prince of Nassau. But the picture was not to bring cheer to Philip for long. The force of gravity of his distant territories was against him and in June he wrote: "I believe that everything is a waste of time, judging by what is happening in the Low Countries, and if they are lost the rest (of the monarchy) will not last long, even if we have enough money." He was right. The great, sombre decline of Spain had begun, it became a country that didn't count any more, where old times were perpetuated, so that until recently crossing the Spanish border was like entering another continent, and even more like stepping into the past, as if it were actually possible to travel in Europe like a contemporary of Stendhal's, to see what the world had looked like before progress, with all its merits and demerits, set in.

There is an old Castilian saying: "*Si Dios no fuese Dios, sería rey de las Españas, y el de Francia su cocinero*" – If God weren't God, he would be king of Spain, and the king of France would be his cook. Philip himself does not appear to have thought his position in the least enviable. Time and again one has the impression that here was a lonely man labouring under the crushing burden of his possessions, linked with the far corners of his empire by reading and writing. He ruled for forty years, and until six weeks before his horrible death he kept up his correspondence. Muleloads of his letters were deposited in the royal archives, where they remain stored for posterity, thousands of sheets in the handwriting of the spider.

The cover of Geoffrey Parker's book shows a curious bust of the king. He is at the height of his power, his hair seems darker than on the portraits I have seen, the lips fuller, the head too large above the stone ruff. For a moment I am reminded of the oversized head of a dwarf, which is not surprising in view of his fondness for that special type of little people. In his letters to his daughters he often referred to the dwarf Magdalena Ruiz, who was their favourite. Parker devotes a whole passage to her:

> In the Prado Museum there is a painting of Isabella with her hand on the head of her faithful dwarf, who had been her servant since 1568 (when the princess was two) and died at the Escorial in 1605. She had epileptic seizures, she was heavily addicted to alcohol, and she was capable of staging tantrums in front of the king himself. "Magdalena is very cross with me," Philip told his daughters in one letter, "and she has gone off saying she wants to leave." She was a favourite with the crowds, and whenever she appeared in public she would be greeted with shouts of "Whip her, whip her" in an attempt to provoke or frighten her. Magdalena could always be relied on to do the wrong thing – to fall over; to overeat (especially strawberries) and be sick; to be seasick before anyone else – but that was all part of her charm.

Bells ring, guards call out, the palace is about to close. I walk down the passages dragging my feet, as if there is an invisible force slowing me down, as if those four centuries are trying to pull me back, to hold me prisoner in the web of stone.

XI

The Black Virgin in Her Golden Grotto

The Virgin talisman ~ Approach to Guadalupe
Saint Jerome of Guadalupe ~ The Hieronymites in history
Zurbarán recalled by Guadalupe ~ A guided tour
The black Virgin ~ Zurbarán treasure trove

JERKED BY A BELL, A ROPE, I am dragged up from the depths of sleep. The world has shrunk to a room filled with the clanging of that bell. That's not how church bells in northern Europe sound: a few deep strokes, like a giant wading through water, and then some agitated, nervous chimes, as if another, smaller man is trying to catch up with him. The room, I see, is small, low-ceilinged, the walls white-washed, the furniture of dark stained wood, there is a polychrome tile with the Holy Virgin of Guadalupe (a real goddess in my room at last), a floor of red tiles. Perhaps I'm someone else, a professor at the Latin school which this parador once was. But no, I'm not someone else, and it's not for me the bells are tolling, it's for the monks in the monastery across the road. The pealing bells lend structure to their day, they interrupt, announce, invoke, set a fixed measure of time. My own day stretches out ahead of me empty, I have no duties, I can do as I please. When the clamour subsides I can sense the form of silence which must have been there all the time: the gurgle of a fountain. *Wada lubim*, Guadalupe, hidden water. The Black Madonna goes by an Arabic name.

14 February, 1493. The *Niña* is tossing in a storm, the sails are torn to shreds, the great swell of the ocean with its relentless progression of rollers, plunging, soaring, collapsing, determined to shake off that absurdly light craft. What kind of obeisance can one make in the sights of approaching death? A candle weighing five pounds. In his logbook Columbus noted: "I have let Fate decide which of my sailors should

make the pilgrimage to Guadalupe to offer that candle to the Virgin."
They collected as many *garbanzos*, chick peas, as there were men in the
crew, and among the peas one was marked with a cross. The peas were
put into a sailor's cap, which was thoroughly shaken. Columbus had the
first draw, and he pulled out the pea with the cross.

Cortés, the conquistador, spent nine days in prayer at Guadalupe;
after the battle of Lepanto, Don Juan of Austria, bastard son of Charles
V, half-brother of Philip, came here to donate a lantern captured from
the Turkish flagship. The black statue has been dressed anew countless
times, but her expression never changes; Cortés' prayers have evaporated, Columbus' candle, once worth so many men's lives, has been
burnt, the lantern is still there.

Guadalupe is miles away from anywhere, there are no main roads in
the vicinity, it has lived quietly through the centuries in the shadow of
this monastery. You sense this as you approach the town: suddenly you
plunge into the deep shade of a eucalyptus-lined avenue, like entering a
cool grotto after a day in the heat. But there have been other signs,
earlier on. My attention is caught now and then by a blue sparkle in the
bushes, a lightning flash of blue, and it is only when I stop the car and
wait that I discover what it is, an azure-winged magpie, the envoy from
the tropics which is found only here, in this part of Spain, as if to underscore the exceptional status of the place. Thus too, waiting patiently on
the bank of a muddy stream in the shade of an old, high bridge, I also
get to see the brown shape of an eagle folding itself and diving like a
missile, the awesomely big wings then spreading again, as it wheels off
towards the Sierra with the prey still writhing in its talons – it is already
too far away for me to see what it has caught.

Inside my room I can hear them, those different times. The muffled
patter of more than one pair of feet, and I open the shutters to see a
mule coming down a steep hillside path. A man is straddled on top,
a knotted cloth with invisible wares between his knees. By the time I
go outside to the terrace where breakfast is served the *esteras* have
already been lowered: sun-screens of woven straw, thick and fibrous,
smelling of earth.

The parador is low and white, an ancient Latin college built around a
courtyard with roses, geraniums, a fountain, with the early-morning
freshness that will soon be gone. From there to the centre of town is a
hundred metres: the church, the monastery, a triangular plaza, another

fountain, less ornate this time and with a horse drinking from it, on each flank a wicker basket laden with pitchers containing oil and wine. A woman sits at the corner with some flat baskets at her feet, a Franciscan monk strides across the square and brings a shiver of fear across the skin of my back, a forgotten, bony, boyish back, so deep down under the other one that I didn't know it was still there. It was the same brown habit belted with the white cord that used to wake us at six in our dormitory with the ear-splitting clanging of a bell, the same habit that rustled in the wrathful gloom of a hundred confessionals, that meted out punishment, wished us *felix studium*, taught me Greek, humiliated and harassed us, kept guard in the dormitory to prevent anyone from stirring; it was the same shiver all right, but there was a hint of triumph. Not everyone has the privilege of seeing his childhood so emblematically represented, all wrapped up in a brown parcel secured by a cord with three knots.

The inhabitants of Guadalupe were Hieronymites, late disciples of that wondrous and contradictory saint who was portrayed an infinite number of times, as cardinal and doctor of the church, as hermit in the wilderness, as self-chastiser, as translator. Among his attributes are a skull, a lion and a cardinal's hat, yet he was never a cardinal and the lion is legend (he is held to have taken a thorn out of the beast's paw). And there were those who doubted his saintliness, for all the beating of his breast with a stone. "He did well thus to use that stone," Pope Sixtus observed. "Without it he would never have been numbered among the saints." The genius who translated the Vulgate was possessed of an irascible temperament and an ego uncrushable by any stone. He was a savage polemicist and as such wielded a virulent pen, he was one of the greatest philologists of antiquity, a masterful stylist, patron saint of all translators who came after him, someone to be invoked by those wrestling with the infernal problems of the alchemical process whereby the gold of one language is transmuted into the gold of the other. In that capacity the author of *De optimo genere interpretandi* also belongs to my own literary πανοπτικον (as he would say, the place where one can be observed from all sides, or where one can observe everything). No better book has been written about him – and about translation as art – than Valéry Larbaud's *Sous l'invocation de Saint Jérôme* (1946), but the man who emerges from those pages does not match the image that was cherished by seventeenth-century Spaniards, including Zurbarán. They saw him first and foremost as the eremite, the recluse, the anchorite, the breast-beater. This was the ascetic Spain of the Counter-Reformation, austere and at the same time brimming with religious fervour, a *chaud-froid* of renunciation of the flesh, mystical exaltation, and ostentatious splendour. The Hieronymites have almost died out, there are but a few left, and those only in Spain. Monastic Orders tend to disappear like rare birds. Their feathers were white and brown, chiaroscuro, brown scapulars on white tunics. But their monastery (now run by Franciscans) still stands, and even today it exudes the spirit of the Order: severe and rich. The intellectual tradition established in the fourth century by the founder – translator of the Bible from Hebrew and Greek into Latin – had earned the Order a privileged relationship with the crown of Castile. Hieronymites served as father confessors and advisers to Castilian kings. The black Virgin of Guadalupe is the patron saint of Spain, and the wealth arising from all those privileges is still visible today. Charles V's last abode on earth, in Yuste, was built as an annexe to one of their monasteries. It still stands, and there are seven monks still living there.

The precise year I first visited Guadalupe escapes me, but I know it was a very long time ago. The temperature was above thirty degrees, the earth was parched, the air shimmered in the heat. I drove through the sweep of land between Tagus and Guadiana, land that grows desert-like far from the rivers, and then abruptly offers solace again. An oasis by a stream, a clump of trees, the shade of stone oaks; I remember poppies, cornflowers, and I also remember thinking back on what I saw and realizing how much the scorched earth, the stony, barren landscape and then the sudden splash of colour – how much all that has to do with the art of Zurbarán, how the plethora of monks sometimes makes you forget there are other colours besides brown and grey and white and black, until he himself reminds you with the green and blue and another blue and yet another blue and gold and red and pink in *The Adoration of the Magi* at Grenoble, or with the fiery martyr's red of Saint Laurence in the small painting that once hung high and barely visible in the Carthusian monastery at Jerez de la Frontera, where it formed part of an altarpiece whose components have been scattered by time. Compare the red in the embroidered sleeve of the kneeling king with the blood-red of the dalmatic worn by the saintly martyr in that portrait showing him with his iron grid, the instrument of his torture and death, but lost to the world, sunk in prayer; compare it in turn with that other, deeper

The Adoration of the Magi, by Zurbarán

Saint Laurence, by Zurbarán

red of the strange curtain with stiff, almost cloud-like billows in the portrait of Bishop Gonzalo de Illescas at Guadalupe. The colour of that curtain, which so dramatically cleaves the space of the painting, is muted. There is a tinge of brown, of black, of dried blood; just visible behind it is a strip of blue sky, the same blue exactly as those magpies you only see in these parts.

I can spend hours looking at this painting, to the point of bafflement about whether the curtain is actually hanging before or behind the bishop who seems imprisoned in a protracted, indivisible instant. It is not certain whether he is sitting indoors or out, in a monastery or on a stage. The artist has draped the bottom edge of the white habit on the floor, and this subtle touch makes the space under and behind the chair forbidding and obscure, almost engulfing the curious little dog in the foreground. Also the front side of the tablecloth is shadowy, although it catches a fraction more light; the true colour of the cloth is revealed only when your gaze comes to rest on the surface of the table upon which the bishop's books are so clearly displayed, along with the indispensable gleaming skull and the hour-glass retelling the story of death and the

brevity of life – the same story the bishop may well be writing at this very
moment, for, above those still life objects, riveted in place, seeming to
defy the very existence of time and the passage of time, he looks at you

Bishop Gonzalo de Illescas, by Zurbarán

with the vacant gaze of the writer oblivious to those around him, a man in pursuit of an idea, a formula, a word. His pen is poised in the air halfway between the open volumes on the table and the closed book lying on what you might call a windowsill, beyond which extends a no less indeterminate space, framed by the black silhouettes of two columns which divide the interior (which may not be interior) from another world beyond, a *public* world in which the writer looking at us without seeing is distributing bread or money to the poor and infirm. It must be the same man, you can tell by his pale blue mozetta, the short mantle, and the monastery must be the same one as that in which he is posing for the portrait, so that the visitor observing this painting in the monastery of Guadalupe feels lured into a subtle trap and may even fancy that, any moment now, he himself will step out from behind that theatrical curtain. And perhaps he will. Who knows? On top of the closed book there is an apple, complete with the twig broken from the branch of the tree. There is a single leaf left on the twig. The apple is provocative, it is the apple that someone in Mantegna's *Camera degli Sposi* has let fall or is about to, or the apple that will be balanced on a man's head in order to be pierced by the arrow of a Swiss archer, the kind of apple that is eaten on pain of everlasting loss of innocence. I wish I could slip casually into that painting and take it in my hand, but that apple, emblematic and at the same time real, must lie there forever on the border between interior and exterior, as if it is quite alone in challenging the idea that is taking shape in the head of the man as he writes, the idea that presently – when he has turned to the paper before him – will take the form of words on that same, painted sheet of paper. But by then the painting I am looking at will have ceased to exist.

Then I proceed to do what all the pilgrims do, I climb the steps to the church. Already I am being lifted from the earth a little, although actually I must do it myself. The façade is hard to describe, there are too many peculiar elements, there is too much contrast and too little symmetry for a quick classification. The church is built like a fortress, but in the flamboyant Gothic whirlpools over the entrance portals, in the four dissimilar sections of the balustrade and in the rosette, the sunlight seems to be swirling in self-consuming rings of fire. The Arab influence is at its most obvious in the rosette, and if you stare at it for a while and then shut your eyes you will be left with a blazing labyrinth printed on your retina; without the help of a camera you have made your own living, moving picture, which you must contrive to store in your interior archive without damaging it.

I enter the monastery to the left of the church, and wait for the guided tour to begin. This time it is a group of Spaniards from the countryside, their faces filled with reverence. They crowd together in front of the tempting display of rosaries and figurines, medallions and postcards; trophies which they will take back to their homes in some remote province to remind them of the taste of faraway places for the rest of their lives. The guide is a layman, he has a dusty grey complexion and talks down to us from his privilege of sharing in the sanctity of the site, a scholar, for the stream of dates and names gushes forth at great speed. He has a record to break, it seems, so I get no more than a glimpse of all there is to see, a mere smattering of the Arab cloister with harmonious pavilion in two styles, Gothic and Moorish, or, as my Spanish guide-book says, "*el gótico de elevada espiritualidad con el árabe sensorial y humano*". I can believe it: elevated, spiritual, humane, sensual, for before me I see high aspiration and beauty combined, and I hear the self-absorbed trickle of the fountain, but I am not permitted to linger here because the guide has already herded the others into the museum, and is waiting for me like a sheepdog.

The space we now enter is furnished with glass cabinets filled with embroidered chasubles, mantles and *capas*, all of which were at some time worn for ceremonies. They present a strange spectacle, because they seem to be standing there like people without heads or feet, a regiment of decapitated priests in gold brocade, and as they are all turned in the same direction they seem to be actually looking at you. The cape, *capa*, the mantilla, the pelerine, the chasuble, each round item of clothing with a hole in the top symbolizes the dome, the tent, the round house – and the hole (for the head) is the chimney. The term used in the *Dictionnaire des Symboles* is "Heaven-directed imagery": the priest vested in mantle or chasuble ritually marks the epicentre of the universe, he perches on the axis of the world in his heavenly tent, his head in the afterlife in the company of God, as whose deputy on earth he serves. The tents are empty now, the heads that once rose from them have long since exchanged this life for another, up or down, who can say. They have left behind their golden dwellings, an empty village of gold and orna-ment, totems, richly embroidered with scenes from the lives of the saints. The monk Jerónimo Audije de la Fuente covered the *capa rica* with superbly fine embroidery, and my eyes are dazzled by the orgy of gold, the interlaced tracery of dancing leaves, the abundance of fruit, the radiance of the sunflowers on that satin field.

Beati / qui in / Deo / moriun / tur – blessed are they that die in the Lord. The men in these clothes (but these are not clothes, these are carapaces), the men who made them and wore them have long since vanished, their bodies melted from their deadly shells, carried off by the same, cheerful, vigorous Death that is portrayed in their embroidery. Priests, deacons, subdeacons, vestments for a requiem mass "with three señores", the mournful trio stand erect behind their panes of glass. An embroidered Death rises gleefully from the coffin, the scythe looms behind him. Is there such a thing as black brocade? The figure of Death is stitched in stiff silver on a black, intricately woven ground. In his right hand he holds the ominous, bleached bones, his taut little rib-cage attached to a sturdy spine which rises straight up from the golden casket. I count no fewer than twenty skulls on a single vestment. What emotion did the embroiderer feel when he put the final stitch in the twentieth? "The choir books weigh 50 kilos," the guide explains, but by the time I arrive at the illuminated manuscripts he has already swept on to the next room, we are whisked past the altar cloth donated by Henry IV of Castile, past the cross-eyed ox and squinting ass in the open *cantoral* of which I will never see a page. The infant in the manger appears to be pierced all over with darts of straw, but they are rays of gold bursting from his small naked body. Giving in to the persistent voice singling me out to hurry up, I tear myself away and am overcome by an almost physical sensation of futility. All those books, so randomly opened, all those pictures sealed from view, shut away, forbidden, as that man now shuts the door behind me. Gone, lost.

In another space the harsh voices of Spanish boys can be heard blurting out the Ave Marias, a vestige of something deep inside me makes me hum along with them. We walk through the nave and aisles of the church, I see the flags of all the countries of Latin America, the octagonal dome overhead, the ornate grille enclosing the choir with the elaborately carved seats, the polychrome altar sculpted by the son of El Greco, the Renaissance desk which belonged to Philip II and which has been incorporated into the altar, and then high up above, in the centre, she with the blackened face, the idol, the Great Mother, dressed from top to toe, shrouded in draperies, diamonds, pearls, gold, the focus of all attention, flanked by two Corinthian columns. Later on I get a better look at her. It is impossible to tell whether she is standing or sitting because of her voluminous cloak, and it's as if the old, undoubtedly plain, Romanesque image from the twelfth or thirteenth century has retreated behind the statue. Only the small black face, almost hidden, is visible behind a double horseshoe of pearls, above which floats an outsized jewel-studded crown. The right eye seems to veer away, the other seems more inward-looking. A straight nose, small mouth, a stiff little black hand peeps out from the garment, a golden sceptre held between the fingers. The guide beckons, and I follow a dozen shuffling Spaniards up the forty-two steps of red jasper, *for all the world a pilgrim*, and then I find myself in a cramped space crazed with ostentation, the *camarín* (little chamber), where the idol is dressed, undressed and dressed again in the presence of her biblical precursors, the Strong Women: Judith, Rachel, Abigail.

But now something odd happens. The guide has gone, his place has been taken by a monk. We stand packed together, in that dazzling treasure-chamber shaped like a Greek cross, surrounded by the Strong Women under their inverted, stylized scallops, surrounded by Luca Giordano's fluid paintings of scenes from the life of the Madonna, moments in another myth that has lost its self-evidence. Not for those around me though – a couple of nuns, some elderly people, a young boy. They are waiting, I have been given to understand, for the Great Trick, but it is not time for that yet. The monk, who is quite old, concentrates his attention on the boy alone, to the exclusion of everyone else. The child is not in the least embarrassed. The pale hand emerging from the wide sleeve of the brown habit rests on his shoulder and steers him past the statues and paintings, the voice speaks of kings, treasures, gems, artists. It is a wonderful story, how the image was carved by Saint Luke, how it was lost in the mists of time, and rediscovered in the fourteenth century by a shepherd after a cow dropped dead by a stream and miraculously came to life again, how the Virgin appeared to the shepherd and how King Alfonso XI heard about the vision and vowed to build a sanctuary for her, how she then became the virgin queen of *Hispanidad* (Hispanicism, everything Spanish), what sort of miracles she performed, and all the names of the people who gave her the ever more sumptuous, gaudy, gem-encrusted robes in which she is dressed on feast days. And then – he still hasn't reached the end of his story – he opens two little doors made of gold with enamelled scenes. As we gaze at the Madonna's embroidered back and past the statue down into the church, he pushes an invisible button and slowly, with a gentle purr, the statue turns round to face us, shockingly close. It crosses my mind that in the church below they can only see her back at this point, and I look at my watch to check the time because I'd like to witness this scene from below, to see what is the reaction when the lady high above the altar suddenly turns her back on the assembled faithful. But where I am now there is deep emotion, the nuns kneel, there is much sighing, the women touch the hem of the robe, they cross themselves, the child is wide-eyed, and the priest, his pale face caught in the beam of the floodlight, is triumphant: *ballerino assoluto*. Did it again!

It occurs to me that I have seen something like this only once before, in Ingmar Bergman's *Smiles of a Summer Night*, when the lord of the manor presses a button to make his mistress's bed slide into his room to a fanfare of little trumpets. A disrespectful comparison, since that lady was a mistress of such different sentiments. But things can get worse, for the next day I went back to experience the miracle again.

This time it was not the Protestant Ingmar Bergman who sprang to mind, but the anticlerical and blasphemous Spanish master of my best hours, Buñuel, although I have never heard anyone fart in one of his films. For it was a fart that I heard. A long one, coursing through the entire range of the twelve-tone system, albeit at the instruction of a composer from an earlier time, with *andantes* and *prestos*, *lentos* and *accelerandos*, a wonder of unflagging expression. This time it was not the old monk of the previous day but a high-minded young man who found the proximity of the secular fold with their meaty smell almost too much to bear and who, for lack of a child on whom to fix his attention, talked over our heads, as if that was where his discourse belonged, half a metre above our brains of *profanum vulgus*, and the *vulgus*, a bunch of stooped, gnarled peasants with broad medieval faces of the kind that will have disappeared from the face of the earth in a hundred years' time, were drenched in reverence, drinking in the nectar of words raining from above. I waited for the button to be pushed so that the black statue would gyrate again and stare, and when the moment arrived everything proceeded as it had the day before, the sighing and the crossing, the kneeling and the touching of the holy hem, and at that instant there issued from one of the old women, no longer belonging to this world, a fart of fear, a helpless response from low to high, tumbling and sliding, rising now plaintive then triumphant into the twenty-metre-high dome above us in the *camarín*, the ultimate fart, never to be surpassed, gathering shaky momentum, growing triumphant, culminating in baroque jubilation, and then slowly, as if unwilling to let go, dissolving into that ultimate form of music, the bars of rest in a composition.

It is at such times that the differences between cultures become apparent. To the Spaniards in our group, for whom death, both their own and that of animals (and by extension the consumption of food and attendant bodily functions), is part of everyday life and therefore generally draws only fleeting attention, the incident is of no consequence. A brief smile on the peasant faces, a brief reprimand from the two daughters of the wind musician, a cloud of forgiveness around the heads of the Franciscan, that was all. But the only two representatives of less earthy races, the author of these words and an attractive Englishwoman with reddish hair, had the misfortune of letting their eyes meet and could not stifle their laughter. Steadying ourselves on the jasper and marble balustrade with gold ornaments, we fled from the inner sanctum, because those who deny the presence of excrement and death in their daily lives by focusing on the benefits of counselling for the dying, on euphemisms and air-fresheners, cannot but capitulate in the face of such a demonstration of corporeality.

This shared fit of the giggles did not become a love story, alas. We pull ourselves together and rejoin the tour in the treasure chamber, back in the not-real world where *I* am more at ease than my fellow pilgrims: the world of art, of ambiguity, of noble deception.

Through the *antesacristía*, the anteroom of the sacristy proper, we walk past the disdainful, down-turned mouths of Charles the Hexed and Marie-Louise of Orléans – she corseted like a queen bee, he with shoulder-length hair framing his face, a marshal's baton and a black gleaming beetle-like carapace to camouflage his fatal weakness. (He was the last of the Spanish Habsburgs.) They are both watching the entrance to this treasure-trove which shelters the Zurbaráns. Maybe this is not all that respectful a description of a sacristy, but the place is stamped with an oriental luxury which, if not in harmony with the deserts and the solitary quest for God, is entirely compatible with Saint Jerome's forty-fourth letter (to Fabiola) in which he describes in great detail and with numerous illustrations the vestments worn by the levites in the Temple at Jerusalem, and what they symbolised. Synagogue et Ecclesia. Valery Larbaud was later to express surprise at this juxtaposition. "Did Jerome clearly take stock of this passage of eastern into western thought, of this fusion, as it seems to us today, of these two traditions in Catholic orthodoxy?" A marriage of Temple and Cross, this was to be just the thing for the master who was working on the Vulgate right up to his death in Bethlehem.

The sacristy was built between 1635 and 1645 by a Carmelite friar who remained anonymous, but who knew what he was about. It measures twenty-eight metres long, seven and a half metres wide, with a height of twelve metres.

On entering one is seized with a sense of dizziness; it is only after a while that one notices the pictures. Garlands, flowers, fruit, bows, pilasters, entablatures (cornisamentos), transoms, and dinteles, frescoes, gilt and jasper, the colours of the chasubles and stoles catch one up in a whirlwind until the moment when the eye is arrested, seized by the claustral silence emanating from the eight large canvases painted by Zurbarán for the sacristy. For two solid years the painter lived and worked here on these illustrations which depict scenes from the stories of religious men long dead: lives, miracles, encounters. Silence is the only word, a great peace inhabits these canvases, and even today one is struck by the instant when the painter intervenes: here the bishop reflects on the word he wants to set down on the paper; in the next picture Christ passes and rests His hand with infinite delicacy on the forehead of Father Andrès de Samerón; in the next we have Father Cabañuelas on his knees, attired for Mass, lost in his vision. Not a breath to indicate movement, there is nowhere for time to flee to, the candle-flame does not waver, the host does not skim, it rests suspended in the golden air; the pattern embroidered in the chasuble harmonises with the one in the carpet covering the altar steps, the design is just as complex, just as motionless, down to the smallest thread in the fabric and in the multicoloured embroideries: here eternity reigns. Behind the priest, the acolyte looks out at us. He appears not to notice the miracle taking place before his eyes; his gaze is as empty as the square behind him, rimmed with classical buildings, which suggests that the miracle took place on this earth and not in some other place. But what sort of a world is this in which some obscure figure may wander across a space that looks covered in snow?

And suddenly I dream of the silence which must have reigned here while Zurbarán was painting: the silence of the monastery, the silence of the village which was even smaller at the time, the silence of the empty countryside all about. The only noises are those made by the animals, the wind, human voices, the monastery bells, the monks' chant.

Two low decorated arches give access to Saint Jerome's chapel, in an extension to the sacristy. Here the brothers' exemplary lives are displayed at their apogee; but now it is the Founder of the order himself who is to serve as model for his future disciples: one moment negative, the next one positive, one moment as a sinner and penitent, the next a saint. And it is precisely the nature of sin that throws such an odd light on the Spain of Zurbarán's day, and on the paintings' protagonist: the first painting shows the linguist (Saint Jerome) scourged by angels for having shown too much interest in pagan (classical) authors. Kneeling on the ground like a wretched supplicant, he lifts his face to Christ who radiates utter peace and prepares to watch through half-closed eyes and see how the two angels are going to administer the chastisement. "Are going to", for there is as yet no trace of the lashes to be seen on the bare back; the angels have raised their scourges (they look simply like branches) to a uniform height and in less than a second will lash the vulnerable pallor of this back; the whistle of the lash may be heard.

A muscled back, a male back, which would have been unthinkable without the Renaissance, the Renaissance that was to retrieve authors banned in Italy and turn them into their new saints, and all this more than 200 years before Zurbarán. Spanish paradoxes! It is a strange canvas; I do not care for it and yet I cannot help scrutinising it. The position in which the supplicant saint is placed, in a different plane from that of the Christ figure, reinforces the impression that the scene does not concern him. Nor do the angels seem all that much affected by what they are doing, they could just as well be engaged in threshing wheat; nothing dramatic is to be read in their faces, they are fixed in their postures, like two large male birds with women's hair beneath a stormy sky charged with clouds from which a couple of absurd putti (an aberration of the religious evolution) are watching the spectacle – or maybe they are not, that is not obvious either. These blows about to come hissing down, for whom are they intended? Are they meant for Cicero, for Seneca or some of those other authors the saint had included in his texts without mentioning them by name, so much so that later

The Temptation of Saint Jerome, by Zurbarán

generations assumed these were his own writings? Or do the blows attest
Jerome's own self-laceration in spite of everything, his sense of culp-
ability – in our own view so unlikely and unjustified – for having one day
yielded to the morose pleasure of a vulgar tongue? What is here depicted
is the vision of the person thus scourged; the painter had nothing to
invent for this picture, any more than for the *Temptation of Saint Jerome*
in the same chapel, one of the most beautiful and mysterious of
Zurbarán's canvases.

Here the saint is an old man, a stranger to the world, his features have
changed; in a gesture of rejection he stretches out his long, scrawny,
senile arms towards the group of five young women busy with their
music-making. Half his face is in shadow, which prevents us really seeing
his expression; we can guess at it, however, from the eloquent way in
which his arms repel the seduction in an intense supernatural light: go,
leave me alone in this desert, alone with my sacred books and this skull
that prefigures death, be gone, let this chalice pass from me. The man has

turned his face away, but what would he see were he to look? These women are not lascivious temptresses: the same mystical effulgence that falls on the saint's anguished arms throws light also on the serious, sad faces of these musicians. A storm would seem to be raging in the darkened sky: the eleven versions which my dictionary gives of the word *tenebrae* all suit here: obscurity, night, blindness, a dark place, a cavern, prison, dark spot, mystery, ignorance, spiritual blindness, melancholy. What are these luminous women doing steeped here in this double darkness, that of the rocks – barely discernible – beside which the man is kneeling clad in a loincloth of purple colour (the cardinals' colour) who is mortifying his flesh, and that of the sky, lowering, menacing, tormented? And what is the source of this light that does not exist in nature and throws a pitiless radiance on this static, leaden group? Bodies, faces, objects, the so-very-palpable wood of the harp, the lute, the guitar; the neck of the guitar player – it might have been sculpted – that feels so soft and diaphanous beneath the fingers, the insolent luxury of her heavy silk dress, the black orifices of the skull, the luminous, dog-eared page of the book which the saint was reading before the women disturbed him in his voluntary solitude.

In this detail the saint parts company with the writer in the representation he gives us of his vision; the women are dancers who surprise the hermit in his hut isolated in the middle of the desert, and make him escape towards the dangers of this wild region. One asks oneself what sort of picture would have resulted had Zurbarán stuck with the writer's vision. Perhaps the sensuality would have shocked the monks who commissioned the painting; the sensuality is here attenuated because static, but the painter would have imbued it with movement. But who is to say? Now the only person dancing is the kneeling saint; his arms move in a lyrical fashion deemed to express fear, defensiveness, a touch of choreographic genius. In a moment he will get up and start dancing to the sound of the feminine music that we cannot hear, a dance of rejection, negation, of mortification.

Who was this painter who vanished behind his canvases, who could paint the voluptuousness of silk to the point where even today we can feel it beneath our fingers, as real and palpable as the disgust for the world that goes inseparably with the coarse texture of homespun?

Behind each of Zurbarán's paintings one perceives this burning passion; the erotic component in Hadewych's mysticism or that of St John of the Cross finds here its ecstatic painterly equivalent; but one cannot depict the carnal so perfectly without having observed it, felt it, lived it, just as one may not depict spiritual ecstasy unless one has first abandoned oneself to mysticism. Or do I deceive myself? It took me time to *see* Zurbarán's work, and even more time to love it. There is no time for dallying here; as far as the tour guide is concerned these paintings – which incidentally are more colourful than most of Zurbarán's works – are simply a feature of the sacristy. I buy a postcard of one of them on leaving the church.

I sit down on the steps, where yet another group has assembled for a tour, and look at the picture. It shows a monk, Pedro de Cabañuelas, who was suddenly assailed by doubts while celebrating mass: what if it were not true that bread and wine are changed into the body and blood of Christ during consecration? Not a single thought on earth passes unnoticed, for punishment follows forthwith, the Eucharist rises, paten and all, into a golden grotto of clouds where it floats, radiant like the white light itself, thereby illuminating the priest's tormented features and his crimson chasuble, picking out each pattern in the Oriental carpet on which he kneels and every detail, fold, pleat, billow of the acolyte's white habit and dark brown scapular. The instruction in delicate gold lettering "*Tace quod vides et inceptum perfice*", which translates roughly as, remain silent about what you have seen and proceed with the mass, comes down from the heavens and sinks into the gaunt, incredulous skull. Cured. In the background a square, half hidden by elegant columns, leads through three equal arches to a world where no one lives, and a few faint figures of monks linger in that fantasy architecture which is bathed in a light that could only be caused by a permanent, all-enveloping flash of lightning.

Enough. I slide back into ordinary life, the life of low houses and balconies with geraniums, the cobbles, the gurgle of the weak fountain on the village square, the cafés filled with men in black, the diminutive woman with her home-grown tomatoes, laurel, lemons, the tobacconist with the lottery tickets that never win, yesterday's newspaper – the unchanging everyday world which has paid for the treasures of the palatial monastery behind me. I go into a shop which is empty but for the counter and buy a bag of *churros* for seven pesetas, and then I climb up the ancient streets of the *barrio alto* and beyond until I am high above the buildings. I rest for a while on a low wall under an olive tree, and watch dusk take over from daylight. Swirls of mist are approaching from the right and dark clouds gather over the low brown plain set in a wide circle of mountains. In the small town far below, a lamb bleats, a dog barks, children's voices ring out. Grey clouds slide out from under a high cover of paler grey, a man's voice urges his donkey on with cries of *huí, hará*, I watch them as they inch their way down a steep path, and then the two-toned Angelus rings out, and I realize how irrevocably I, too, belong to a late form of Antiquity.

XII

A Moment in the Memory of God

A civilization obliterated ~ Trujillo, city of the conquistadores
Ghosts of another age in Mérida ~ Holy Week
A civilization recorded

T HE TEMPERATURE IS WELL OVER 30 °C, the landscape of
Extremadura has adjusted itself to the heat, the car radio has
adjusted itself to the landscape and is broadcasting a mass with a
lot of loud singing and false notes. It is three in the afternoon when I
drive into Trujillo, and I'm in luck, because the town totals a mere
10,000 inhabitants, all of whom are asleep. Through deserted streets I
drive to the Plaza Mayor, where the last survivor tucks a parking slip
under my windscreen wiper before retreating into the shade on the steps
by the church of San Martín. The only living creatures that still move at
this time of day are the storks on top of the spires and towers, stepping
gingerly on their ragged nests, at home in their own African heat. I am
standing in front of a vigorous equestrian statue of the conquistador
Pizarro, his sword thrust forward to stab his Inca adversaries, and so he
must remain until it is his turn to be murdered, since the sculptor has
forgotten to provide him with a scabbard for his weapon. The clock
rumbles, so something must have happened to time, but on the square
nothing changes. I stroll along the crumbling palaces of the conquistadores, find myself back where I started and catch sight of the huge
medieval castle rising high above the town. The prospect of climbing
up there being too daunting, I seek refuge in the shade where the
parking attendant now dozes, and shell some roasted sunflower seeds.
An inordinate amount of shelling for a few tiny seeds – food for people
with little money but plenty of time.

A good map lays bare the history and hence the soul of a place,
like an X-ray. Wounds, old scars, repairs, additions, they are all clearly

recognizable. Trujillo is not a big town, it makes a small map. Churches, monasteries, noblemen's mansions, they're easy to pick out as they are shaded purple, and they join the chorus telling of now old, then new aristocracy, the strategically placed monasteries clustered about the town like the signs of the zodiac. It is only when you translate their names that the oddness strikes you: the monastery of the Incarnation, of Mercy, of Conception, the church of the Blood, of María la Mayor, Mary the Greater, and then, a little distance away, the Albacar, the old bastion of the castle, and to the west, by the triumphal gate, the Alcázar, the fortress, the palace of the Bejaranos, the Alcazarojo of the Altamiranos, the fortified house, *casa fuerte*, of the Escobar family. It goes on and on, until I have spelled out all those names of men who were nothing when they departed but whose return from Peru, Ecuador, Bolivia, laden with gold and silver, was rewarded with the ranks of count, knight, duke and marquis, and who built grand houses which they proceeded to decorate with their newly acquired crests and quarterings. The gold and silver booty would be funnelled into the monasteries and cathedrals and the unsuccessful wars of their rulers, the New World would cast off the yoke of the Old, the palaces would become the homes of bats, storks and nuns, only the names would survive, sometimes with people of flesh and blood to bear them, in history books and registers of noble families, and in dusty, sweltering cities scattered all over the conquered continent at the other end of the world.

It is true to say that history is never more than an interpretation of certain facts, and that there is always a parallel version in which the same facts present a different face. What is victory and conquest in one history book is defeat and oppression in another. But our knowledge of the facts and of the outcome, added to diminished personal involvement of the future spectator provided by the distance in time separating us from a particular event, can create a feeling of almost divine omnipotence, as if knowing how things turned out enables us to survey the past from a lofty position of superiority. Walking about Trujillo's depleted blazonry is like reaching the end of a blood-curdling novel and then turning straight back to page one, to the time when the same town lay there, dun-coloured and unprepossessing, when the grand houses had yet to be built and the adventurers had yet to depart in search of gold and the world. In the course of the story the palaces will be erected, the enterprising townsmen will be granted aristocratic ranks and honours with which to prefix and suffix their names, and at the same time, in faraway lands halfway across the globe, an entire civilization will be destroyed within a few years, the devastation being so great that the few remaining pieces of the puzzle are only now, after centuries, beginning to be painstakingly reassembled.

At one end of the scale the Inca empire, ruled by an absolute monarch, grouped into units of ten, each unit responsible to the next largest unit; a state of farmers without personal property – an authoritarian socialist society, to be sure, where everyone was allotted land in keeping with the size of his family. First he would harvest one third for the Sun (the State), then he would help the old, the sick and others who needed help to gather their harvest, then he would harvest one third for himself, and the last third was for the imperial Inca, who ruled his empire through a caste of royals and inspectors who travelled constantly through the land. The road they travelled was the longest in history, longer than the Roman road from Scotland to Jerusalem, and it was marked every two miles with staging posts for the ever-ready *chasquis*, the relay runners. In this way a distance of 2,000 kilometres could be covered in five days.

Pizarro leaves Trujillo with 130 men, forty cavalry and two small cannons, and arrives in this society of planned agriculture, stupendous monuments, untold quantities of gold and rigid organization. What happens next is one of those things that gives history that nightmarish quality, that makes it all so freakish, when a small miscalculation causes irreparable damage. But now, more easily than then, the insanity can be summed up: two civilizations failed to understand each other's *signals*, whereupon one of them simply ceased to exist, was obliterated.

The last of the Incas, Atahualpa, is in what is now Cajamarca, taking a cure of hot sulphur baths. He has vanquished his rival and brother Huascar, he is a god in his kingdom, his spittle is not permitted to touch the earth and is therefore caught in the cupped hands of virgins, his raiment of vicuña is never worn twice. He is planning a triumphal entry into Cuzco, the capital. Pizarro captures Cajamarca during the Inca's absence and sends a messenger with an invitation to Atahualpa. The latter arrives with 6,000 men, and within thirty-three minutes a centuries-old empire lies in ruins. The divine Inca is carried to the main square of the city on a golden litter, the feet of the son of the Sun are not permitted to touch the ground. Servants sweep the street ahead of the procession. But Pizarro has ordered his soldiers to take up positions in the surrounding buildings and he himself, a towering figure on his horse (an animal unknown to the Incas), rides towards the Inca. The Dominican monk Valverde holds out a Bible to Atahualpa; he doesn't know what it is and lets the holy book fall to the ground. This is the signal for attack. The two small cannons are fired, the Indians panic, 2,000 unarmed Incas are massacred, Atahualpa is taken prisoner. But it is only in *our* minds that he was defeated by fewer than 200 Spaniards and forty horses. He, however, was defeated by beasts with feet of silver, creatures that were semi-human, centaurs. Or in the shape of a legend of white gods who were fated to return. His downfall was not brought about by the power of his adversary, but by an interpretation, and by the time the Incas realized that it was too late.

The Inca empire was a colossus with feet of clay, but it was also a colossus with a head of gold. When that head rolled, the body became the pawn in any game Pizarro wished to play. In exchange for his freedom the captive Atahualpa offered a ransom in gold, enough gold to fill the room in which he was imprisoned from floor to ceiling. Pizarro accepted the offer, messengers were dispatched, the gold was gathered, the blood-gold that the Spaniards made so much of in the subsequent centuries. Once he had collected the ransom, Pizarro held a mock trial during which Atahualpa was charged with idolatry and polygamy. He was condemned to burn at the stake, but because he – having at last come down to earth – agreed to convert to the incomprehensible Christian faith of his captors, a less harsh sentence was considered appropriate. Having undergone the baptismal rites, the last of the Incas, emperor of an empire where the sun had set for ever, was strangled by the garrotte.

Pizarro then travelled to Cuzco, the navel of the Inca world 3,400 metres high up in the Andes. That city, and all the other splendid Inca cities of South America, was devastated, reduced to ashes. The Incas of South America never recovered from the humiliation; they lost their culture and their language in one blow, like, to paraphrase Spengler, a sunflower beheaded with the flick of a cane. Pizarro in his turn was also murdered, and as he lay dying he just managed to dip his fingers in his blood and make a cross on the ground, a cross of blood to mark the end of his own life. Some fifteen years ago I saw his last resting place in the cathedral at Lima, Peru: a leathery mannikin, the skeleton poking through the skin, the beard that had struck terror into the heart of the

Inca like devil's horsehair sprouting from the decaying jaw; the colonial dilemma on display in a gilded coffin.

Trujillo now seems very similar: a grave in which the living reside. I can hear them but I cannot see them, muffled Spanish sounds behind thick wooden doors with iron cladding, mournful songs behind the coats of arms, murmurs that follow me as I make my way up to the castle. There is no one in sight. The crenellations, the square towers, the wall which still encloses most of the town, sombre, fierce and useless, colonized now by grey-black crows. Below, the plain stretches as far as the eye can see, on the surface of the plain the heat, and in the middle, the long, straight road to Cáceres, on which I will soon travel.

What does a foreigner do in Trujillo? He roams the shadowy alleys, retraces his steps down to the Plaza Mayor, admires the medallions of Francisco Pizarro and his Indian wife Yupanqui Huaynas gracing the palace of the conquistador's son-in-law Hernando, who had them installed when the title of Marqués de la Conquista had been conferred on him. Pizarro looks none too happy, the grandee of conquest, his long El Greco-like face held firm between two excessively ornate Renaissance columns, the high, rounded cheekbones, the extraordinary hat, the flowing beard looking white in the carved stone overhanging the eagle that separates him from the modest virginal face of his Indian conquest, home at last.

A crowd of Lolita-age girls twitter in the dark entrance portal of the palace of the dukes of San Carlos. One of them lays a finger on her lips and pulls at the handle of a bell which clangs somewhere down the hall. Slippered footsteps approach the door, they sound like nervous sighs. A nun in white opens the door, the girls scurry away, the nun swoops past me like a white bat in an attempt to grab one of the girls, but they're too quick and their high-pitched shrieks vanish around the corner, triumphant. The nun now strikes classical poses, eyes upturned to heaven, arms raised, a lot of *ay! ay!* and deep sighing, but when the tour is over I have still seen nothing. The palace, which remains the property of the eponymous dukes, has been robbed of its soul, it has been over-restored. Only the exterior is original, a barred fortress that the duke has leased to the nuns under the protection of his family coat of arms, which straddles two walls, secured by the imperial two-headed eagle, one head on each wall, glaring left and right at an enemy that will never show its face again.

I spend an afternoon wandering the faded treasure trove of the past, the robbers' lair which was itself plundered by the mysterious enemy at whose hands names fade and weapons are rendered obsolete, facts remain facts and yet undergo subtle changes, a city is relegated to the past in a forgotten province like pulverized memory.

That very day, having travelled 88 kilometres in distance and 1,500 years in time, I sit down in the Roman amphitheatre of Mérida. The sky is red, the play is called decline, but the stage is empty and I sit alone, high up, in such a seat as a humble Roman foot soldier might occupy. I stare at the large flagstones no longer trodden by the feet of actors, I hear the absent laughter at Plautus' witticisms, I yearn for Rome, and I think all the other appropriate thoughts. But it's just too much, two separate histories are too much for one day. I look, *bête et méchant*, at the statues of gods who have lost their heads but not their poses, climb down those far too large steps from the *cavea* to the orchestra, give a shout that echoes shrilly and shoo away a pair of doves, stroll across the proscenium, past the *aditus maximus*, inspect the grey, gleaming twisted columns.

It is hard to believe, but for a moment I am alone among the 5,500 empty seats. The eye of the imagination fills them with people wearing togas and tunics, and the owner of that fanciful eye dreams about really seeing them, Romans in a western province, 2,000 years ago. I remain there quietly, in the midst of these shades from the past, and stay until the watchmen in the distance announce loudly that the gates are about to be closed and I saunter past the surviving mosaics towards the exit. Three cheerful figures, portrayed in fragments of coloured stone, are briskly treading grapes. Stone men, stone grapes, stone juice flowing into conical jars, in which it will be left to ferment, and with my stone hand I will raise the stone wine of that mosaic to my mouth, a mouth like theirs, of small, chipped, pinkish little stones, and in my petrified drunkenness I will see them, the *naumachiae*, naval battles with fully manned war ships, real ships on real water, brought here over canals now dry, dry but surviving yet, just like the cages for the wild animals, the gladiators' quarters, the remains of the race track. I trace my finger along the grooves that together spell Caesar's name and try to work out how many years it is since I had to study his military prose, but then the watchmen ring the bell and call out that the Last Judgement is upon us and chase me out of paradise.

Trujillo, Mérida, Sevilla. Andalusia has drawn me towards her, but now shows her harshest face, the temperature has risen above 40 °C. Who gets no snow makes it himself: I have never seen a more dazzling white than the white houses of Zafra and Llerena, I have bypassed the Great City, the white spider's web of Arcos de la Frontera, everything frozen in the heat, the compacted snow of the igloos full of harsh Spanish sounds, I have driven through the low Guadalquivir valley down to Cádiz.

Sunday afternoon reigns when I arrive, complete with palm trees, the sigh of the ocean, the proximity of Africa. The day is languorous, grey warships float in the subdued water, nothing moves, this is farewell to Europe. I try to remember when I was here before, I remember a military procession, shuffling boots, monotonous drums, gold, holy idols hoisted into the sunlight. But that is a radiant memory, the city I visited then had a vibrancy I miss now.

On the boulevard I walk under a fig tree so huge that a hundred people could take shelter beneath its canopy. Men slouch on the tiled benches, listening to a football match on transistor radios. The *Artillería* building has been abandoned, the windows smashed, I catch a glimpse of three lonely little ships sailing in the distance where the air is surely cool, and then I drive back to Seville ahead of the day trippers, back into the heat which does not go away even after dusk, but seems to come to a standstill in the spacious parks with frangipani trees and in the white-washed patios cluttered with incessantly watered plants. Gypsies shatter the heat and silence with their clapping. Plaintive cries, wailing, fans, mantillas, the drumming of heels, tormented expressions, and that insane feeling that there are some places in the world where things are sustained for your sake alone, to help you remember. You need only step inside to witness that music again, the familiar expressions of pain, the long-drawn-out, Moorish, plaintive tones, the quivering dancers, all of it false perhaps and yet true, the sound of this underbelly of Europe being torn off like a strip of a flag. The words are so protracted that they have become mere sounds, the convulsed movements of the dancers speak of torment, the guitars pluck their notes from a memory that is not mine, it is merely wafted in my direction from another continent and another time. The same feeling is still there the following day, when I am lured out of my cool hotel near the cathedral by the bleating of loud boys' voices and the thudding roll of a drum.

Sure enough, the first thing I see is a huge *paso de Semana Santa*, its bearers concealed beneath it except for four times four pairs of small shuffling feet. This float is covered with a blood-red cloth, and the unwieldy black cross on top is loosely draped with a demure white shawl. A riffle of castanets now rises above the drumbeats, but I can't tell where the clicking is coming from until a bevy of very small girls in Sevillian costume turns the corner.

A crowd gathers from all sides now. Golden legions for those with a fondness for boys, grave-looking lads weighed down by the cross, their football-players' bodies hidden under monks' habits. Each group has its own *paso*, its own symbols. The poor bodies that belong to the feet underneath must be suffering tortures of heat. This may still be Catholicism, but it is the fanatic, flagellant variety, strange and dire, extreme like the heat and the landscape of Andalusia. I escape into the cathedral, where the sound of drums and castanets pursues me like the rumble of distant thunder, for hours on end.

What can one do when the temperature rises to 40 °C? Do as the Sevillians do: sigh, and wait until the sun has set to go out in search of coolness in gardens and churches, to stroll along the Guadalquivir, but at a slow pace, until night spreads itself out like a black cloth over the city and river, over the twelve-sided tower where the merchant ships set sail for the Indies, over the palm trees and rose bushes, the lilies and the cypresses in the gardens of the Alcázar. Murmuring voices and murmuring water courses, crumbling columns and trimmed hedges, the croaking of frogs among the water lilies, whispering and shuffling of feet, real flowers and the flowers of the arabesques, the letters in your guidebook jostle and merge into a grey blur of absent, meaningless text. The paths are sprinkled with petals, as if for a grand wedding. A bird, unaware that the night is falling, whistles a butcher boy's vanished tune. The air is scented with a different climate, as if it couldn't be otherwise, as if among the memories of houris and Moorish princes the Spaniards were led as a matter of course to the momentous discovery of the tropics: a logical sequence.

Trujillo, Seville. The hard men came from Trujillo, while their heritage, the inventory of their estate, is to be found in Seville, in the *Archivo General de las Indias*. If the clock, the hour-glass, the skull in the hand of the monk are to symbolize the passage of time, the archive itself presents a far more eclectic metaphor. Time has passed, yet it is preserved. Bound in volumes, recorded in writing, bundled and tied with string, room after room stacked from floor to ceiling with time. A more suitable building than this *lonja*, this exchange built by Philip II would be impossible to find: an immense icebox of granite guarded by lions, in which is housed the colonial past, every sigh and every comma, until the end of the world.

You climb the wide marble staircase slowly, and then find yourself in a spacious room where a warden sits behind his desk like Mussolini. He makes a note of your name as if you too are to be added to history, and next you step into a vast hall where every inch of wall space is taken up with bulging, dark brown portfolios, the ties invisible at the back. I ask whether I may see one of the portfolios, but it is not allowed, that is only possible in special rooms with special permission. Scholars from all over the world come here to sniff around, to browse, to conduct secret investigations, because these portfolios contain everything to do with the colonies – per geographical region, per historical period, everything. EVERYTHING: cadastres, letters of supplication, custodial sentences, decrees, financial accounts, reports of military campaigns, letters from governors overseas, negotiations, plans for the layout of new cities, maps. That must be what God's memory looks like: every centimetre, every second of every man and every spot on the face of the earth, described and recorded.

Even as I stand in this room His thoughts are drawn to Santo Domingo, and my finger touches His thought as it runs over the spine of portfolio number 744 of the *Sección Quinta, Audiencia de Santo Domingo*, but the numbers continue all the way up the wall to where I can no longer read them. And this is just one room, devoted to one island. Other, larger rooms preserve the memories of Peru, Chile, Cuba, New Mexico, Florida, in clerical handwriting and coloured maps, soldiers' letters to their loved ones and ledgers, the memories of everything that linked the Spaniards, in a case of mistaken identity that is perpetuated to this day, to what they thought were the Indies.

And so I move past the inaccessible centuries and seconds, with the feeling that all this cannot really be possible. To give the visitor some idea of what is to be found in the world that is securely locked away, there is a selection of maps, books and letters on display under glass. A blue bird with ragged wings flies over the Río Tinto, a split banner in its beak. *1730: Plano del puerto de Acapulco*, with its settlement and army of San Diego. The depth of the harbour is indicated on the map, so now I know how deep the water at Acapulco was in 1730. Or is, for on this map time has stopped at 1730, just as in the next cabinet, showing the "expansion, situation and dimension" of the *Alcaldía Mayor de San Salvador*, it has stopped at 1778. Nicaragua: map of the course of the river Matince, with its shores and lands situated between the Moin and the Pacuaré. Letters from Magellan, Vespucci, Columbus, the escutcheon of La Paz, the course of the Orinoco, a dazzle of heraldic configurations, maps with childish colours, troop movements and decrees, records of everything that happened after Pizarro of Trujillo and Cortés of Medellín had killed the Inca and Aztec rulers and had obliterated their centuries-old empires, when they founded a new empire which would fall apart into a variety of different countries four centuries later, but which would still be suffering from the sickness of its conquerors. When I step outside hours later, my brain is scoured like the outside of a spaceship returning to earth after many years.

XIII

Winter Days in Navarre

Basque tension in San Sebastián ~ Desolation in Olite
The birth of the Gothic arch ~ Alone in Sos del Rey Católico
Fluid stone in Sos Sangüesa ~ Company in Sos del Rey Católico

S AN SEBASTIÁN LIES ON THE Bay of Biscay like a somewhat
bizarrely painted lady of a certain age reclining on a sofa. She has
known better days, murmurs in theatre boxes, royal admirers –
all that belongs to the past now, but the traces of former glory are still
in evidence, and for someone who falls for that she is still quite attractive. The good thing about the impoverished rich is that they take better
care of their remaining possessions. As there is no money to buy anything new, the lamps, the wardrobes and the engravings of the old days
are still in use. San Sebastián is a huge storehouse of Art Nouveau and
Jugendstil, odd-looking bridges with lamps of the kind that you find
nowhere nowadays, hotels that, in Brussels, would have been demolished long ago, wrought-iron railings a collector would like to be
hanged from.

It suits me fine. I have escaped from the snares and entanglements of
the world to go on a nostalgic winter journey in my ridiculous battered
purple car. I haven't decided yet on my itinerary and so I have taken a
room at the Hotel María Cristina on the Paseo de la República
Argentina. A child in uniform leads me through a civilized garden into a
hall vast enough to massacre three royal families in. I like things that are
time-worn, but even in this field it is as well to be a connoisseur. It
all depends on what it is that is showing wear and tear. An interminable
parade of kidskin boots and court shoes belonging to pimps, poets,
mistresses and bankers has given the Persian football field under the
chandeliers the patina of a time forever lost, which is only accentuated
by the discreet repairs done in the twenties, thirties and fifties. The brass

stair rail, though, is still in place, and brass polish is cheaper than a new carpet. The doorman's shirt is as white as snow, but as he shaves carelessly on most days, like today, the collar is beginning to fray. The leaves of the ficus are a bit dusty, too. My bed has fancy brass ornaments, and the passions it has borne in a long life make me roll into the soft rabbit-hole in the middle. There are mirrors in the room in which my supine reflection would fit twenty times. The passage of time has woven a dull sandy shade into the red velvet of the curtains. My clothes hang, wall-flowers in this ballroom of a wardrobe. There is no doubt in my mind, this place was once the abode of giants, and tonight they will come to get me and will stuff me into their gigantic trouser pockets or hurl me out of the window, over the statue of the gazing navigator whose name I cannot make out, into the Rio Urumea. A ripple, and then nothing.

The streets of the old town are paved with big stones. The streets are narrow, poorly lit. A singing, strolling Saturday evening crowd fills the bars, wine splashes into glasses, the walls are covered with Basque slogans. The atmosphere is restive, as in garrison towns or provincial capitals on the edges of the kingdom; Spanish and yet not Spanish, and it seems to be a different era. I go into a restaurant. I can read Spanish, but part of the menu is written in code. *Txangurro. Kokotxas.* I order the second, and am presented with a brown earthenware dish containing a curious, greyish, shiny substance that tastes of fish. I inquire what it is and am told that the dish is known exclusively in these parts : it is the throats, or the necks, or something of that nature, of hake. The taste is delicious, but it makes me feel very far away. I am the only outsider in the restaurant. A married couple, a party of seven women, two soldiers, a pair of lovers. Snatches of conversation drift across my table, I hide my English book under the menu and try to look as Basque as I possibly can.

When I go out into the street there are people everywhere. They proceed in clusters from one street to the next. There is a certain tension in the air, incomprehensible songs are sung, I walk like a shadow close to the walls and suddenly find myself in front of a big dark building, and I can hear the sea. Ahead of me a small, spooky park with cropped, horribly mutilated trees, an army of monsters in battle formation, slightly bent by the prevailing wind. Antique globe lanterns, only a few of which still work, stand among them like commanding officers. Beyond the clipped privet hedges I can hear the suck and pull of the surf.

Somewhere down below must be the famous beach of San Sebastián, la Concha, the shell, a crescent moon in the firm embrace of the bay.

Next morning I was able to get a better look. The building I had stood before is the Casa Consistorial, the sad ochre of the walls now darkened by the rain. The bench I have been sitting on bears the slogan NO A LA MILI, SÍ AL DESARME. No to conscription, yes to disarmament. The army of black, wet trees is still standing to attention, stunted, leafless plane trees straight out of a dwarf's nightmare. All over town the walls are scrawled with liberty and amnesty, and in front of those walls, on every street corner, stand policemen in grey uniforms. They have pushed up their plastic visors; they are armed with machine guns, rifles, revolvers. I am beginning to understand the tension of last night. The police are there wherever you look, and they're on edge. On the *paseo*, in the squares, next to the bookshop. Hundreds of them. In front of the gate of the Gobierno Militar stand two ordinary soldiers, their rifles pointing downwards. I buy a couple of newspapers and step into the dismal mix of formica, mirrors, and plastic of Café Barandiarán.

The 101 bus comes past (EAT MORE DONUTS), a crippled shoeshine-man sets up his stall, a VW van belonging to *La Voz de España* stops at the corner and the driver hands the traffic policeman a newspaper which he stuffs into his inside pocket, the Coca-Cola clock slurps at the bottomless pool of time, I read my paper and look at the palm trees all tied up for the winter and the empty Sunday morning pavements and wish that my entire life were a provincial Spanish Sunday morning, and I the sort of man who belonged there.

Irura, Uzturre, Tolosa, Lizarza, Azcárate, Latasa, Irurzun. I drive through the rain into the hills. Now and then I catch a glimpse of the mountains on my left, when I stop the car I can hear the river. Before each village and by each bridge over a mountain stream there is a sign-post with a name, and I spell out the words and say them aloud as I drive past. The road is still full of bends, the mountain landscape green. When I leave behind the foothills of the Pyrenees the land will spread out wide, it will be low, undulating, empty. Iron clouds will hang over the rusty fields of the old kingdom of Navarre. There is no traffic, tourists do not frequent this region, and it is thinly populated. Old, old, is the ambience that clings to everything I see, timeless time, the empty back rooms of history. Fortress-like churches with abandoned storks' nests, the shifting outline of an earth-coloured herd on a distant slope, nothing more. I am on my way to Olite, but in this landscape that seems forever to repeat itself I feel like a pilgrim to nowhere. The same, the same, the same, the windscreen wipers drone, and the effect is that of a prayer wheel, the same, the same.

Olite. The Spanish government has established one of its paradors here, in the fortified castle of the kings of Navarre. On this windswept winter's day I am the only guest.

In the early years of the ninth century the emirate of Córdoba reached up to and beyond the River Ebro. The people of Navarre fought passionately against domination by both the Muslim emir, who had almost the whole of Spain in his grasp, and Charlemagne.

For centuries Navarre remained independent, and under Sancho the Great (1000–1035) the kingdom extended all the way from Catalonia up to León and Asturias, but after Sancho's death decline set in, and from 1234 to 1512 the kingdom on this side of the Pyrenees was ruled by French dynasties. The castle where I am now staying was built by Charles III in 1406, and by that time the history of Navarre was already so old that its origins, somewhere before the seventh century, are hazy: the first kings owned large herds of cattle and maintained their own small armies. The parador takes up only part of the vast, rambling castle. High walls of sand-coloured brick, fifteen towers, that seem to crush the village. The *castillo* was built by French architects and Moorish craftsmen. Once there were hanging gardens behind the ramparts, but even the memory of them has vanished now. Today a raw wind blows over the plain, a wind that comes from afar and has met no one in its path. The rain lashes against the walls, I walk down through the empty streets and wonder whether anyone actually lives there. The village itself lies on the plain like a coin on a pavement, the wind plays on it like a flute. No, today is not a feast day in Olite.

This is the kind of afternoon on which discoveries are made. Simply because the life you have chosen to lead is out of step with those around you, you see something that others don't get to see that afternoon. Not something that wasn't there before, it has always been there, but once the assistance of an old man with a bunch of keys is obtained, and you see the sight *alone*, you feel you are rewarded for being there on your own, for letting your capricious nature decide that you should visit this particular forgotten village in this unsuitable, miserable, blustery weather, which is why on this afternoon you and nobody but you will have the privilege of prising a morsel from between the teeth of time.

The old man I have hunted down to unlock the palace chapel switches on a couple of lights so that I can get a better look at the interior: a high retable on the main altar, shielding a Gothic Virgin Mary. There is something odd about all those little paintings – the faces look blank, weathered. Two men, their triple-tailed lashes raised high, are whipping Christ who is tied to a column with a rope, the end of which is held loosely in the right hands of his tormentors. The expression on the victim's face is not that of a man being whipped, nor are there any wounds to be seen. The look in his eyes is somewhat vacant and mournful, his gaze is directed at a point in space where our eyes are sure to meet. That is all. A greedy witness to the scene clings to a column with both hands, but a little pug-like mongrel lies asleep at Christ's feet as if to draw attention to the utterly impossible position those feet have found. One of them points forward, the other, half invisible, is twisted the wrong way. I look at all those eyes avoiding me, only the Moorish king, a black man wearing black velvet slippers and yellow-and-black striped stockings, returns my stare, as if he and I are the only ones to have any business here; the rest, wise men, soldiers, kings, martyrs, are locked in a silent world of their own, as if they have always known that the drama they are enacting would be invalidated by time and that they would one day be seen by people who no longer understood what they represented, as if determined to resist their transformation from article of faith into work of art and thus locked themselves up in the authenticity of adoration and suffering.

Any attempt to describe these parts is doomed to include the word "empty", it is unavoidable. This is clearly illustrated by the Michelin map of Spain number 42: leaving the red N121 at Pitillas, you take the thin, yellow C124 which crosses the winding Aragón river at Carcastillo. From here down the map is white, and white means empty. No roads, just a few peaks, such as Los Tres Hermanos, the three brothers, Balcón de Pilatos, and the ruined castle of Doña Blanca de Navarra. Why should Los Tres Hermanos have been named after three brothers? Are there three peaks? Did three brothers die there once upon a time? Riddles, and no one knows the answers. The famous Trappist monastery of Oliva is not far from Carcastillo, but that isn't saying much either. It lies between nowhere and nowhere, yet the severe Cistercian buildings have been inhabited by monks for nearly a thousand years. As I approach Oliva I catch sight of a band of monks with rakes over their shoulders, trudging across the fields. My car dissolves beneath me, the telegraph poles disintegrate, the ridiculous tower that was added to the church in the seventeenth century crumbles, I am left standing in the middle of a country lane, dressed in a peasant smock, and the scene is unchanged: I watch a medieval procession of men in fluttering habits until they disappear round the corner of the monastery.

A bell peals thinly, but the sound is shredded by the wind. Many years ago, in a different and yet the same life, I wanted to be a Trappist monk. I paid several visits to the hermitage of Achel on the Belgian border. I would be roused for matins at two in the morning, and it was the sight of those ghostly, silent white figures meditating and striding about with skirts flapping, the sound of Latin canticles between the facing rows of choir stalls, the all-enveloping silence in the library and the idea of staying in the same place for ever, *stabilitas loci*, that convinced me: here was the place for me, this was the life. Not a moment to lose. I presented myself to the abbot, kissed his ring, and told him of my resolve. He didn't appear to be very impressed, and went to a bookcase, selected the life of Abelard – in Latin – and handed me the book along with a pencil, a Latin dictionary and a note pad. "Why don't you begin by translating this text," he said. "When you've finished we'll talk again."

Others have always known me better than I know myself. The same man who wanted to stay in one place for the rest of his life now travels the world ("my monastery is the world", Harry Mulisch said to me when we visited Achel together years later), and yet, somewhere in that cubicle in Achel (a chair, a table, wooden walls, all bleached and pale), the life of Abelard still lies open at page 10, and each time I set foot in a Trappist monastery the same holy shiver runs down my spine.

Gerrit Achterberg wrote a famous poem titled "Ichtyologie", which opens with the lines: "A coelacanth has been found in the sea / the missing link between two fish. / The finder wept in wonderment. / Before his eyes lay, finally connected / the long-interrupted chain of evolution." The discovery of this fish with little paws brought to light the hierarchical relation between "man and lizard and of the lizard buried deep in the dust, beyond the reach of our instruments". The poem concludes with: "This being so we can pretend / that the upward progression takes the same course / so that we may look on God's table."

I was reminded of that poem when I stood in the cold courtyard at Oliva, in full view of the façade of the church. Not that I was weeping in wonderment, but still, the emotion you feel when suddenly you see very clearly (or think you do) how things fit together. So what did I think I saw? I hardly dare write this down, but I thought I saw the birth of Gothic art. Time melted once again and trickled away, and it happened exactly where I was now standing. The main entrance of the church is decorated with a Romanesque arch, or rather with a curved stone relief in the façade comprising thirteen arches all aligned with the Romanesque arch and becoming progressively taller and wider from the inside out, a scaled-down portal. But what concerns me is the shape of the arches: the two sides of the perfect Romanesque arch come together in the faintest imaginable angle, a dent so faint as to be almost invisible, to seem almost accidental, an upward thrust that is turned to stone in flight, motionless like a rocket photographed just after blast-off, when it hovers above the launching pad. The angle may be almost indistinguishable, but however small the break in the perfect circle, it is nevertheless a radical break with all that went before, the curved line can never be perfect again, from now on the angle can only escape the rounded line, soaring higher and higher until it has become the Gothic arch of Amiens and Chartres. Cold and drenched to the skin, I stood gazing at those arches and not a hundred scholars with their seals and berets could dissuade me from my claim that this is where the moment-ous occurrence took place, here and nowhere else, and should the pressure become too great I might concede that it took place elsewhere, too, but nowhere in such a lucid, exemplary fashion.

Professor Michelin, with his customary shortsightedness, hadn't noticed, he just rambled on about the "transitional buildings con-structed by the Cistercians in the thirteenth century, in which *Romanesque features are still manifest*", but I know better, it happened today, here, in this place, and I was a witness. I linger for a while in the polar chill of the dimly lit church. A morose pigeon flies messages from column to column. The floor of one of the lateral naves is sand rather than paving, there are holes and scaffolding, and I think of the monks who gather here before dawn for matins and I shiver, this time from the cold.

Towards evening I arrive in Sos del Rey Católico, where I will spend the night in the parador of the Catholic King. Scenario for a lone traveller. A car on a deserted country road. Night is falling. A village on a hill. Car turns off country road and climbs winding track to castle. The plain lies below, lashed by the rain. Man in car hesitates about seeking entry. There are no other cars. Then he plucks up courage and lets the heavy knocker fall against the high, wooden door.

The porter, in grey uniform, awakes from his torpor. The wind moans in the high chimney. I am, once again, the only guest. I follow the porter down the corridors. A stone floor. Simple wooden furniture. Rustic wrought-iron lamps. Woven curtains. No radio. No television. No neighbours. The silence, which had been shattered by my arrival, piles up again and closes around me.

A few hours later I go downstairs. Not a soul. I locate the dining room. Two girls from the village, in grey waitress uniforms and white aprons, watch me pick a table from among the thirty unoccupied ones. Bread, and a pitcher of wine. Inevitably, my gestures now take on a ritual quality. So I break the bread, what else can I do? Am I now raising my glass, or am I merely bringing it to my lips? The girls watch and whisper in a corner. I eat garlic soup with bread, and then dried cod prepared in the manner of Navarre, baked in the oven with sweet red peppers. When they disappear into the kitchen I catch a few words, then it is quiet again. After dinner I go to the drawing room. Lamps with parchment shades, big leather armchairs. I am served coffee and green chartreuse, and settle down in a corner to read as if I'm my own grandfather. The lights in the bar are switched off, the girls go home. The shutters rattle in the wind, they are still rattling when I go to bed a few hours later. The place is deserted and I, the lord of the manor, have taken it upon myself to switch off the lights one by one on my long way upstairs.

I was in Sangüesa once before, is it twenty years ago already? I even wrote a piece about it at the time, which I have never managed to find again. In my memory that village is eroded down to one moving feature that I am determined to see again: the Romanesque portal in the eleventh-century church of Santa María la Real. The little church seems a bit lost in the village, you have to stand in the middle of the road to get a good look at the tympanum, but I experience the same ecstasy all

The west portal of Santa María la Real, Sangüesa

over again. Sangüesa was a popular resting place for pilgrims on the Great Way to Santiago de Compostela.

What I myself do or do not believe is immaterial: to the sculptor who transformed the dead stone into a living, rippling stream, the scene he depicted was as clear as it is to me today, across centuries of battles, plague and change. This is still a world that I belong to, by virtue of understanding. The carved figures, the proportions, are almost absurdly naïve, the whole scene is borne by a number of hieratic figures, of Gothic appearance already, elongated by comparison with the other figures: Mary Magdalene, Peter, the mother of Jacob, a gruesome hanged Judas. The damned souls way up on God's left are thrust backwards into hell, Ensor-like masks and an outsized sheep appear on the scene, tucked away in the stone picture a tiny mannikin lies asleep, knights with shields like overturned beetles, Moorish geometric shapes – twenty years have gone by in a split second and here I am again, just as before, gawping like the village idiot for hours on end, like someone who longs to be taken by the hand, petrified, turned around, changed into a dwarf, lifted up and placed among the others, to have perched there for the past eight centuries like the rest of them, a carving on a church portal in a forgotten Spanish village visited by no one.

These are slow days. I drive along the reservoir at Yesa, a deathly quiet lake guarded by a ring of chalky mountains: the Sierra de Leyre. For the

Follow the scallop: the Pilgrims' Way in the Spanish Pyrenees north of Jaca

A Roman bridge north of Jaca

The fortress of Alcañiz

first time in days the sun comes out and dazzles me as it bounces off the shimmering disc of water, but in the primordial crypt of the Leyre monastery – archaic, curiously uneven columns, robustly hewn, low capitals decorated with the Y-shaped ram's horns that signify the doubly chosen – the air is colder than the night. It is the perfect season for this kind of journey. Pamplona has shrunk to the size of a provincial capital, the keepers in the magnificent museum of Navarre are emerging from their winter sleep, Jaca lies docile at the feet of the snow-capped Pyrenees. Each evening I return to my hotel in Sos – and it is as if from being the only guest I am turning into the only inhabitant, until I myself break the spell and drive off towards the south of Spain. First a long ride across the surface of the moon, then eastward along the wilderness of the Ebro valley until the earth turns red. Olive groves dot the slopes, I notice the small blue flowers of wild rosemary along the roadside, and at the end of the day, silhouetted against the roaming, sailing clouds, looms the fortress of Alcañiz.

That evening I am not the only guest in the dining room. Four Spaniards occupy a table in a corner at the back, and a solitary Englishman sits a few tables away from me. I know he is English because the only other car by the gate had an English licence plate. His table is set under a flag with the coat of arms of Don Martín Gonzales de Quintana, mine under that of Don Alonso de Aragón y de Foix. The level in our carafes of wine sinks at the same rate. He reads and writes, I write and read, and we avoid meeting each other's eyes, like dogs that know they share the same disease.

XIV

Walter Muir Whitehill

Serendipity in a bookshop
A Dutchman's problems with nomenclature
The face of eleventh-century Christian Spain
Attempts to follow Muir ~ Changes since Muir
The permanence of the Romanesque sets

STERNSTUNDE, A WONDERFUL WORD in German, defining a particular moment in life, a "starry hour" that has been or will be so important that it will change life's course. The notion presupposes a stroke of enlightenment, a sublime flash of insight, a shock of recognition, and I am much too intractable a character to believe in that kind of thing. Surely whatever it is that has suddenly required illumination must have been there already, in a state of latency? How else could you recognize the moment?

So there was nothing very special about my pulling out that particular, rather dull-looking volume from among all the others on the shelf. The cover was a faded orangey brown, and the book a photographic reprint of a volume published by Oxford University Press in 1941. Had they nothing better to do, you can't help thinking, and at the same time it is an optimistic, cheering thought: while the Battle of Britain was raging a volume as big as two bricks appeared on the subject of eleventh-century Romanesque architecture in Spain. Evidently there were some things that refused to be destroyed, a form of redress for a number of remote and sometimes forgotten buildings that had put up with the world for a thousand years. The book was priced at eighty-odd guilders, and the contents looked equally forbidding: drab, vague and even some downright poor photographs of crumbling buildings, disused churches, ruins, as well as a large quantity of detailed and, to the layman, daunting plans of the churches concerned, which one was obviously supposed to analyse. Now and then it can happen, you are quietly observing the aesthetic qualities of a Romanesque tympanum, when one of those couples shows up wearing walking outfits as stiff as armour, guidebooks firmly clasped in scrubbed hands, muttering relevant phrases aloud to each other and scrutinizing detail after detail – the sort you find sitting next to you at a concert with their faces buried in the score. I'm not one of those people, am I? So much for the *Sternstunde* factor, then: from that moment on I was indeed to be one of them. That particular book would bring forth a mass of other books, I would splurge on the expensive, handsomely produced Benedictine books on Romanesque art published by Zodiaque and be exasperated by not knowing the Dutch equivalents for the terms employed therein – and, being frequently unable to discover, I was to be frustrated with the realization that I had lost my former ability to take simple pleasure in a pleasing sight, with having completely to re-think my old notions about what was considered beauty in the Middle Ages, and with the knowledge that I would lug all those kilos of printed matter with me on my crazy detours through remote regions of Spain in pursuit of Walter Muir Whitehill.

Was there no fun in it then? There was plenty, and also a funny kind of elation. It was like playing detective. I was following someone who did not know he was being followed and who himself was busy tracking down things he knew had to exist but which he had never seen. Sometimes his "churches" turned out to have been converted into farmhouses or cowsheds, or simply to have crumbled into desolate heaps of debris, in which case he would continue on his way, complaining bitterly. I was in a somewhat better position. In the first place I had *him*, although neither his technical expertise nor his eyes. I never became a technical expert, although I do know now what a voussoir, a corbel and a cushion capital are. You learn, and that probably has something to do with an addiction to words, because I can't stand it when something has a name, in my own language no less, and I don't know what it is. On the other hand, you find there is a name for *everything*. Every type of arch, niche, bracket, moulding, vault has a name. It is a pretty discouraging thought, and I'm not sure anyone can fully empathize with my situation: imagine you are in one of those deathly quiet churches, you have gone to considerable lengths to obtain the key from the proprietor of the bar next door, and there you stand in the wordlessness of such a building with a man at your side whose only concern is to get back to his game of cards, and you take an excruciatingly long time studying Muir's ground plan, knowing the man with the keys thinks you're either mad, or one of those obnoxious scholars, or both. The best thing is to try to convince the man that you have no intention of making off with his church, and with a bit of luck he will leave you alone.

But that is only the beginning. The silent and usually cold building starts to bombard you with messages. That's the symbolic side, which was as clear as crystal to medieval man. But that other, possibly foolish obsession on my part to do with words and nomenclature, is also challenged. I don't know if I can describe the feeling convincingly. Once you know that everything has a name, you want to know what that name is. Suddenly you are not content with fuzzy indications like "the top of the column" or "that flat bit there in the corner just like the other three just under the dome". But that is where the trouble starts. Since the decline of the Netherlands as a world power, Dutch has ceased to be a world language, and the avid Dutch traveller's path is strewn with thorns. The exemplary *Glossaire* that Zodiaque always provides in its books, in which everything from lintel to steeple is identified, described and recorded in drawings and photographs, gives lists of terms in five languages, but mine is not among them. That means a lot of browsing in Haslinghuis' *Bouwkundige termen* (Architectural Terms) and riffling through the batches of mimeographed terminology lists I picked up at the university library. Quite often the appellations in different languages do not correspond exactly. The terms are by no means always equivalent. On the other hand it can be quite fascinating to try to fit the puzzle together, although this effort is nothing compared with the awesome thoroughness with which Muir undertook his explorations. Like a latter-day Sherlock Holmes he journeyed, usually on foot, from church to church, pored over documents and tombstone inscriptions, and in footnotes about dates and interpretations fought duels with old Spanish gentlemen who, twenty years earlier, had done exactly what he was doing. Of course footnotes are not the proper place for insults, but there is often an undertone of singular obsessiveness, with daggers of suspicion lurking in the diplomatic prose. When Muir states "Sr. Puig i Cadafalch and M. Gaillard, having related the capitals to other early Catalan sculptures, inclined to believe that the building was begun in . . .", then you can bet your life that Muir has discovered some bloodstain or other which proves beyond any doubt that the murder cannot possibly have been committed before 2.00 a.m.

My love of Romanesque art did not of course come out of the blue.

Many years ago, in Vézelay and Conques, in Maastricht and Sangüesa, I had already come under the spell of . . . well, of what precisely? The simplicity? The sincerity? The strange fantasies? I do not know. Not really. Perhaps it was just that this art is *sui generis*. But that isn't wholly true either: certain architectural forms were clearly inspired by Roman basilicas, the first monks brought plant and animal motifs with them from the Middle East and the Orient, and the religious symbols of Christianity had already existed for hundreds of years. Yet this is the first great European art movement since the classical period, and as such it expresses a character and world view all of its own, it is so totally enmeshed with what people thought and believed – which amounted to the same thing in those days – that it is fair to say that Romanesque art is a world view expressed in stone. Whether we can still *read* the image thus created is another matter, but I will return to that later.

What did Spain look like in the eleventh century? Three dingy maps reproduced in Muir's book can provide an answer, and they make one thing at least very clear: the struggle for influence and power went over the land like a steamroller, first this way, then that. The frontiers shift as in an animation film. On the earliest map, dated 1050, the *taifas* extended far northwards. The southernmost tip of the kingdom of León reached as far as what is now Madrid, the likewise Christian territory of Aragón was still tiny, and spread, like Navarre, over both sides of the Pyrenees. The Moorish kingdom of Zaragoza suddenly turns up on the third map, León has annexed Castile, and the Catalan block on either side of the Pyrenees constitutes such an undeniable linguistic and cultural entity that Muir, writing in this century, still ranks the two large abbeys of Saint Martin du Canigou and Saint Michel de Cuxa as Catalonian. I have travelled a lot in these parts, so it is familiar ground, but because of all the marriages, inheritances, alliances and rivalry, the non-Islamic part of Spain in the eleventh century remained an unseemly chaos of dynasties and borders dancing giddily to and fro. A few things are, nonetheless, quite clear: the needle in the compass of Spanish history turned slowly but surely away from the Latin and Arab influences towards the "modern" European north. Instrumental in that process were the settlement policy of the Benedictine Order of Cluny, and the ever-swelling stream of pilgrims from all the corners of Europe to Santiago de Compostela.

There was a vast difference between the two Christian parts of Spain in the eleventh century, and that difference remains evident in the architecture. In the west you had the kingdoms of León and Navarre, where vestiges of Visigothic tradition lingered on. The kingdom of Aragón lay isolated in the mountains, while in the east the Catalan duchies which had gained independence from Charlemagne were separated from the other countries by Muslim-held land. Thanks to the sea and to the easy access to Languedoc, the Catalans looked to the Rhone valley and Lombardy for inspiration, and consequently to an earlier Romanesque style, with less exterior ornamentation. Catalonia, unaffected by the increasingly international outlook that the pilgrim's way to Santiago de Compostela gave to the western territories was oblivious to the more "developed" architectural styles of western France.

Ironically, Walter Muir Whitehill conducted his investigations in an equally complicated period of Spanish history. He seldom refers to the political situation – no doubt to protect friends or to keep open the possibility of returning to Franco's Spain – but the dates tell their own story.

All in all Muir Whitehill spent nine years in Spain, and part of that time in the splendid Benedictine monastery of Santo Domingo de Silos, which in those days could only be reached by walking from Burgos. The monks in the Middle Ages had Tibetan aspirations, their monasteries cling to rock faces, they teeter on the brink of ravines, and even today there are some, like Saint Martin du Canigou, which you can reach only by climbing up the mountain on foot. Muir himself travelled with two bibles: the *Historia de la Arquitectura Cristiana Española* by Vicente Lampérez (1908) and *L'Arquitectura Románica a Catalunya* by Puig i Cadafalch ("now [1941] out of print and obtainable only at a fantastic premium"). He admires both, but with all his careful measurements, scrutiny of details, and considered opinions he also reveals their shortcomings, and comes to the conclusion, inevitably, that he is now writing the definitive book on the subject. "A singular obsessiveness", as I said earlier. Muir spent the war years in the comparative calm of the United States, while "proofs continued so methodically to cross the Atlantic that in 1941 I received bound copies, containing slips stating in twelve languages: 'Arrived safely – thanks to British convoys'". He proudly states that "in spite of war, frontiers and occupation the book was reviewed in France".

The odd thing is that during all the journeys I made across Spain chasing after Muir – not that I followed him methodically, and certainly not thoroughly because for that I would have needed nine years too – I had no idea what he looked like. I have never seen a photograph of him. I suppose it is even conceivable that he is still alive. Sometimes, when I was clambering up a mountainside, or waiting patiently for a key which never came, I tried to picture him. Tall and spare in a corduroy suit? Or short, stout and bouncy with that typically English kind of gingery hair? In any case taking measurements, muttering to himself and disagreeing hotly with the dead Lampérez. As late as 1968, when the first unrevised reprint appeared, he wrote proudly that no information of essential importance had been contributed since his book was first published thirty years before. Sometimes I suspect him of not really wanting anyone to follow in his footsteps. He could at least have provided a map showing his routes. He does give some vague indications in his footnotes, but often they're not enough, not even if you've got a detailed Michelin map in front of you.

My first venture in Muir's wake was a disaster from the outset. I was staying in Vic, in Catalonia, and had been given to understand that one of the hundreds of churches discussed by Muir was located in the vicinity. "Ajuntament de Tavérnoles, comarca de La Plana de Vic", is the information he offers. The church itself was called Sant Pere de Casséres. Tavérnoles I could find, but there was no sign of Casséres, even on the detailed map. After a lot of asking around I finally found myself in the right area. It was raining, it was a miserable day in all respects. Muddy paths went off in various directions, it had to be one of them, but the farmer who gave me directions said: "I suppose you want to see the church?" I admitted to being one of those pitiful lunatics. "You can't get there by car," he said, "you'll have to leave it here. The church is a farmhouse now, but there's no one there any more, so you can't get in anyway. *No hay nada!* There's nothing to see!" Yellow, muddy clay, black autumn rain. I slithered down the slope backwards with each step I took (how about that for a footprint!) and acknowledged defeat. By way of retribution for my faint-heartedness I climbed up to le Canigou in more than 40 degrees of heat, and performed other chastening feats, but I still feel bad about it and one day I will set eyes on that squat farmhouse in the photograph: a blackened, dilapidated building with a sudden bulge in the stable wall – could that elegant, semicircular form be all that remains of the apse built by the pious Ermentrude, viscountess of Cardona, in 1006?

Travelling with a forty-year-old book to guide you has its disadvantages. Where Muir encountered ruins, I find modern buildings, and vice versa. So it happened, in another year and another season, that I actually tried to avoid one of his churches. I was on my way from Jaca to Olorón. I was coming to the end of my trip, I'd had enough. But there was this indistinct photograph of a crumbling church set against a bare mountain wall, and a detail of a bricked-up portal with an arch of billet-moulding with a couple of farm-gates stacked against it. The grotesque ugliness of it all gave the photograph a certain seductive quality. The text was straightforward.

> The romantic little church of Nuestra Señora de Iguacél in a remote Pyrenean Valley to the northeast of Jaca, was entirely unknown to archaeologists until its publication in 1928 by Professor Kingsley Porter. One could not wish for a more fundamental monument for the Romanesque chronology of Aragón, for an inscription over the west portal, cut into the very stone of the building, states that the church was built by the Court of Don Sancho and his wife Doña Urraca, and finished in 1072.

And then, in one of those perfidious footnotes:

> The church of Iguacél is three-quarters of an hour on foot beyond the village of Acín, which is about three hours from Castiello de Jaca, the nearest point on a motor road. The church stands completely alone, and *in 1928 the priest of Acín had the key*.

But when I finally arrived in Acín, where I would ask the village priest from 1928 for the key of the church at Iguacél, I had, for the first time, the feeling that a neutron bomb had hit its target. The world had vanished, or rather, the people had gone. Empty houses, through which the mountain wind whistled, a collapsed church, a cemetery with toppled gravestones. It could have been Russia: a village without souls. What now? To go back was to give up, but without the key I would not be able to see the inside of the church. All right then, I'd settle for the exterior. It was raining, and I was walking in a valley of stark beauty. The last flash of red in the trees, a gurgling mountain stream, the thousand-year-old path winding ahead. There was nothing about the shape of those mountains that could have changed, I would walk about in a laboratory of preserved time and would meet no one, that was certain, on my way, except the successive ghosts of professors Porter and Muir, and of course Count Sancho, architects, masons and monks. The landscape is utterly deserted here, brother raven, sister gale, the perpendicular rain, and at the very end, that church, the same colour as the stony ground.

The original significance of churches is of course that they keep the air within their walls sequestered from the air outside, from the secular air of the world. From the moment of consecration there arises, inside, an atmosphere of mystery, of a place where God lives and His creation is made visible.

The church as the representation of a higher reality is not an astonishing concept, and that such a concept gives rise to a symbolic world is something you know if you have ever been in a Greek, Buddhist, or Shinto temple – in all of them you see those magic sequences of overt and covert meanings, where each image and each object acquires its rightful place within the esoteric system. What is so appealing about Romanesque art is that it is the first all-inclusive expression of such a system in its own world. A Romanesque church is cosmogony pictured in stone. All is meaning, morality, metaphysics, and it is not Christ on the cross who occupies the centre, as in Gothic art, but Christ in Majesty, lord of the universe, chronocrator, creator of that strange element in which the creation is vested: time. Within that concept everything had a meaning, from the wall to the lintel, from the vault to the baptismal font. The hunt, the seasons, the constellations, the symbols of guilt and punishment, resurrection and eternity, the bear and the snake, the raised tail and the pineapple, the chevron and the crossed girdle, everything had a meaning and everything was legible even for those who could not read, a language of numbers and signs you clung to in a universe in which, all being well, you felt at home or at any rate felt was yours, and in which the temporary world and your temporary existence was no more than a passing phase.

There is another notion, which presents me with much greater problems, and which I find impossible to articulate, namely that everything about those churches that I regard as *beautiful*, as art let's say, was by no means experienced as art when it was created. The man who carved these images in stone, images that still move me to the farthest corners of my twentieth-century soul, was no more than a mason or a carpenter in the eyes of medieval man. In *Die Theorie des Schönen im Mittelalter* (The Theory of Beauty in the Middle Ages, Cologne, 1963) Rosario Assunto observes: "*Kunst ist keine von den anderen unterschiedene Tätigkeit, sondern der Aspekt des Handelns, der die anschaubare Schönheit seiner Erzeugnisse zum Ziel hat*",* but I find it hard to come to grips with this notion. It is worse than East is East etc., I simply cannot detach myself from my own way of looking, I would have to become another man, a man who is a thousand years old but who is nonetheless oblivious to the ideas that have evolved during those thousand years. If I have ever come close, it must have been in that deserted valley in the Pyrenees. There was no sign of life, no one to be seen, I just stood there in front of that closed door with burning zeal and without a key. Another frustrated soul had managed to bore and scratch a tiny hole with a sharp object, but all I could see through the hole was part of a wall of rough-hewn stones. Now something odd happened. I had not, after all, come empty-handed. "There was supposed to be a man who could do magic," I muttered, echoing the poet Ed Hoornik, and in the shelter of the arch (symbol of heaven) over the door I read Muir's detailed description of what was to be seen – but not by me – two metres from where I was standing. In that other kilo of print, *Aragon Roman* (Zodiaque, 1971), I saw photographs of the austere barrel vault, the wondrous grille and the earnest, mournful faces of the mother and the child with the smooth, raised knees, rigid and hieratic as an idol from a sunken world.

The afternoon darkened, a gust of wind chased through the few trees. Perhaps Professor Muir was getting impatient in the kingdom of the dead. I turned to follow him, my invisible guide, as I had followed him to the castle of Loarre, where the whole of Aragón lies at your feet like the dusty hide of a bull, and to the pale swirl of mist in the main square in front of the cathedral in Santiago. All those roads! All the way over the drab shroud of the Castilian tableland to the church of San Martín de Frómista with its 350 corbels carved in stone and its well-nigh Rhenish stature – disproportionately large now in its forsaken village. From the low, chill, primordial crypt of Saint Michel de Cuxa with its single

---

* Art is no different from any other occupation except in that aspect of its activity that aims at something resulting in aesthetic beauty.

petrified palm-column, to the mysterious royal Asturian graves in the pantheon at León, from the wind-lashed gallery of San Esteban de Gormaz, in a landscape of pigs and mire, to the bird's nest of San Juan de la Peña clinging to the rock face. I was grateful to Professor Muir. He had unlocked for me a new world, and I had got to know certain empty, strange regions of Spain much better. I had received gifts of honey and bread, cheese and wine from monks who, in their millennium of circular time, had regularly come across the representatives of linear progress. They had endured a thousand years of the same rules and still lived in isolation, their backs to the world. What I had learnt about eleventh-century architecture would seep out of my system in due course, but the stone-built manifestation of that self-absorbed thought process, itself almost a cloister, unique in each place and yet enigmatically the same, is an image that will stay with me forever.

XV

Perhaps the Dove Knows

In the kingdom of Asturias
Fuente Dé – the jigsaw puzzle of Spanish history
Unsubjugated Basques ~ The cradle of the Reconquest
A memorable glass of orujo ~ Santa María de Lebeña
Connections across 1,000 years ~ A summit in blue

T HE WALL FACING ME IS as white as paper, or as white as snow. It is a Spanish wall: this is the Picos de Europa. It's May, and snow is still falling. The parador I'm staying at lies at the foot of a steep cliff, but that sounds too cosy. Teeth of a dragon, mandibles of a god, a crest with jagged, frayed edges, scars from old wounds. These are the mountain passes and valleys of the kings of Asturias, who changed the course of European history and consequently of the world. That sounds intriguing, if also like an overstatement, but he who writes such things is in harmony with his surroundings. Nature in these parts plays on an immense pipe organ. The sea is 30 kilometres away to the north, the mountain soars to 3,000 metres, the granite décor of a theatre without performances, a semicircular backdrop of gaunt, rocky bluffs that make a nonsense of all else. The road ends here, and behind the unassailable walls live the eagle, the brown bear, the cock-of-the-wood. The parador is called Fuente Dé after the Río Deva, which rises in the mountains above; the river has to fight its way to the sea, carving the gorges I drove through yesterday.

It is not time that has stood still here, although one would like to think so, it is the mountains. All that has moved is history, and all that has breathed are the seasons. Hot summers, harsh winters and the activity of man in between. Always the same: hunters, shepherds, farmers, descendants of Cantabrians and Goths. Never subjugated by Moors, Saracens, Mohammedans, Muslims – whatever you wish to call them. It is from here that the reconquest of Spain began. Reconquest is the proper word, but the prefix "re" encapsulates a long work of nearly eight centuries culminating in the victory of the Catholic Kings at Granada, and which began when the first Asturian king, Pelayo, defeated the Moorish troops at Covadonga in 718. The valley where this battle took place is now something of a national shrine. Covadonga is a key word in Spanish history.

It is complicated enough, and trying to make sense of it all is not everyone's idea of fun. The more you read, the more pieces fall into your hands, then one day you find yourself hunched over a jigsaw puzzle that extends far beyond the confines of the room you are in; you are surrounded by dozens of other rooms in which yet more pieces of the puzzle are stored in cupboards, boxes, wicker trays. Suddenly you see yourself as the lone fool in an absurdist play, muttering, shifting the stage props around, chasing after whatever's missing and yet drowning in what is there. So there I am. My opposite number is the historian, not even the history philosopher, no, just the academic, a drone as big as a man, working his life away in archives and monastery libraries which he leaves briefly once every so many years to announce, with modest jubilation, the discovery of another piece of the puzzle hitherto missing, a piece that expands the puzzle even further.

Near Fuente Dé, Picos de Europa

The more detailed the story, the greater the mass of facts and motivations, a blend of chaos and logic, irrational decisions, stupidity, enigma. If there were an eye capable of transcending the limits of time, an eye magically equipped to unravel the tangled twine like a divine, ideal computer, the outcome would be an understanding that everything, including the irrational elements, had followed a logical course from the beginning. Logical? Yes, but only because things turned out the way they did, a retrospective logic that fits the tangle of insanity into a system. Everyone has had such a vision of this eye – Hegel, Humboldt, they all aimed at ultimate illumination – whatever name might be given to it, even *purpose* is permitted. No one wants to acknowledge the slimy morass of facts and incongruities as their natural habitat, because then who would you be?

The Visigoths gradually moved southward into Spain, and they ruled Spain from Toledo. A glance at their laws, their form of government, their elected kings, their script, their churches – a few of which still stand fully intact in the Spanish landscape – is enough to extinguish any notion of the barbarism which is nevertheless associated with their name. In 475 they broke the old *foedus* linking them to the Roman Empire and

San Pedro de la Nave, Zamora

established an independent state, which burnt like straw three centuries later. What started the fire? Dissent within the royal house, growing impotence of the state, crippling taxation on behalf of the lords of the land, a wave of anti-Semitism that damaged the economy. This one paragraph spans three centuries.

It is the fashion nowadays to characterize what happened next as irony. I will not do so; I will just describe the situation. A knock on the door, someone comes in with a newspaper. Remember: I'm in a room (surrounded by a surfeit of history books, the fool in the play with his ever-expanding jigsaw puzzle) in the early kingdom of Asturias, cradle of the reconquest of Spain from the Arabs who had crossed over from Morocco. We'd got to 718, the year in which, so the history books/myths/legends tell us, a king who was, if not the king of Spain, was anyway a Spanish king pre-eminently *Spanish* gave the impetus for that countervailing movement.

The newspaper has a photograph of the heirs to the throne of Spain and Morocco on the front page. Philip of Bourbon and Greece welcomes Sidi Muhammad. Place that photograph next to your history book and you will notice a mirror effect, which you can by all means dismiss as the irony of history, but which you can also treat as a piece of your puzzle. The photograph conjures up the battle of the Guadalete in 711, at which the Berbers/Moors/"Moroccans" defeated the Visigoths/Christians/ "Spaniards" and pushed the remnants of their army back into the mountains of Asturias whence seven years later, at Covadonga, sprang the first successful retaliation.

What is it that triggers these thoughts? Just about everything around me, from the Basque words on the signs along the motorway (*itxita* closed; *irterra* exit; *hartu ticketa* get your ticket) up to and including the Mozarabic church I have been looking for in the valley of the Deva and in the pages of the *Liébana Beatus*, which I saw in the monastery of Santo Toribio. Even today the Basques dominate Spanish history, albeit in a negative sense. On a map I have which shows the political situation in the seventh century, the Basque country is indicated with grey dots: that was a region the Visigoths left alone. The Vascones were never subjugated, and Felipe González still finds them hard to deal with. Franco still had enough power to outlaw the Basque language, but the Basques of today are not content with the nebulous independence represented by token signs in Basque scattered along the motorway, not they.

They'd rather destroy the Spanish state, by whatever means, including assassination. The number of votes won by Herri Batasuna (*Pueblo Unido*), the political front of ETA, shows that 15 per cent of the Basque people are still prepared to use violence. So there's nothing paradoxical now about winning seats through elections which are only possible thanks to democracy, and then shitting on that very democracy by refusing to take up the seats in parliament.

I have driven in a loop around Santander, along the Costa Montañesa, sea to my right, mountains to my left. At Unquera I take the N621, a yellow road that follows the winding course of the Deva up into the mountains. On my right rises the Sierra de Cuera, and at Panes a gorge 25 kilometres long stretches ahead. At the end of it lies Lebeña, and my church. It is the kind of landscape history puts to use for troop movements, ambushes, cross-fertilizations, intermingling.

I am following the river upstream, the road zigzags ferociously, now shut in by boulders, then offering sudden views of arcadian dales, farms with slate roofs, mountain-country. There is very little traffic. The car radio gargles and splutters with election results, fresh history which, eventually, will be condensed along with all the rest into the indigestible soup of one page of print, all those millions of words, facts, gestures, images and promises which took as much time as they needed to come to pass, only to be crushed and pounded and compressed into a single book, a single chapter, a single page, a single sentence, a microdot in a future that will no longer be ours. There is something noxious about the tenacity of these thoughts. But what did you expect? Better look at the flowers along the road! You don't even know their timeless names, those words by which they have been designated since voices have been heard. Brother thistle, sister poppy, swaying in the soft mountain breeze.

With the Picos de Europa to the west, the Sierra de Peña Sagra to the east, this region lies between the Cantabria of antiquity and Asturias. Names like a song. *A way through*. It was from here that the vast, empty lands between Ebro and Duero were recaptured, León being accessible by way of the San Glorio pass, Castile by way of Piedrasluengas. This is where the stream of Christians fleeing across the depopulated plains sought refuge from the new African rulers advancing from the south. It was not until later that they were given a name: *muztarabes, muzarabes*, in the Spanish of today: *mozárabes*. An anachronism, as the events preceded the appellation. Christians who had lived in an Islamic environment. The term is applied to a liturgy, to an architecture and music, to a style. The shapes and patterns of the Middle East flowed into Spain via the invasion from North Africa: horseshoe arches, mythic beasts from Persia, stylized plants unknown to the temperate north, geometric, obsessive forms, symmetry and repetition, they were all transported over these mountain passes as pollen by human bees, they were carved in stone and traced on vellum, there for all to see, preserved.

It is like being released from prison when, after rounding a final bend in the road, the village of Lebeña suddenly appears, in a valley of profound stillness and an archaic sort of green made more intense by the rain which is now beginning to fall. I drive the car to the church of Santa María. Apple trees in blossom, not a soul in sight. "Where the narrow pass opens onto a ring of grassy mountains, you see on the left, across the river, the small church and the village in the distance. If the priest is not there, ask after the key of the church in the village." But the priest is never there in these villages, the species has died out. Some places are visited once a week or once a fortnight. There are too few souls that need ministering to. The door is locked. I walk to the village, a huddle of houses, alleys of cow dung and soft mud, steps hewn out of stone. By a door I see a pair of low, black clogs mounted on three stubs. It rains a lot here. As in a film I can feel someone's eyes fixed on me, and before she can dodge out of sight I have caught a glimpse of a small white-haired woman through a chink in her door. I ask where can I get the key, and she points to a house down the way. The village appears to be abandoned, there is not a sound. I climb the rough stone steps and knock on the door. I hear shuffling, an old man appears. I ask if I may have the key and he says "yes", but I must come in first. Would I like some *orujo*? Do I know what *orujo* is? Yes Sir, I know, and I also know that there is no escape. A rustic version of marc, grappa, liquor distilled from the skins and seeds of grapes, after pressing. Residue, dregs, slough, waste which, as legend has it, is left for the ungodly.

We go inside. His wife, stooped, wears black. On top of a dresser I notice a photograph of a pair of very dead people, even when they were alive they were already dead. There is a style of portrait photography that can actually do that, anticipate death. They stare out from a void at the curious stranger standing before them, in the parlour of their already so elderly children. The husband does not pour himself a drink, it is the stranger who is about to be poisoned. The room is small and very dark. The wife rests her feet on a footstool, the rain gently rattles the window. Everything is just as it should be, as in legend, no other forms have penetrated these parts. Yesterday, in the tenth century, he helped build the Mozarabic church, today he receives a visit from a thousand-year-old stranger. Where do I come from, he wants to know. "From Holland." "The prince with the beard," the man says to his wife, and to me: "Your prince, the one who married the queen." I stare at him. "The one who fought so bravely against the Germans." "That's the husband of our previous queen. Now there's a different prince." He is unperturbed. Princes succeed each other and spawn other princes. "But the one we have now doesn't have a beard," I say. "The one who fought against the Germans did have a beard," he says.

Silence in the room. The clock behaves like an hourglass and pours another minute.

They don't have a prince, they have a king, he says.

The only one whose hands aren't stained with blood, she says, *que no se ha manchado las manos con sangre*. With this line from a *chanson de geste* it is impossible to see anything but hands and blood. Truly a sentence that is the sum of its words. He fought in the Civil War. On the right side. That's why he has trouble walking.

I sip the *orujo*, which cuts through me like a knife.

His brother fought in Russia on the German side, in the Blue Division. He was wounded, too. Spain, the contrasts. He says these things in a monotonous voice, there is no differentiation of emotions in his statements. He. His brother. Russia. The Republic. Wounded.

Another *orujo*? No, thank you.

He brings me to the church. I ask myself what I would see if I weren't looking at the building with an historical eye. A lovely rural shrine, ancient, in a deserted corner. You can spot it from the road, you can pile it on top of all the other delights, and drive on. But it's too late for that. I have in the back of my car a book from the Zodiaque series, *La nuit des temps*, publication no. 47 from the abbey of Sainte Marie de la Pierre-qui-Vire. The whole series – more than one hundred volumes already – is devoted to Romanesque art, and this is the second volume which deals with pre-Romanesque art in Spain. They are hefty tomes, more than 400 pages each, full of splendid photographs taken by someone for whom evidently no interior was too obscure. The sleuths who write these books

Santa María de Lebeña

leave no stone, ornament, document unturned, forcing you to look with eyes you didn't know you possessed. The volume I have brought with me this time is devoted exclusively to Mozarabic art, all the churches and chapels I have encountered over the years in hidden crannies of Spain (as in Berlanga de Duero) are in it, complete with ground-plans, diagrams, historical details. The same goes for this church.

The old man unlocks the door and we step inside, into the pungent, old air, which seems to resist our intrusion. The interior is shadowy, I have some difficulty recognizing details, but gradually the edifice gains ground, the architecture defines itself in the gathering light, but while I am determined to look with an eye for technical detail – because that's what I came for – I find that my nature prescribes that I should feel. Hardly anything can have changed here, and when I reach out to touch that physical *sameness*, the stone, the stone configurations that have stood here inviolate, autonomous for a thousand years, my mind fills with romantic fancies, which, I must confess, take far less effort than the meticulous scrutiny of all the influences, variations in height, voussoirs, architraves, corbels and forms of vaulting listed in the book. A saintly Sherlock Holmes has been at work here, he has measured and compared, crawled over the floor, discovered Asturian traces, Visigothic nuances, Mozarabic clues, he has exposed vain attempts by anonymous villains to rub out traces, he has drawn straight and curved arrows on diagrams to indicate "*l'orientation des hauteurs croissantes des supports-colonnes*", but I do not speak his esoteric detective's lingo and my dictionary lets me down time and again. The old man observes me leafing wildly through my books, glancing swiftly from photograph to capital, pacing the floor in obedience to the plan, and also how I give up, how I surrender to sheer admiration. Leaving trapezoidals, western accretion, Greek cross, aisles and apses to the saintly sleuth, I sit down to marvel at the capitals with their oriental vegetal motifs carved by a nameless hand a millennium ago, at the Arab arches which have been etched in my system ever since I saw them in Isfahan, Kairouan, Córdoba; I am rocked in the kind of silence that goes with the absence of other people and which is so hard to come by today.

I have put away the book, but I have my guide. He doesn't know as much as the book, but this has been his church for a lifetime. He limps to the altar, dragging his bad leg, and points to the big slab of stone on which the altar table rests. "*Los Godo*s," he says, the Goths, and in his mouth the word takes on another meaning, as if those alien Nordic tribes still exist, as if they might yet launch another invasion from the north, from where I come, and maintain their happy-unhappy kingdoms until such time as they are conquered again by the Moors.

He points to the decoration in the stone, a large wheel encompassed by six smaller wheels. "They were dug up here," he says. I have seen the same geometric patterns outside, in the long stones supporting the ridge-beam: corbels. I look at the slab under the altar. The big wheel is standing still, but it seems to be turning. From the silent centre spring sixteen curved lines, a fluid swastika. Wheel, eternal movement, eternal return, the world a wheel within a wheel, said Nicholas of Cusa. How did the people who lived here relate to this Celtic echo? Swastika, rotary motion, flowing this time, around a motionless centre, turning counter to the hands of the as yet uninvented clock in the Carolingian way, or with crossed, world-hungry hooks chasing after the representation of time, like the emblem of Hitler's diabolical millennium. Signs, pictures that expressed what they thought, what they needed to exorcise. But what did they think, poised as they were on the dynamic junction of thought systems vacillating between faith and superstition, tradition, heresy, innovation?

The stone here gives the answer, and withholds it at the same time. I run my hands over those rhyming grooves as if to set them in motion, and my guide smiles. "*No se mueve*," he says. "It doesn't move." But is he speaking the truth? Sixteen arms depart from the central point, branches, rays, beams, garlands, curved lines, elegant spokes, what can you call these things? Nor is the number sixteen random. Gratuitous decoration did not exist, everything *said* something. Sixteen, four times four. But what am I getting at? Nothing, I just want to listen. Not what *I* have to say about these numbers and forms is true, only what they purport. Wheel, circle, swastika, sixteen, four, they all start whispering at me, cabbalistic singsong, esoteric buzzing, Byzantine gurgling, heritage upon heritage, Mozarabic jubilation, Coptic whistling, Mesopotamian humming, Celtic murmurs, not one of them excludes the presence of the other in this self-fructifying everyman's-land.

I am defenceless, also the lintel, the column, the arch, the cross, the acanthus leaves and the eastern mythic beasts on the capitals, the geometric stylized flowers on the high, narrow friezes pelt me with their forgotten meanings and demand to be read as they were once read, recognized and understood the way they were recognized and understood in an era when four was not exclusively four times a unit of the same, but betokened – as it had since the shadowy depths of prehistory – reliability, solidity, fullness, when the titles of kings included a four, "lord of the four winds, of the four seas". But I stray from my stone, towards sixteen as the doubling of eight, towards Hod, the eighth sefer of the cabbala, the radiance, the glory, towards the significance of the four consonants in the unpronounceable name Yahweh, Y for man, H for lion, W for bull, another H, the eagle, and then I flee from all those obscure significations across the threshold that was once the boundary between holiness and the secular world, and stand outside again under the soothing patter of the rain on the trees – which profess nothing here because they were made by no one.

Yet it is odd: something has a meaning and at the same time it doesn't. Not to me, but to those who built the church, carved the images, drew the ground plan. What divides us is time, what connects us is the stone artefact I am leaning against, sheltering from the rain which is unchanged. Thrush, dove, crow, they could have connected us, I think, because at least the animals have remained exactly the same. "That's because they can't think," mutters the countervoice, but: take that dove scratching about among the twigs under the apple tree and put it back a thousand years. Perhaps it can hear the sound of chisel on stone now that they are building this church against the expected end of the world, perhaps it hears the Asturian murmurings of the men hacking the stones to size in accordance with the idea they have brought with them from the Caliphate of the Ummayads. It hears or does not hear, just as it does or does not hear me conversing with the old man at my side. Does not, I think, for it has other concerns, it has to forage, build a nest, be a dove. Then, as now, it would blend into the surroundings, no one could distinguish the wear and tear of a thousand years, it has not changed its language, its behaviour, its feathers, its meaning has not changed, it is its own perpetual archetype, welcome among doves and men, busy repeating the daily fatigues of all doves: a dove-ish existence. Dove, *Taube, paloma*, the bird that existed long before it was promoted to Spirit and pronounced holy, although there are sure to be some scholastics around which insist that the Idea of the One was vested in the Other.

Not being a scholar myself, I do not know. I shelter in the porch of the church at Lebeña, and then I sit in my room in Fuente Dé at a table covered with photographs, notes, books. I have to go out, before darkness falls, and take the cable car up the daunting mountainside. I must not look up to the summit, or I will be too frightened, the cables rise almost vertically, the stone book covered in scrawls and scratches ascends before my eyes, I am so scared I cannot look, until I sense a shimmering whiteness behind my closed eyelids, and feel a jerk. We are at the top.

The room in which I sat writing peacefully moments ago has become so minuscule that I will never fit into it again. Before me a white snow-covered plain stretches away. I see a far-off horizon of peaks among which sail dreamy clouds. I think I can hear the stone groaning, but it is only the silence that I hear, so tense that sooner or later it must break. Is that the worst? No, the worst is the blue, so absolute, so utter, so removed from the earth that I ought to invent a new name for it.

What comes to my mind is not a new name, but something that still links me to my tiny quarters below, to a book lying on my table, to a miniature in that book. An angel with red wings. Feathers like swords. He raises his startlingly red trumpet to a band of blue sky, to a sun and

a moon which are two-thirds red, one-third white. It is the angel of
the fourth trumpet in the Apocalypse, the one I saw yesterday in the
monastery of Santo Toribio, 15 kilometres from Santa María de Lebeña,
the monastery where Beatus once lived. But that's another story. The
cable car operator confers with his base on the phone: Andalusian
accents, out of place in this thin, wintry north. I am the only passenger,
he signals that we are off. One last look at that fierce blue sky. No eagle,
no angel, but only when I am on the ground again can I breathe normally
again.

XVI

Kings, Saints and Heretics

Zero and the millennium ~ Beatus' words become pictures
The Apocalypse ~ Beatus' commentary
Pictures reach Santiago ~ Oviedo
Santa María del Naranco

WHAT WAS SO UNIQUE about the final years of the nineteenth century that a special name was coined for that period? *Fin de siècle*, farewell to the old century, with spleen, ornamentation, fatigue, innovation. For the end of our century another epithet will have to be found, *fin de millénaire*, why not? After all, a great deal will come to an end in a few years' time, if not in reality, then at least in digits. The arbitrary measure of a thousand rolls gently towards its full figure. If we're lucky we will live to see it, and although I have never taken particular interest in the *fin de siècle* I can't help feeling the same glee, now that the end of this second millennium is in sight, as when the mileage recorder on my dashboard approaches the 100,000 mark. It's all those zeros that do it.

Zeros have a particular aesthetic appeal. The Mayas used the zero a thousand years before the Europeans did, and took the round snail's shell as its token. The Egyptians had no sign for it, which is a pity, because zeros are so round and perfect, empty and yet full, they contradict themselves so vociferously that they give the figure 1 preceding them a curious added value – although that added value itself has depreciated considerably by comparison with a thousand years ago. This was inevitable. People in the Middle Ages believed not only that the earth was a mere thousand years old (even Kant, seven hundred years later, was still thinking in terms of millions), they also believed, as the thousandth year after Christ approached, that the end of the world would soon be upon them. The exact moment depended on whether you were counting from Christ's conception, birth or death. We, with our such long short memories, know that the end did not come. Which takes the sting out of the angst. Our chances of destruction have both increased and diminished, but no one expects Armageddon to come about on precisely 1 January 2000, or indeed in the year 2033, when I will be, or would have been, a hundred years old.

A thousand years ago people were a lot more afraid than they are today, and in the mountain landscape I am now driving through, between Cantabria and Asturias, there lived and wrote in the eighth century a monk whose commentaries on Saint John's Apocalypse kept the whole of Europe busy for several hundred years. The monastery was then known as Liébana, now Santo Toribio, the monk's name was Beatus.

I have left the main road to search for the monastery. Sombre, rain, no one in sight. A door with a knocker. I expect to hear padding footsteps, but there isn't a sound. Distrustful now of the dry thud of the knocker I bang on the wood with my fist. The sound reverberates in the passage beyond, but there is no response. *Knock, and it shall not be opened unto you.* The building is unprepossessing, rectilinear, it can't possibly be the same structure as in Beatus' day. I walk around it, discover a side entrance which is open; it leads to a courtyard. *Seek, and ye shall find.* The monks, or whoever live there, have taken the easy way out: the walls are hung with regularly spaced reproductions of the pictures in Beatus' book.

Beatus himself never saw those illuminations, they were supplied by the monks who copied out his commentary in their scriptoria. Fear and art, sisters in despair, the stylized Mozarabic representations still strike fear into the heart. Stylized fear, but fear all the same. Fear of monsters, plague, fire, hunger, ruin, fear of the prophecies. Beatus' book was the bestseller of the end-time, it dealt with the end of the world. The proximity of doom so filled the minds of artists and readers alike that those illuminated manuscripts of Beatus' commentary are still referred to by his name, as if they are a genus of their own: the Beatus Pierpoint-Morgan, the Gerona Cathedral Beatus, the Beatus of Liébana, which is displayed before me now. I said "bestseller", but I hate that word. Umberto Eco uses it in his essay on Beatus,* and although it is inappropriate in that there were no "sales" to speak of, not in our modern sense, his point is clear: the 650 pages penned by Beatus would have even greater repercussions in the centuries after his death than in his own day.

* *Beato di Liebana: Miniature del Beato de Ferdinand I Sancha*, F. M. Ricci, Parma, 1973.

What was it all about? "The book survives the book" is one of the quotations Eco gives in his essay. And Eco himself adds, elsewhere in the text, that the world is a book that demands to be read like a book. The world as a forest of signs demanding interpretation, every meaning complemented by and derived from another. Who could be more familiar with such a world than the master of signification himself, a saint in the church of Borges, Calvino, Barthes. Eco – you can feel the delight with which this chief clerk of modern semiotics, this possessor of fabulous knowledge of Antiquity and the Middle Ages – intercedes as an echo (the pun is childish but irresistible) among all the other echoes roused by Beatus' "commentary".

But that early commentary, too, was an echo in its own right, not only of the Revelation of Saint John but of all the commentaries that had been called forth by those twenty-one chapters up to the days of Beatus, from Tertullian and Augustine to Isidore of Lyons and Isidore of Seville. And, asks Eco, what was the Revelation itself? A book in the Jewish tradition, an echo of Ezekiel. And did Ezekiel's texts arise out of nothing or were they the echoes of Syrian texts? And so on, all the way back to the beginnings of writing. What a fantastic, perverse construct: Eco, agnostic, Italian of the Gramsci century, the man who writes so persuasively about film, television and cartoon strips, and at the same time Eco the Clerk, the man who devoted his PhD thesis to Saint Thomas Aquinas and who has thus absorbed all that went before, and who now joins the hallowed ranks of patristic authors and commentators not to explain, like them, what the Book signified, but to explain what they thought it signified, and why.

A mirrored script without end. In the silence of your room you can hear the turning of stiff pages in the thousand libraries and scriptoria which together form the library and the scriptorium of the world, you can hear the scratching of pens on paper and you observe the accrescence of texts over other texts, the origins of the interminable manuscript that only Borges and Eco can read.

"Palimpsest" is the title Umberto Eco gives his essay on Beatus. He is not inspired by the style nor by the originality of Beatus, for he possessed neither. "The hero of our book was an epigone with a tendency toward cultural confusion, who employed a syntax which can strike fear even into someone accustomed to the most extraordinary corruptions of Medieval Latin." Beatus repeats his own explanation ad infinitum, he loses his way in "circuitous analyses", he mistakenly attributes texts to one Jerome instead of to Priscillian, he omits, substitutes words, contradicts himself, uses the same quotation first with an accusative and then with an ablative, in short, he drives hordes of posthumous clerks to distraction and yet he has produced a bestseller: the commentary made such an impact that Beatus' fame only increased in the centuries after his death. In his obsessive quest for hermeneutic clarity he was, in a sense, already scripting the illustrations of his work that would be made by others: every seventh horn, every fourth eye, every terrifying stage in the apocalyptic nightmare was set down in infinitesimal detail, and those graphic descriptions gave rise – first in paint and later in stone – to images *without* words, and *images* were what the medieval mind related to. People who could not read learnt the texts by rote. Assistance, explication, interpretation were offered by the image, and the image was Beatus'. I'm simplifying things, of course, but I have less space at my disposal than Eco (and Beatus). The exegetic representations on the capitals and tympanums of the Romanesque churches along the pilgrim's way to Santiago de Compostela were often, as in Moissac, borrowed from "illustrations" generated by Beatus' commentary: the ideas that left the gate of this monastery as words, returned centuries later to Spain as images carved in stone.

Beatus wrote his commentary for a purpose: he was determined to stamp out a certain heresy. We are, once more, in the Spain of the eighth century, or rather, in the geographical area which is now called Spain, and which was then for the most part occupied by Arabs. The north is free, and there lives Beatus, abbot of Liébana (730–85), chaplain to Queen Osinda who is the wife of King Silo of Oviedo (Asturias). His opponent is Elipandus, archbishop of Toledo, caught, as the Spanish saying goes, between "the sword of Islam and the Carolingian wall". Toledo, the old Visigothic capital, is now an important city in the Caliphate of the Ummayads, and this ancient *urbs regia* lies half-way between al-Andalus with its subjugated Christians at one end and the free land of Asturias and the Carolingian Empire at the other. It is a capital in the cosmopolitan sense of the word, with different cultures existing side by side, observing each other, stealing and borrowing from each other. The Christians are proud of their Visigothic tradition, and at the same time they are open-minded when it comes to the Arab world, in a way that will ultimately prove to be a blessing, because of the cultural legacy that was preserved by Arab scholars in translations from the ancient Greek. In this atmosphere of Mozarabic Christianity there arose the heresy of *adoptionism*, centred around Elipandus and his ally Felix, bishop of Seo d'Urgel (which incidentally was not under Arab influence). I am too paltry a clerk to expand on all the ins and outs of the heterodox speculation, trinitary uncertainty and theological hair-splitting of those days. What interests me is the spectacle, the mechanics of that period, because the role of time and politics therein was so fantastic.

Adoptionism, in brief, is the doctrine that Christ was merely adopted by God the Father, and consequently was not himself God. First the general picture: how slowly that theory found its way to the far distant north where Beatus lived, and how long it took him to compose the 650 pages containing his accusations of heresy, and for his indictment to reach not only Elipandus ("who belongs to the body of the devil") but the whole of Christian Spain and the Christian world beyond the Pyrenees (*allende* in Spanish), to the court of Charlemagne himself. Indictment and rebuttal were separated by weeks or months. The speed of the dispute was dictated by the speed of horses and horsemen: that was the only sort of time there was.

Elipandus is outraged, he denounces Beatus as *in*beatus, as "*Antiphrasius Beatus*", he's a "*carnis lasciviae deditus*" (a swine, let's say), and an "*antichristi discipulus, ab altario Dei extraneus, pseudo Christus et pseudo propheta*", and these charges too are conveyed in leather satchels by horsemen across Europe, all the way to the thrones of Pope Adrian and Charlemagne. I am a child of my time: I want pictures, a shot of Charlemagne's confidant and secretary breaking open the seal, and another, taken at the same time in Rome, of the pope dispatching a message to Elipandus in Toledo, while Beatus sits in his monastery, "*cette haute Thébaide cantabrique*" (where I still stand), scratching his commentary on the Apocalypse with a view to proving that Christ in Majesty, whom he invokes word for word, exists in the "fullness of his consubstantial divinity and lineage".

Beatus emerges as the victor, Charlemagne convokes two councils and a synod (I want to see pictures of that, too, how they set off, how they travel, where they sleep, what they say), and Elipandus and Felix and their followers are condemned. Not that this has any consequences for the protagonists: the wartime bishop Elipandus takes no notice of

Charlemagne's councils. Not without reason, in fact, for there is a certain political "logic" to these events. Charles and the Asturian king are keen to assert the independence of the northern Christian bishoprics from the archbishop of Toledo, who after all resides in Arab territory. The caustic phrasing of the verdict, added to the avowal that the Spanish Christians' misfortune of having to live under the Moorish yoke is a fitting punishment from heaven, leads Spanish Christendom to turn its back on the Carolingian renaissance.

In such a story there are no loose ends, it is all a great tangle of different sorts of twine – that of the interests at stake, of the ideas, persons and power relations, that of nature. Beatus' commentary, written to quash a Christian heresy in the eighth century, became *the* book of the tenth century, not for that reason, but because of its millennial overtones. At a time when famine swept across Europe, the same words took on new meaning, the suffering and dying recognized themselves in the prophecies of horror because the horror was all around them.

It was an "empire" in name more than reality, the form of government was erratic and disorganized, travel was dangerous, banditry was rife, the population was racked by plague, malnutrition and chronic famine. There is no more heartbreaking evocation of life and death at the close of the first millennium than that given by Raoul Glauber, monk of the Benedictine abbey of Cluny, in his *Historiarum libri quinque, IV: De fame validissima quae contigit in orbe terrarum*. The passage quoted by Eco is too long to be included here in full, but a few fragments are enough to make any television programme about Ethiopia look tame in comparison.

> Interminable rains turning the earth into a quagmire in which no seed can be sown, so that it is to be feared that the whole of humanity will perish . . . when the time for harvest arrived the fields were completely overgrown with all kinds of weeds and insidious grasses . . . if there was any food for sale the prices soared . . . after the people had eaten the wild animals and birds they managed to catch, they were forced to search out all sorts of cadavers and other things too horrible to relate . . . things got so bad that the people were driven by hunger to eat human flesh . . . Travellers were attacked by men stronger than themselves, their limbs were cleaved, cooked, and eaten . . . many who had found

shelter were slaughtered in the night and served as food for those who had taken them in . . . others lured children with an egg or a fruit, murdered them, and then ate them . . . and often the dead were exhumed to alleviate the hunger . . . people became so used to eating human meat that it was boiled and sold at the market as mutton . . . whoever was caught doing this was burnt at the stake . . . many people dug up a certain kind of earth that resembles loam, which they mixed with the little flour they had to make bread so as not to starve . . . you saw pale and emaciated faces . . . but also many people who were bloated with hunger . . . the human voice became shrill, like the cry of birds in distress.

Wondrous are the ways of a text. Once Beatus' commentary had made its theological and political mark and been superseded by so many other, now possibly forgotten, commentaries on the Apocalypse, the images that the monk in Liébana had so graphically evoked continued to simmer for a couple of centuries, until they became divorced from the text in the apocalyptic wilderness of the tenth century, and went their different ways: minutiae ceding to miniatures, verbal images ceding to a visual idiom of lines, colours, symbols so forceful, so novel and astonishing as to electrify European figurative art for good. I have said it before: having departed Spain as words, the ideas returned as images over the pilgrim's way to Santiago de Compostela, and then gushed forth again from the same Spain in Mozarabic guise, scattering in all directions, only to return once more by that same Milky Way, "*vía láctea*".

The pilgrimage to Santiago de Compostela is one of the arias of madness of European opera, a gigantic migratory flow, a movement of millions of extras, an unceasing stream of scallop-bearing pilgrims from all corners of Christendom, who found shelter and sustenance at Mont Saint Michel, Tours, Vézelay, Le Puy and Arles on their way to the Pyrenees and beyond, until they reached the *camino* to Santiago. What that massive adventure signified in terms of religious zeal, political, social, economic and artistic influence is almost impossible to imagine. For centuries a whole army was permanently on the move across Europe, where the foot was the unit of measurement. Everyone who joined, whether voluntarily or as imposed penitence, abandoned hearth and home to the vagaries of circumstance, the dream of every romantic soul, not in those uncertain times, but in later ones. Thus the pilgrimage became a myth in its own right, and as the links between northwestern Spain and the European north continued to strengthen, the desire for reunification with the Arab-occupied parts of Spain deepened.

The fiery resplendence of Santiago and all it inspired came about because people *believed* they had found the grave of the apostle James in that town, events therefore that were set in motion by something that perhaps never took place at all. On that shadowy conviction and on the obstinate independence of the Asturian kings since the semi-mythical Pelayo, hinged a momentous European mass migration which gave successive generations of Spaniards the motivation and the means to resist Arab domination, to reconquer the rest of Spain from Islam, and thus to turn a tide that could have swept all over Europe. Seen thus, it is no exaggeration to say that the course of European history, and hence of the history of the world, was changed in the valleys and passes of Asturias. But I must retract the "changed", because there can of course be only one history: the history of what happened. One can speak of change only vis à vis an imaginary history, a history which might be: a non-Christian Europe, a Europe engulfed by the wave of conquest like other large parts of the known world at the time.

The Spanish historian Claudio Sánchez-Albornoz takes this a step further: it is thanks to the Spaniards, he says, that Europe was not overrun. He quotes Livy: "Spain, *Hispania*, was more suitable than Italy and more than any other land on earth to wage war and to persevere by virtue of the nature of the land and its inhabitants." He draws from this a number of fantastic conclusions: by sweeping down from Asturias and Navarre after crossing the no-man's land between the Duero and the Ebro, and then driving the Moors out of reconquered Castile over the next seven centuries, Spain succeeded not only in keeping Europe apart from the political sphere of the influence of Islam – while preserving for Europe and her ultimate renaissance all the treasures that scholars, writers, philosophers, physicians and Arab translators had salvaged from the Greek and Hellenistic heritage – but also gained from seven centuries of fighting the experience and mentality that led to the discovery and conquest of the western hemisphere. He sums this up with a paradox, which he decides is not a paradox after all, but reality: "*Si los musulmanes no hubiesen conquistado España en el siglo VIII, los españoles no habrían conquistado América en el XVI. Paradója? No,* *realidad.*"* You can turn it around, and then it becomes a paradox after all, or a fantasy. If the Spaniards hadn't put a stop to the advance of Islam, it is not inconceivable that not only Europe, but also the Americas would have been Islamic. It is hard to imagine because it did not happen, but how inconceivable is it? "That's nothing to do with us," says a voice. "The world is everything that is the case."

"Everything we know is the case?"

"Everything that is the case."

This must be true. Things we don't know about are also the case. Or not?

It is time to give my eyes their due, I decide. That's what I have come here for, after all. I have knocked on the monastery door once again, heard a muffled radio and later, women's voices, I have even pressed a small white button discovered next to a shuttered window, but I continue to be excluded. Women's voices? Aren't they supposed to be monks here? I go back to the courtyard. Did Beatus walk here? Is this where he had his brainwave about James of Compostela being the refulgent head of Spain ("*cabeza refulgente de España*"), which gave the impetus for the cult, the pilgrimage and all its global ramifications, as Sánchez-Albornoz suggests in *Dípticos de Historia de España*? I look at the reproductions once again, one by one, but they irritate me because they're just an excuse for refusing to let me in. I am being taken for a ride, fobbed off with reproductions and, now that I have come so far, I want the shock of the real, I want to run my finger over the parchment when no one is looking. Nothing can beat that sensation, a thousand years melting away under the tip of your finger to reveal the monk in his scriptorium hunched over his cabinet of horrors, the East driven back into the East, the fantastic visions of Patmos spurred on by the Mozarabic imagination, angels blowing their scarlet trumpets, shipwrecks, horsemen announcing death. Back in my car, in the rain, I read the words that go with the vision . . . "and see, a dun horse, and he who rode it, his name was death; and hell came in his wake . . ." Then I drive away, into the green, everlasting landscape, leaving Patmos' bad dream behind.

I am now crossing the same mountain passes through which the ragged armies tramped southwards over the Puerto de San Glorio, and then past

* Had the Moors not conquered Spain in the eighth century, the Spaniards would not have conquered America in the sixteenth. Paradox? No, reality.

Riaño up through the evil gorge of the Desfiladero de los Reyes. Not surprisingly, there are still bears here. The mountains themselves look like sightless, savage beasts, the earth is grey, black, brown, yellow, the wind blows where it pleases and buffets the car, the weather is determined to wear down these mountains, a crazily contorted tree clings precariously to the grey rock face, spectres, figures roaming in the mist, black stripes against the mountain side, "the devil has shat here", the peaks are hidden in the clouds scudding along at the same speed as my car, greasy and gaunt, there the Beast cooks his infernal stew. An inn, a woman in black, a plate of beans, a church, two stone guards wearing tricorn hats, where was all this?

Hours later I arrive in Covadonga, where Pelayo won the battle for Spain. Sacred ground, but corrupted by the trade in piety, wrong church, wrong image of a sword-wielding hero. Touring cars, day trippers, souvenirs, a stone marking the spot where SS MM and AA RR the queen of Spain Doña Isabel and her august spouse, Don Francisco de Asis and the *serenísimos Señores* the prince of Asturias and María Isabel, infanta of Spain, stood on 28 August 1858, and beside it a stone commemorating a hundred years of *nocturnal veneration* of the Virgin who led Spain to victory, but I have an appointment with kings older than these belated nineteenth-century Bourbons and leave the mercenary ghost town.

I spend the next day in Oviedo, I drink cider and eat *fabada*, beans, with red sausage and black pudding, *chorizo* and *morcilla*. The taverns are wonderfully dark, the people cheerful and free-spirited, they are their own masters, here you can stroll and read and roam, here you find none of the macabre pathological carnage of ETA which pollutes the land. Slow days. In the archaeological museum I peer at the arms and the names, the pearls in the crowns, the anchors on the cross, the runes on the graves. I am the only visitor, and I trace the illegible words with my fingers, trace the Celtic, Visigothic, Asturian motifs as if I myself have chiselled them, I caress the stone, the time-worn fragments smashed out of their context by war or rage or arson, lintels, capitals, broken columns from invisible, vanished churches, interrupted sentences, maimed texts, truncated names and mottos, the work of humans, heritage.

In the cathedral are displayed the crosses of the early kings, *La Cruz de los Angeles, La Cruz de la Victoria*, atavistic, sacred objects from the days of Alfonsos II and III, Asturian kings from the early ninth and tenth centuries. The first cross has become self-contradictory, utterly simple,

Greek in shape, the transverse beam wider at the ends, cedarwood overlaid with gold and filigree, set with *cabujones* and *camafeos*, uncut gems and cameos; the second recalls the Carolingian jewels of the Rhineland treasure troves, gold surmounted by a scattering of gems like drops of hardened treacle, tiny, exotic representations of plants and animals in stained glass.

How insane that most people visiting Spain never venture beyond the burning glass that is the east coast. I have travelled around here for all these years, and there is no end to it. Beyond the Pyrenees lies an entire continent, mysterious, secluded, unknown, an ensemble of lands with their own histories, their own languages and traditions, it takes years to discover that past, to piece it together, to come to terms with it.

This church too is a confluence of different times and different styles – who has seen the paintings of Sebastiano Conco, the veiled fresco of Francisco Bustamente in the dome of the sacristy, the sceptre of Enrique de Arfe, the baroque retables of Juan de Villanueva? And this is just one church in one small town in a remote western region, far from the routes travelled by most people; and it isn't even the best specimen, for the loveliest church is situated at a little distance from the town, in the hills. It is the Santa María del Naranco, one of the oldest Christian churches still standing. It was built under the rule of Ramiro I (842–50) as *aula regia*, and was later converted into a church. There are actually two churches in the hills; close together, they date from the same period and are both in the pre-Romanesque, Asturian style.

It is still early when the female guide lets me into the Santa María, swirls of mist hang in the valley, in the distance lies Oviedo. The building is quite tall, but despite the big, roughly hewn chunks of sandstone of which it is constructed, it creates an impression of delicacy, of refinement and grace. What sort of kings were they? From where did they get the inspiration for their buildings? One is reminded of the elegance of Rome, the charmingly twice-opened façade smiles at the so-called darkness of the Middle Ages, I know of no building like it. Down below are the baths "for the watchmen", solid and basic, but the upper level, which you can reach only by an exterior staircase on the north front, is what my guide so charmingly calls *diáfano*, transparent. She's right, the building is made of stone but it is diaphanous, light and air have unrestricted access yet they are altered, modified, and this affects the visitor, who temporarily finds himself in a different sort of light, a different air, which makes him pensive but also elated, joyful, glad that some things survive to tell their stories and pose their riddles.

Santa María del Naranco, Oviedo

The guide focuses her attention on a newly arrived visitor, leaving me free to wander down the western gallery, to sit and look at the town in the distance, the town of the Asturian kings, and think such vague thoughts as: so this is the place, this is where an idea was conceived, transformed, suppressed, but it is too far away, too shadowy, swathed in layers of yet another history which is and is not part of the earlier one, an episode that took place just fifty years ago, when the anti-Republican colonel Arando had to defend the right-wing city of Oviedo with 3,000 men against the onslaught of Asturian miners.

> *Fuego, fuego,*
> *Entrar a Oviedo*
> *Coger a Aranda*
> *Y echarlo al agua*

chanted the children to the tune of a chocolate advertisement, "Fire, fire, on to Oviedo, seize Aranda, and throw him in the water . . ." But Aranda had a hundred Hotchkiss machine guns, which enabled him to lay a ring of fire over the surrounding hills, and he endured a siege which lasted ninety days and cost thousands of lives. He saw the fall of his stronghold on the Naranco mountain and the Republican soldiers pouring into the suburbs, until a cry was raised that was almost as ancient as Spain itself: "*Moros! Moros en la cuesta!*", Moors on the hill, whereupon Franco's Moroccan troops rushed down from the Naranco mountain, past the church where I'm sitting now, and entered the town. It was a misty day, as so often in the northern land of Asturias, and that night the vanguard of the Galician troops emerged from the mist, their bayonets stained with blood, to finish the job.

A light mist, the same or another, rolls across the plain, from the church comes the sound of soft voices, in the stone wall I see two apocalyptic horsemen charging headlong at each other, I think of the ETA bomb that killed nine young people yesterday, of the Moors on the hill, of the socialists who were defeated in that epic struggle and who now have a majority in parliament, and then of past wars and early battles which are fading from memory, of the king who built his royal *aula* here, of Beatus and his imagery, the Christians in the north, the Arabs in the south, the gathering and dying storms of war. History, everything that was the case. No loose ends.

XVII

The Past is Always There, and Yet It Isn't

The psychology of travel ~ A traveller's library
The author is moved by Euryclea ~ The kings of León
León's royal pantheon ~ León's cathedral of light
The traces of war

IT HAPPENS WITH EVERY TRIP, or rather, it happens to me on each extended journey. The time I spend away from home stagnates, coagulates, becomes a sort of mass that closes up behind me. Then I'm off, under the sway of a different order, the order of travel, the elusive element of not belonging, of collecting what is different. I have tried to find a word for this, and all I can come up with is: *extension*. That, according to Spinoza, is one of the two attributes of God, so I must take care. I am extended by everything I see, consume, amass. It is not a question of higher knowledge, it is more like sedimentation, an accretion of images, texts, of all the lasting impressions that come my way from the street, from television, conversations, newspapers.

I could simply say that I am gaining weight, that I am swelling up with innumerable trivia, unfinished thoughts, news about the region I happen to find myself in, but I must find some way of relating to that extended, thickened personage. A somewhat bloated individual who has no thought of home and who happens to be elsewhere for a while.

Elsewhere. A room in some hotel in León, capital of the land between Asturias and Castile, the land of castles. A stone floor, a view of a court-yard and a row of shabby apartments, indiscriminate noises coming from stone rooms (that's why the sound of Spanish television is essentially different from that of other countries, you hear it as you walk down any street), a bed with a mattress gravitating to the centre of the earth, my suitcase, a picture of a child and a flower, portrayed with the usual perversion of lack of talent, a table with my things, newspaper cuttings, notes, maps. The rest of my extension is in my head and it is cherished there because I take it that even the pettiest of worldly phenomena reflect the whole, that the structure of existence is as manifest in a page of local death notices as in the attempts of certain philosophers to throw a net over so-called reality. The advantages for the free-floating spirit are clear. I am entitled to combine the Holy Virgin with Homer, the dead author Borges with random sums I make in my head, a recipe for dried cod with a treatise on heresy, and that is precisely what I intend to do. I have a room and a typewriter at my disposal.

The Virgin and the blind poet, that's straightforward. As a baptized Catholic, I share a past with her, she and I go back a long way, all the way to that baptism in fact, because my name is C. J. J. M. Nooteboom, and the M – as every anti-papist will tell you – stands for Maria. That name is my companion for life. Besides, I was educated at a boarding school run by monks, the gymnasium *Beatae Mariae Immaculatae Conceptionis*, of her Immaculate Conception. The Virgin and I went our separate ways after that, but she is part of my heritage, and in the countries I am especially fond of she manifests herself in the most extraordinary guises, so we run into each other quite frequently. Most recently yesterday, when I took leave of the coast.

I do not know all her feast days by heart, but in the village where I made a stop before travelling on through the mountains southwards, to León, the quayside was crowded, and I was just in time to see her embark. This time she was Santa María del Carmen. Mary of Mount Carmel in Israel (that's where girls called Carmen get their name from), patron saint of fishermen. The fishing boats in the harbour were all decked out with flags. Her statue was being carried on board the largest ship by sailors and fishermen, followed by a pair of monks. The statue sways high above the men's heads, lurches from side to side on account of the unsteady steps of her bearers, and yet is motionless. Swaying, that is what it is, one hand outstretched to the sea, the rays of the setting sun sparkling in her crown. Idolatry, grumble Nordic voices, and that's precisely what I find so pleasing, because the figure hovering so stiffly and so movingly above the tanned faces, is not only the Star of the Sea from my boyhood litanies, she is also the daughter of Isis and of Astarte, of Aphrodite born of sea foam, and today she is Amphitrite indeed, goddess of the sea, wife of Poseidon.

Each of us has his affectations, and one of mine is that I always pack a volume from Loeb's Classical Library whenever I travel, as a mainstay, a breviary, a talisman if you like. They are attractive little books, the size of your hand, lightweight though they can run to 500 pages, green for Greek, red for Latin, the classical text on the left and the English translation – which can be centuries old, like that of Augustine – on the facing page. Nostalgia comes into it, and a pinch of smugness when you sit reading in your hotel room or on a park bench about being privy to inside information, about your privileged access to a far older world. Quite often I cover the English with my right hand to see how well I can read the text on its own, without the translation, and just as often I am disappointed, the four decades separating now from then have had their effect, although there are moments of grace when the secret language all of a sudden reveals itself, the code having melted away so that I can find my way unaided in the Greek or Latin text.

They must all be dead by now, my teachers who presented themselves at the monastery gate in their youth to join the Order. Perhaps they had dreams of converting heathens in remote parts of Africa or Asia, or simply of a life of adventure. Their superior decided otherwise, or who knows, perhaps they were just too talented in the classics. Their vow of obedience left them no say in their destiny: teachers they would become, whether they liked it or not, and teachers they would remain for the rest of their days.

My Latin master was Father Ludgerus Zeinstra, followed by the letters OFM for *Ordinis Fratrum Minorum*, which we used to translate as *Ohne Feine Manieren*, German for "without fine manners". At my next boarding school, the Augustinian one, we translated the OESA following the name, which stood for the Order of the Hermits of Saint Augustine, as *Omnia Emunt Sine Argento*, those who buy everything without money.

He was fat, Ludgerus Zeinstra, and old. White hair. Bare old man's feet in sandals. Caesar, Livy, Cicero, from that mouth I first heard the metrical beat of Ovid's verses which I still know by heart. His habit was always dusted in ash from his pipe or cigar, I can't remember which. Here my extensiveness fails me, even though he contributed so generously to it – I can't conceive of my life without Latin, I feel as if the part of me that stayed behind in that world is actually growing more robust as I get older. Who knows, the slow homecoming has already begun.

All I remember about my Greek master is what he looked like. He was shorter than Ludgerus, more nervous too, in my imagination he was asthmatic, but it may just have been his enthusiasm. He kept jerking his head and gulping air with rapid, upward movements, as if he needed oxygen. We called him Pa. It sounds like a term of endearment in retrospect, perhaps because my own father had been dead for so long by then. We read Herodotus and Xenophon, and he turned Thermopylae and *Thalassa, thalassa* into spell-binding performances, I would sit motionless at my desk. He was not very good at keeping order. When he was on duty in the study room we would count his footsteps under our breath until he reached the front and greeted us with *felix studium*.

Felix studium indeed! Get up at a quarter to six, then Holy Mass and an hour of study before breakfast. Still, it must have been in those pristine hours that Homer first slipped into my consciousness, and even today, I know it sounds silly, but I am almost physically in love with the Greek alphabet, I delight in mouthing the Greek syllables, even when the precise meaning of the words escapes me. It is like the meditative mutterings of Buddhist monks, sounds that have an effect that is not directly connected with a statement, just text pure and simple, and I the clerk pronouncing it. And the feeling this always gives me, is that my life would have been somehow second-hand if I'd never been obliged to spell out those texts which still link me with all manner of things, from the texts on Spanish walls to that effigy bobbing above the sailors' heads, and then setting out to sea, followed by a whole flotilla of white boats.

Within the extension nothing is coincidental. Both the fact of my sitting here observing the spectacle, and the fact that I have brought with me the *Odyssey*, which I had not read for such a long time, are equally inherent in my extended being. It was with the impetuosity typical of last-minute preparations for travel that I picked Homer, it could have been Lucretius, or Livy, but it happened to be him. What I wasn't prepared for was to be moved to tears, which only happens to me when I see a sentimental movie, at the point where boy meets girl, or at some other cardinal moment in the gamut of theatrical atavisms. To be moved by a book, that hadn't happened to me for a long time. It began at the end of the first part, with Euryclea, who had been purchased in her girlhood for twenty oxen by Odysseus' father Laertes, and who, as they say, became part of the family. She brings Telemachus, Odysseus' son, to bed "with blazing torches". Why is this moving? The absence of his father, the ever-present suitors pestering his mother to remarry, the goddess Athene's urging the boy to undertake his great journey which bore all the marks of an initiation, all that and more. But most of all it is the picture of the old woman leading the boy to the palace, "where his chamber was built in the beautiful court, high, in a place of wide outlook, thither he went to his bed, pondering many things in his mind". Euryclea herself is only briefly described, and yet the scene is unforgettable, if only because it is so visible:

> He opened the doors to the well-built chamber, sat down on the bed, and took off his soft tunic and laid it in the wise old woman's hands. And she folded and smoothed the tunic and hung it on a peg beside the corded bedstead, and went then forth from the chamber, drawing the door to by its silver handle, and driving the bolt home with the thong. So there, the night through, wrapped in a fleece of wool, he pondered in his mind upon the journey which Athene had shown him.

Of course the explanation for emotion is never the same for any two people. Identification, that is what it must be, the description has transported me inexorably into the intimacy of that room where I do not belong, and I participate, both intrusively and invisibly, in the thoughts of the boy who will depart the next day to search for his father. Some images have the value of a seal: they accompany all future versions of the *éducation sentimentale*, the hunt for the father, the quest.

The emotion increases with Telemachus' appearance at the court of King Menelaus, who returned from the Trojan war, and who may have news of Odysseus. So here is a man who knew the father, but who does not know that the youth before him is the son. Only we the readers know that, we listen along with the son to the loving description of the father, how the king laments the fate of the son who, unbeknownst to him, is sitting right there beside him. It is his not-knowing that makes his words true, and in this case the truth is the emotion:

> So he spoke, and in Telemachus he roused the desire to weep for his father. Tears from his eyelids he let fall upon the ground, when he heard his father's name, and with both hands he held up his purple cloak before his eyes.

In the small centimetre between this paragraph and the one before, I get up from my chair on the quayside, watch the fishing boats sail out of the harbour towards the inky sea fraught with dangers from which the fishermen seek protection in the female figure they have taken with them, just as Menelaus was protected by Eidothea, "daughter of Proteus, the old man of the sea". I do not wait for her to return, and drive over the Puerto de Pajares to León, 150 kilometres away. I see her again that evening, in the hotel lobby where I have joined the other guests watching television. I see her a dozen times. All the long coast of Spain she has embarked today in ever different, ever similar guises, at Murcia and at Cádiz, in Galicia and Catalonia. Homer is near at hand in these parts, only the names have changed.

León. Coming from the north over the high mountain passes, from Asturias where the Christian kings recruited their armies. From the east and the west, over the pilgrim's milky way to Santiago. And from the south, from the empty plains of Castile between Ebro and Duero, where around the year 1000 al-Mansour emerges, the scourge, a name which has an ominous ring even today.

León, founded at the time of Nero's death in AD 68, was once the garrison town of the Seventh Legion of Imperial Rome, which gave it its name, Legio Septima. The legionary eagles witness the wars in Hungary, in Asia Minor, in the Alps, in Mauritania, until finally, in the third century, it is the only legion left in Hispania, protector of the gold and the gold convoys of El Bierzo in the north. The assorted tribes have by then been brought to heel and herded together, the Latin language has imposed itself on the earlier vernaculars, bringing the story of Christendom within reach of a population that never worshipped the gods of Rome.

The bishoprics of León and Astorga were created as early as the third century. The new religion brought with it an aroma of curious words, such as "love" and "equality", words which were well understood by the oppressed, the slaves. Rome bore the seeds of her own downfall. It was these Christians who, four centuries later, would stop the spread of another new religion, Islam. The fall of the Imperium was followed by a witches' ball. Marauding Germanic tribes, the unaccountable momentum of people streaming over the Pyrenees. Alani, Suevi, Vandals; plague and famine, the first martyrs, persecution of Christians, then the emergence of the Visigothic kings and their conversion, and again Christianity.

Only an impassioned dynastician can learn the steps of the dance that follows. The Asturian kings transfer the seat of power from Oviedo to

León. This corner of Spain, with Navarre, is the only part of the country not occupied by Arabs at that time. But who were these kings, where did they come from? The first one we know by name is Pelayo, who ignited the Reconquista in 718. But before then? Military leaders, gentlemen farmers, local chiefs, men who fight their way to power. Only after Pelayo is some light shed on the vagaries of the Asturian monarchy and the ensuing developments in León and Castile. A dynasty when graphically represented always looks like an inverted pyramid. In reality the pyramid is a construct of flesh and blood, with the latest potentate at the summit, on top of the dead who have hoisted him to power with their tangled strings of alliances and marriages. It is all clotted together with weaponry, escutcheons, quarterings and each reshuffle represents couplings and sirings, love between interested parties but always with real people, men with power, women dying in childbirth, spurned brothers, feuds, betrayal, names that always stood for land, land which was lost when they divided and which was won along with people and power when they united.

The names are Alfonso, then Fruela, and Aurelio, and Silo, Mauregato, and Bermudo, then another Alfonso, and Ramiro, and Ordoño, and then Alfonso again, and still we are only in 886. And they have nicknames, the Chaste, the Hairy, the Horrible, the Deacon, the Great. Alfonso the Chaste (791–842) has the first shrine built at Santiago de Compostela, he conquers Lisbon, beats back Arab attacks and seeks contact with Charlemagne. His son Ramiro builds the splendid *aula regia* at Oviedo, his son Ordoño has to deal with Moors and also with Normans.

We claim to live in apocalyptic times, but these people lived out their lives under the constant threat of annihilation. The next Alfonso is Alfonso the Great. He conquers, more or less for good, the area up to the Duero and has himself crowned Emperor of Spain. His three sons depose him, the empire is divided, the crowns fly through the air, those of León, Asturias, Galicia. After this the choreography becomes almost too intricate to follow. Ordoño II takes over the kingdom of León from his brother Garcia, and makes the city his official place of residence in 924. He defeats Abd ar-Rahman and is defeated by him. His successor dies of leprosy. Now the lights in the dance-hall are dimmed for a while, a great whispering of names rises from conflicting sources. Conquests, losses, dependence on the Caliphate of Cordoba. Soldiers from the north fight Moorish troops in Lisbon, León is sacked but is reconstructed under Alfonso V and is granted magnificent privileges. Thirty years on, when Alfonso's son is killed in battle, the three-centuries-old dynasty, which had always claimed descent from the old Visigothic kings, comes to an end. León has lost Castile, the next king marries the loser's sister and proclaims himself king of León and Castile.

This had been the pattern of European history all along, but the contours are now becoming a little more distinct. The crowns grow heavier under the weight of additional territories, but the numbering continues just the same. The next Alfonso is the sixth, and he conquers Toledo. He uses his war booty to rebuild Cluny and marries the daughter of the Duke of Burgundy. In 1135 Alfonso VII is crowned emperor in León, even the Moors recognize his might, but his death in 1157 means that not only kingdoms must be split up but also the numbers of the kings, which makes things very complicated for a bit. Castile and León go their separate ways, each under their own Alfonso, an Eighth and a Ninth respectively. There is treason in the air, for while Castile's eighth Alfonso marches against Seville, stronghold of the Almohads, León's ninth Alfonso is busy negotiating an alliance with the Muslim rulers. It takes a tenth Alfonso, Alfonso the Wise, el Sábio, administrator, poet, one of the greatest monarchs of Spain, to reign over León and Castile once more.

In the meantime rivers of blood have trickled into the earth, and plenty of royal blood has flowed into new streams which are subsequently depicted in new coats of arms, but here my *raccourci* ends. I am in León, everything has vanished, and everything is still there. This is both a city of kings and a provincial capital. The marrow has been excised from the bone, but the perfume of power still wafts towards you now and then from an ancient wall, a tomb, an inscription. León is a city where the past is under seal. You can make it out if you try.

I have come here to see things I have seen before. The cathedral, the cloister next door, the Romanesque church of Saint Isidore, the royal pantheon, a place of slumber behind Romanesque paintings where the semi-mythical names repose, so much lovelier and more mysterious than the icy crypt of the Escorial where the gangrene of the Habsburgs smoulders in funerary urns and monster caskets.

It is dark in the crypt, as if not only the paintings are almost a thousand years old, but the air itself, their very age having produced a special type of silence in which every sound you make is excessive. There are several tombs, some of them quite plain, without inscriptions or decorations, others covered in convoluted script from which an intelligible name surfaces now and then, but which reveals no further secrets to me. Petrified, belated messages in private codes only the scholar can decipher. There are not many visitors, we shuffle across that low-ceilinged royal hall like intruders, we run our hands over the gleaming letters and we contemplate the vaulting overhead, the angels and shepherds with their dazed, saintly look, the zodiac expanding and contracting like the universe according to the ribs of the vault, the rage of the butting goats, the wolf drinking milk, and Christ Pantocrator in his mandorla surrounded by waves. Walls and vaulting become the pages of a book with Carolingian and oriental echoes; we read as we walk along, turning the parchment pages and repeating the histories we already know, the last supper and the raising of Lazarus, the massacre of the innocents, the crucifixion, the apocalyptic vision of the tetramorph, the winged figure of legend which has lost none of Ezekiel's dread:

> And I looked, and behold, a whirlwind came out of the north, a great cloud, and a fire infolding itself, and a brightness was about it, and out of the midst thereof as the colour of amber, out of the midst of the fire. Also out of the midst thereof came the likeness of four living creatures. And this was their appearance; they had the likeness of a man. And every one had four faces, and every one had four wings.

A book evokes an image and the image refers back to the book, *that* is the reflection in which this crypt holds me captive. I know the city awaits me outside, I am free to leave and return as I have done so often, and each time I will visit this place, this book that never ends.

It was King Ferdinand I who brought the relics of Saint Isidore to León. The supernatural powers attributed to bones and skulls, nails and hairs in the Middle Ages have been discussed at length by others, but in this case the fetish was especially meaningful. Not only did it give both the town and Ferdinand's own lineage a certain Gothic legitimacy (Isidore's mother was probably a daughter of Theodoric, the Ostrogothic king), the acquisition of this prize also seemed to reaffirm the existence of a direct link with classical Rome. For in the Middle Ages it was generally held that the entire knowledge of the classical world was vested in Isidore, who was born in Carthage in 560. The fame of this writer-bishop only increased after his death, thanks to the abundance of texts he left behind in the form of *Etymologiae, Sententiae*.

In the Romanesque church that bears his name I sit and think it all over. Visigoths, exegetes, the mysteries of the tetramorph, lion, bull, eagle, man, which are called "the four living creatures" of the

The inner court of the church of San Isidoro, Léon

Apocalypse in the Book of Revelation, the church around me, the royal tombs below, the mutually fortifying reflections which are so potent in this place and which will forfeit their validity in the bustling world outside, while that world would not exist without this ancestry, and yet, when I step out into the street, it is as if I am falling through a trap door into the light, a light that is brilliant and effervescent. Down below, in the resting place of kings, flies the four-headed beast, forever static. As for me, I have drifted into the transitoriness of the modern world in a small provincial town where nothing much happens. A few wide avenues converging on pompous monuments, as in all Spanish towns, and immediately beyond the official centre, which appears to exist solely to give the place a properly urban feel, are the winding little streets, hidden squares, obscure cafés, workshops where you can buy baskets and saddles and everything to do with horses, shops with transparent sausage skins and carpet-beater-shaped braids of dried *congrio*, market stalls with bacon, ham, pungent cheeses and honey. The mood is rustic, homespun, timeless. The men have harsh features and the women wear shawls, they have come from the surrounding countryside to buy and sell in town. Knives, twine, salted sardines and dried beans, wares.

And in the midst of the huddle of low houses rises the cathedral, a ship from a distant past, moored here forever, a quiet reminder. There is always music there, which, although discreet, seals you off from the outside world at once. You were already cut off from the world, but now the effect is two-fold. Last time it was Monteverdi, which is more appropriate to the intimacy of the building. Now it is Handel, the *Messiah* no less, the triumphant hunting cry that I always listen to on my Walkman when I travel by plane because it goes so well with the ecstatic sensation of being 10,000 metres above the surface of the earth. But here it makes me perceive the church differently: the same old mechanism sets to work right away, I long to fly, to rise up into the sky, to soar past those stained-glass windows with the pictures that I would otherwise have to look up in a book because they're so high and so far away.

For whose benefit is the upper section of a cathedral designed? The top of the elevation, the proportion, the spatial effect, was obviously meant to be seen, but probably the last person to have been at close quarters to it was a mason who died centuries ago. What if I were to be in his shoes? And I imagine what it would be like, to wing leisurely past those high cross-vaults, past the windows and rosettes charged with meaning and legend, casting their dappled iridescence on this figure, a tropical angel from the Low Countries dipping and rising along the contours of the vaulted ceilings, swerving past the tranquil retable, looking down on the effigies resting on their Gothic tombs until they are permitted to rise, floating silently through the air which must surely be rarefied at such a height, suddenly to be wafted by the same turbulence that makes the carved robes of the baroque statues flutter so weirdly.

But I can't fly, and so remain earthbound, a failed angel and a timid Icarus, and I look up at the stained-glass radiance from my humble vantage point. There is no church in the world that has more windows in proportion to the mass of stone. The structure should have collapsed long ago, say the experts, and that in itself makes the church a sort of stone-and-glass angel, a form of holiness in its own right. Angelo Roncalli, who lived here before he became pope in Rome, put it more succinctly: "This building has more glass than stone, more light than glass, and more faith than light." I don't know about the last bit, but it is the same light I am walking about in now, since I am not permitted to fly. Tinted, filtered light that exists nowhere else quite like this. You are absorbed by it, buoyed up, and the loss of weight comes pretty close to flying.

A visit to old acquaintances, that is part of it, too. I walk to the middle of the transept, where the southern rosette wheels around me, turn right, and there lies my mitred friend, the dead friend I have come to visit, he of the broken staff and missing feet, the contented, almost oriental smile playing on his stone lips, he is like a Buddha. Not a second has gone by in the year since I was here last, he hasn't moved, the lion at his side still turns his gangrenous head to glare at me with the same desperate rage. In the cloister I find the others, the medallion showing Tamar with a veil on the keystone between the fan of ribs, Death imprisoned in a square, his vacant gaze indicating that he has no time for me yet, and then, in the middle of the sun-baked floor of the cloister court, as if I am able to fly after all, I catch sight of the tops of two dismantled spires, standing there as if they have fallen from the sky. I walk towards them gingerly, as if it is not allowed, as might well be the case. They are not intended for scrutiny of this kind, their proper place is on high, where they may be seen from afar, there is something wrong about standing here and recognizing each shape in its crude, enlarged form. This is meant to be filigree high in the sky, to be hundreds of metres away from my eye, not to be observed and assessed at close quarters. I walk and fly around them and see what the crow sees, and I envy the crow.

The newspapers and television are full of the Civil War, it's a repeat performance of a television series. The government stays aloof, having evidently no inclination to take sides in the old dispute. My room doesn't have a television set, there are usually only a couple of people watching in the hotel lobby, and most of them are impassive, too young to remember, and some of them appear dismissive, as if the Civil War belongs to some prehistoric period or other, that it's over and done with. No doubt a lot of Spaniards have learnt to avoid the subject, because the fighting did not tear only communities apart, but also families.

In the village where I spend my summers, there's a small, weathered plaque on the wall of the church, with the names of six priests who were shot in the war. No one talks about them, but from the names I can tell that they were members of families that still live there. The same memorial plaque is also at the back of their minds, always, and that is of course why this government is not eager for commemorations: commemorating is there all right, but it is done in silence.

Besides, the government is plagued by other problems. Terrorism, further victims of violence. This time the pictures in the paper are not old, they are fresh images of death and destruction. One of the nationalists' reasons for starting the revolution in 1936 was to hold back what they felt was the subversive desire for autonomy on the part of the various Spanish regions. Those who were defeated then are in power now. Other men, other circumstances. But they still have to find answers to the same questions as the problems are essentially unchanged. State versus lands. The dossier begins way back with the Asturian kings, or even earlier. Thousands of names, privileges, *taifas*, duchies, kingdoms, autonomies come up for review. Five centuries ago the Catholic Kings, themselves monarchs of two kingdoms, thought they had founded a single unified state, and so they had. But the cracks remain.

XVIII

A Riddle for Creon

Press cutting of an ETA funeral
Murder as mythology ~ Murder in mythology
Murder, mythology and the role of the state

A GROUP OF MEN AND WOMEN at a funeral. Usually an image of relative simplicity: death is represented by the coffin. A coffin on its own, without a dead body, betokens death, too, as can be seen in some demonstrations nowadays. If there's a dead body, then it's more about death itself, you could say. The coffin I am concerned with is not empty, but the scene is no ordinary funeral, it's a political demonstration. There may be no proof that there is actually a body in the box, but there is circumstantial evidence. The coffin rests on the shoulders of several men, they're not staggering under its weight, but it is certainly not empty. Then there are the faces of the bystanders. No, bystanders isn't the right word, even though they're standing by. Their expressions are too intense for bystanders, they are there for a reason. They are, in a sense, family. One can choose one's family to some extent.

The men haven't dressed specially for the occasion. They're wearing those livid shoes that joggers wear, with thick, ribbed soles. Shirts worn outside the trousers, short-sleeved or with the sleeves rolled up. The women you can see in the photograph are mostly middle-aged, they wear two-piece suits or floral print dresses, handbags swinging crookedly from the elbows because the arms are raised to show a clenched fist. My mother would recognize them as ladies at once. Some raise the right fist, others the left. And then there is the usual décor of paving stones, foliage, a smokestack, random buildings.

The deception of photographs lies in the arrested movement, what happened when this picture started moving is reported in the newspaper. The dead person in the coffin is/was Rafael Etxebeste. What he looked

News photographs for the funeral of ETA terrorist Rafael Etxebeste
(Photograph © Luis Alberto Garcia)

like is to be seen in one of the two accompanying mug shots. A man of
about thirty, balding, more hair at the sides than on top. The side-hair
blends into the black hair of the beard, there is no mouth to be seen, but
something about the shape of the beard tells you that his lips are thin,
turned down at the corners. It is strange how even when you are dead
a photograph can give you away. Big black eyes. A high, pale forehead.
A steady gaze. I saw that face last night on television, along with images
of the burnt-out, blackened, twisted carcass of a car. The death of objects
inspires its own horror. Etxebeste and María Teresa Pérez Ceber were
travelling in that car when the bomb they were carrying, presumably to
blow someone up, went off. Both were killed instantaneously, an instant
which some say lasts an eternity. They had recently returned from
France, where they had been leading a clandestine existence, to join the
summer offensive of ETA *Militar*. The police claimed they had already
been involved in three murders that summer. Not that they called it
murder – words can be put on and taken off just like items of clothing.

At 19.00 hours (punctuality is appreciated, even though bombs sometimes go off prematurely) the coffin arrives in Rentería. That's close to
the border with France, truly this war is not far away. The coffin is
covered with the *ikurriña*, the holy Basque flag, and the ETA anagram.
It's not I who call that flag holy, it's the people who wish to die and kill in
its name, and who, as in San Sebastián and Bilbao during the last few
days, go berserk when it's not hoisted on its own, *without* the Spanish
flag, on the balconies of public buildings. *La guerra de las banderas*, the

war of the flags, is what they call it, and that war would be comic if it weren't for all the corpses. The mayor of San Sebastián decided not to fly any flags at all, the provincial governor, who represents central authority in Madrid, demanded that all three should be flown: the flags of the province, of the Basque Country, of Spain. The governor accused the mayor of "cowardice", the mayor accused the governor of anti-Basque sentiments and of "hating" the people of his province. The issue of the flags sparks off pitched battles in the streets.

Back to the coffin. Herri Batasuna is the name of the political party which maintains close ties with the terrorist ETA organization, but despite that connection the party has a say in local councils, provincial parliaments, and even in the European Parliament (where its representative was the only member not to support the motion against terrorism). Every time a terrorist is buried, Herri Batasuna is there. This is where the schism within Spanish politics, the poisonous and squalid schizophrenia, reveals itself. The body about to be buried usually belongs to someone who, according to all the laws of the Spanish state, is a murderer. Legalists may prefer the term "potential murderer" in certain cases. And yet the state permits graveside ceremonies with full honours, from which the potential *victims* must stay away at all costs. I am referring to the members of the Guardia Civil. Indeed it would be hard on them to have to listen to the graveside rhetoric.

During the funeral I am concerned with here, the leading Herri Batasuna politician in Rentería praised both dead activists, saying that they "had been the bravest of all, for they had done what others would not dare". Then a thirteen-year-old boy danced the *aurresku* by the coffin. "The *aurresku*", was the expression used in the national newspaper reporting the event. Evidently this is such a common occurrence that everyone in Spain knows what the word means. The ceremony thus acquires mythical and religious dimensions, which we are familiar with from other fanatical movements. The *Eusko Gudariak* is sung (the definite article again), there are cries of *Gora Eta*. Nationalism as religion.

The only contemporary parallel I know is the dismal funerals of IRA heroes, where masked men (I know why they wear masks, but the absence of faces somehow detracts from the reality of the scene) fire hand-guns in salute over the coffin. But there are more ancient parallels which offer a better illustration of the dilemma facing the Spanish government. Each dead *Etarra* is a Polynices, the family and fellow warriors are always Antigone, and the state must be Creon. Ever since Sophocles wrote his tragedy people have speculated on its meaning: the exegeses, purely philosophical or in the form of poetry, drama, opera, have erected a cathedral of writings and commentaries, of successive and contradictory Creons and Antigones. Legalists, statesmen, anarchists, old and new Christians, Hegel, Kierkegaard, Brecht, Espriu, Anouilh, Hölderlin, Honegger, Gide, Maurras, Heidegger, they have all drawn their own conclusions from that scarcely thirty-page-long text from the fifth century BC, and those conclusions differ according to the minds and the times.

The story: Oedipus' sons (whom he sired with his mother Jocasta), Eteocles and Polynices, have driven their blind father (who put his eyes out when he discovered that he had killed his father and married his mother) from Thebes. Oedipus curses his sons, who have decided to rule the city together. They quarrel, Polynices gets help from outside and attacks his own city. The brothers kill each other in the ensuing battle. Jocasta commits suicide and her brother, the boys' uncle Creon, is crowned king of Thebes. The new king will not allow Polynices to be given a proper burial, since it was he who attacked the city. He is a traitor, his body must be devoured by dogs and vultures. Creon represents the state, his word is law. Antigone, who had followed her father Oedipus into exile at Colonus, invokes a different law, that of Religion and Nature, according to which the dead must be properly honoured and given a resting place in the earth, or they will roam forever and never find peace. Creon threatens to execute anyone who disobeys his order, Antigone announces that she will ignore it. Both are trapped in their respective stances, both are doomed.

Is it too far-fetched to see some connection here with ETA? On the face of it, yes, because the Spanish state appears to have decided to give Creon the traits of Pilate, he looks the other way and washes his hands. Or does he? It is difficult to read the mind of a state. To ignore the religious aspects of the ETA funeral may be pure secularism, who knows. This is the twentieth century, after all. But it may be a more calculating, more Machiavellian pose: those *Etarras* are dead anyway, and the dead can't do any harm. Just a simple matter to the state perhaps, but not to its citizens. It is not for nothing that ETA lavishes such antiquated ceremonial attentions on its funerals. They also intend to be provocation.

The rituals are widely covered in the media, and are seen by people who have themselves been victims of kidnapping, by businessmen that have to pay "taxes" to ETA, and also by the relatives of assassination victims and hostages, by the parents, wives and children of the targets of ETA violence.

I cannot summon the spirit of Hegel to check whether his prescription is still valid: he calls Creon a *sittliche Macht*, an ethical power, and Sophocles' drama the absolute *exemplum* of tragedy: mutual destruction of impetus, consequence of an inevitable, dialectic collision between the two highest moral imperatives, that of the state on the one hand and that of kin on the other. Next of kin, that's what the funeral-goers in the photograph look like. Kindred spirits, individuals who have sought each other out. Does the individual have the right to follow his own conscience in contravention of the laws and rights of the state, if that individual, acting on his own behalf or in the name of a group, invokes a "law of nature" that he or she holds in higher esteem than the laws of the state?

In the study George Steiner devoted to Antigone – a stupendous inventory of different approaches to the theme (*Antigones*, Clarendon Press, Oxford) – a hundred times more light is shed on the dilemma than I am able to do here. The last *Antigone* I saw, years ago, was Anouilh's. Hans Croiset played Creon, and I remember my strong identification with José Ruiter's impressive Antigone. But Anouilh's is a "different" Antigone from the old Sophocles heroine, and she finds herself face to face with a subtle, "political" Creon, who managed to slip past the German censors (the première was in 1944). Nor did Hegel view Creon as a blind tyrant, but rather as the state, which has no choice, just as Antigone has no choice. Steiner gives a lucid description of their respective positions as seen by Hegel. There are situations in which the state (Creon) is not disposed to relinquish its authority over the dead. There are situations, political, military, symbolic (or all three at once, as in Spain) in which the laws of the *polis* do extend to the body of the deceased, with regard to either a state funeral or the opposite: getting rid of the corpse. The scattering of the ashes of the men hanged at Nuremberg and the official burial of the body of Rudolf Hess with all the dark implications thereof are recent examples of the same dilemma. The myth is by no means moth-eaten.

But let us stick to Spain. Hegel as *étatiste* is not a new discovery. But he understands Antigone, too. Unlike Oedipus, she is not the victim of an inescapable fate, she takes action, chooses, goes against the law of the state. Yet her deed is not political, she invokes laws which, in her view, represent a higher authority than that of any state. Creon has forbidden proper burial for political reasons. For Antigone (and so it seems for the Spanish state) politics stop after death. The dead are exempt from worldly justice, they are elsewhere. It is the duty of Antigone, the sister, to see that Polynices is taken care of in the afterworld. She cannot leave the body lying outside the walls like trash. She elects to ignore Creon's prohibition. Thus her action, though not politically inspired, becomes political. In Sophocles' drama Creon condemns Antigone to be entombed alive. When he wants to retract his decree, it is too late. His own downfall is now inevitable. Two ideas, two mutually destructive human beings. But this is not the end of it, according to Hegel. The conflict, having been exposed with such excruciating clarity, contributes to the knowledge the world has of itself.

You can think what you like about Hegel, and indeed that is what everyone has done. This can lead to surprises, as with two writers who, though on different grounds, tend to be more or less identified with a state: Goethe and Brecht. Both were radically anti-Creon. In Goethe's view what Creon did was a *Staatsverbrechen*, a crime against the state: corpses should not be left out to rot because of the dangers to the health of the citizens. Here we have the governor rather than the statesman. With Brecht, it is different. Man, he asserts, is monstrously great when he subjugates nature, but when he subjugates his fellow man (as Creon did with Antigone) he becomes a great monster. The GDR was perhaps the most Hegelian state imaginable, but that did not stop Brecht from writing it all down (*Anmerkungen zur Bearbeitung*, 1948).

What would happen if the Spanish state/Creon refused Herri Batasuna/Antigone permission to bury the body of ETA activists/ Polynices? I do not know. This is where the failings of the parallel become clear. Antigone can never be "innocent" again, she has read her own story. So she is aware that Creon knows what the consequences of his decree will be: his own downfall. Now she, too, is touched by politics, she manipulates the law of nature, and that is a perversity. Creon need not play her game. ETA knows this, too, its members produce a regular supply of fresh Polynices for burial. What is Creon to do? And which Creon? Hegel's, Brecht's? Or perhaps the Creon of Charles

Maurras? In his view the rebel wasn't Antigone, but Creon. The Creon who "has against him the gods of Religion, fundamental laws of the Polis, the feelings of the living Polis . . ." That is what the play is about, according to Maurras. "Sophocles did not wish to portray for us the surge of fraternal love, nor even, in the personage of Haemon, Antigone's betrothed, that of love pure and simple. What he also sets out to show is the punishment of the tyrant who has sought to free himself from laws divine and human. Who violates and scorns all these laws? Creon. It is he the anarchist. It is only he."

In that respect the Spanish state has options enough. And make no mistake, this is not just a game. I don't suppose González and Barrionuevo, his interior minister, keep Hegel and Maurras on their bedside tables, but still, they will have to decide what sort of Creon they wish to be, and they will have to bear in mind that each Creon creates his own Antigone, and vice versa. For the French philosopher Bernard-Henri Lévy (of the "new right", according to Steiner) it is Antigone who sets herself apart from society by virtue of her solipsism, and it is the priest-king Creon who maintains contact between gods and men. "We may see in the discipline of the Greek polis and in Plato's programme for such discipline an ill-omened apotheosis of servility. But this is not Sophocles' perspective. This is not the vision which can elucidate the realities of sacred kingship in fifth-century Thebes . . . Antigone is a play written entirely from Creon's point of view." González will have little use for sacred kingship. If pressed, there's always a Bourbon he can fall back on.

He will be more likely to identify with Alfred Döblin's Creon, if only because he has not (yet) made the latter's mistakes. In Döblin's novel *November 1918*, Dr Becker is a teacher of Latin and Greek at a gymnasium. He has returned from the war, badly wounded, wearing the Iron Cross, and finds himself facing a class full of right-wing pupils, all except one being in favour of Creon. Becker does not agree. To him the tyrant is Creon "who, in his pride at being, at last, victor and king, believes that he can set himself above sanctified traditions and accepted truths as old as time. . . . If the state is a reality, so, in no lesser degree, is death. It is Creon's stance towards the existential weight of death which is flagrantly inadequate and which entails catastrophe both for himself and the polis."

Priest, king, rebel, statesman, anarchist, coward, politician. But the question remains. How should the world of the living behave towards the world of the dead? What should Creon do, which Creon should the Spanish state opt for? For the time being a new variant appears to have been adopted: he permits the body of Polynices to be ceremoniously buried, thereby running the risk of offending the victims' sense of justice. They, too, have dead relatives to take care of, and can invoke laws from a different, older tradition than those of the state. But perhaps the victims' relatives prefer not to tamper with the domain of death. Who is not wary of setting foot in no-man's land? The alternative would be to claim the bodies and to burn them or bury them in secret, thereby tapping into another seam of bitterness.

Hegel cannot help González, that is not what he's for. He is the spirit of history itself, and he cannot take sides. Like a mystical eagle he floats up there somewhere and from his lofty vantage point he looks down on this human snake pit and observes the mutual destruction, "the partial, the unfinished work which progresses steadily till equilibrium is attained". Consolation from the poet! Until then we will have to kill and bury, and wait until that magnificent abstraction, the *Weltgeist*, the world spirit, looks in the mirror and recognizes itself.

I take a final look at the photograph in the newspaper. The lady in the patterned dress could be coming from a department store, her fist is not after all really and truly clenched. There are always women like her to be seen in city squares. They wave to some Antigone or other, and do not look like enemies of the state. They are the riddle that Creon must solve.

XIX

The Valley of Silence

The cathedral of Astorga ~ The hidden valley
Consecrating Spanish churches ~ Travelling with Frondini
Borges dies ~ The myth-maker's myth completed for him
The myth-maker becomes his own myth

LEÓN, EARLY MORNING. A pale mist lingers over the Bernesga, ragged veils over the quiet, brown water. I have parked my car on the bridge, because the early sunlight is doing strange things to the façade of the Hostal San Marcos. It measures 100 metres across, the façade of this the most handsome hotel in Europe, a building like a statement: a spectacular affirmation of the power of Ferdinand and Isabella. It is always difficult to imagine anything that is centuries old as having been modern once, but the grandeur of their gesture is incontestable. Farewell to the Middle Ages in a small town, which boasts some of the most beautiful early medieval buildings in the world, and which the Renaissance seems to have largely passed by. It is an impressive farewell, a proud salute to a revolution in art. The style is called Plateresque, and for good reason, for the façade looks as if it is made of chased *plata*, silver. If the edifice were a thousand times smaller it would strike you as the most refined *orfèvrerie*, a master silversmith's showpiece, as it is you are overwhelmed by those friezes and pilasters, the lavish ornaments and the disciplined framework in which they are set, the mythological and historical busts in high relief, a European *Ahnengalerie* in medallions.

Later that day I see an echo of the Plateresque style in the vaulted portals of the cathedral of Astorga, another of those monoliths that have been catapulted into a too-small town with a force of such magnitude as we can no longer comprehend. Sometimes it is almost too much to bear, all that mass and weight, all those chiselled mounds lying scattered in the sluggish, empty countryside, on their guard, even a little hostile,

Astorga Cathedral

primordial monsters awaiting extinction. I cannot resist, as usual, and enter that petrified forest of columns towering without capitals into the vaults. It is already hot outside, and I pause, slightly dazed, to get accustomed to the church-shaped light. What's more, I am the only visitor, which reaffirms my humble stature – that of nobody.

A remarkable feature of many large Spanish churches is the *coro*, the choir. The word denotes an enclosed space in the middle of a church, with a rood screen taller than a man on the east side, the side facing the altar. Sometimes the enclosure takes up a great deal of space in the cathedral, and it is there that the canons come together several times a day to sing the office, but the arrangement somehow creates the impression that they have driven the common folk out of the church. If you want to see mass being celebrated you must find a place in front of the choir, because if you enter the church from the back and make your way to the altar, your view will be blocked by the *trascoro*, the decorated rear wall of the choir, a church within a church, from which the faithful are barred. The contrast between this triumphal architecture and the simplicity of Romanesque churches could not be more marked. The *coro* epitomizes the clergy as an institution, the wielders of power in their secure bastion, aloof: the owners of God. Sometimes you step into such a church when the office is being sung. A few old men sing quavering psalms, there are few worshippers, a ship without passengers, going nowhere. Irony. The men in their purple bibs are carbon copies of the priests Buñuel and Fellini have introduced us to: picturesque, benign or malevolent, but belonging to an irretrievably lost past, the stuff of films. Now that they are absent, I venture into the choir with its ninety-seven wooden stalls carved with scenes showing Church fathers and bishops and gleaming with the polish of centuries of sitting and squirming. I stroll around and try to imbibe the atmosphere, but the place is too vast, too triumphant, or else I am too full, the only feature that holds my attention is abstract: the extraordinary geometrical designs at the bases of the columns. I have never seen them before. A riddle after all, and having come to that conclusion I go outside, perhaps I'm escaping. I have been in this land of churches for several weeks now, and it can become oppressive at times, as if all those polychrome statues of saints with their personalized instruments of torture are about to clamber out of their overcrowded retables to come after you, to quarter you, crucify you, grill you, put out your eyes, flay you alive, or worse, to read to you for an eternity from the book they hold and whose pages they cannot turn.

The number of books I take with me on my travels increases with time. Curious editions are irresistible to me. On a street market in León I bought a little book entitled *Valle del Silencio* (Valley of Silence), by David Gustavo López, published locally. I embrace coincidence, and it always comes my way. In the region I am travelling through (where I would not have paused were it not for that little book), there is supposed to be a valley of exceptional beauty, with a very poor road leading to a "medieval" village with a perfectly preserved Mozarabic church dating from the early tenth century. The green Michelin guide does not mention it, the Michelin map doesn't even indicate the road, another map shows a faint dotted line ending at the name of a village: Santiago de Peñalba.

The track ends at Santiago de Peñalba

The road, or track, must end there, as the village is located at a point where various sierras converge: the Sierra del Teleno, the Sierra de la Cabrera Baja, the Sierra del Eje, the peak of the Guiana. Helmut Domke, the author of my German guidebook, *Spaniens Norden*, travelled the distance on the back of a mule, but, so the author of *Iglesias mozárabes leonesas* tells me, that is no longer necessary, as there is indeed a road, although not a very good one, nor does it go all the way to the village. Thankfully, Zodiaque's *L'Art Mozarabe* has the answer: south of Ponferrada I am to follow the country lane to San Esteban de Valdueza for 8 kilometres, then drive 14 kilometres along the river. The motorist is advised to take care, for the road is *étroite* and *difficile* and frequently blocked by *pierres* that tumble down the mountainside. To reach San Pedro de Montes I will have to get out and walk the last 500 metres uphill; to reach Santiago de Peñalba (of the white mountaintop) I must leave the car at the edge of the village or I will never get it out again.

Great beauty defies description. All the family members were in attendance: buzzards, falcons, lizards, butterflies, bumblebees, crickets. And bluffs, ravines, chestnut trees, drifts of heather, the sparkle of the Oca threading through the depths and then suddenly joining up with the road. A few hamlets along the river, old women in black, low houses with wooden balconies, livestock straggling in the narrow, unpaved streets. All the travel books agree that time has stood still here, but there is no question that, on the contrary, everything except time has stood still here. This is what makes it so miraculous. Time must flow, that is its destiny. Tempo also means time, and wherever two tempi diverge, that of nature and that of man, strange things can happen. The disparity arises from the illusion: the traveller sees sights he knows from old engravings, things he knows looked just like this in the past. A man behind a wooden plough, another man with a flail, a woman holding a scythe. The static quality of those drawings or old photographs evokes an *idea* of immobility, an impression that can be banished for ever by wielding the flail yourself for half an hour. The meagre plots of land between the mountains do not call for farming methods that are any different from those of the past, to introduce a combine harvester here would be idiotic.

What remains is the vision. This entire landscape hangs like a cradle in the sky, no one comes here without a purpose. There are no taverns, no hotels, the road is too narrow for two cars to pass, there is just one bus a week to Santiago de Peñalba, last year there were as many as 8,000 visitors, and this vision is for them, and for me: clover and poppies, the studious hovering of birds of prey, the concerto grosso of frogs and crickets, the string quartets of bumblebees, bluebottles, midges and mosquitoes, the shadows and the scourge of the sun, thought, eye, silence.

I leave the car where the road becomes impassable, and climb on to San Pedro de Montes. I am saving Santiago for later. "Walk", say my

footsteps, and as I trudge up the mountainside I am reminded of the
solitary monks who journeyed here on foot as early as the sixth century.
They were fleeing the wide world, the cosmopolis of the Visigothic kings,
to lead lives as hermits. *Tebaida*, solitary resting place, hermitage. Three
centuries later Gennadius came here with twelve men to build a church,
which was consecrated in 919. It has vanished, the sole reminder of its
presence being a stone describing the consecration. Mountain air has
conserving properties, no acid rain here, and I can still read the chiselled
cryptogram: NOBISSIME GENNADIUS PRSBTR CVM XII FRIBUS
RESTAVRABIT . . . *prsbrt, presbyter, fribus, fratribus, nobissime*, now,
recently, *modernamente* as the Spanish guidebook has it, but it was all
a thousand years ago. Again I want to imagine the scene, for the
stone has preserved the names of those who witnessed the event, the four
bishops who came here from over the mountains on a march of many
long days to consecrate the now vanished church, Gennadio Astoricense
(Gennadius of Astorga, where I have just come from), Frunimio
Legionense (of León, I was there this morning but it must have
been several days' journey away then), Dulcidio Salamanticense (of
Salamanca, a world beyond the mountains), Sabarico Dumiense (which,
as far as I can see, can refer only to Tuy). The date takes up a whole
line: SVB ERA NOBIES CENTENA: DECIES QUINA; TERNA ET
QVATERNA; VIII O KLDRAM NBMBRM, their November, our
October, 24 October 919.

Bishop, mitre, staff, an autumn day, chilly mountain air. They
consecrate a church, a man carves an inscription in stone, the event must
be recorded. That sounds active, and the result is passive: I take part in
that historical event and reactivate it by imparting it.

Bishop, mitre, staff. It was only a few days ago that I saw a television
broadcast of a pontifical mass in the cathedral of Santiago. 25 July, the
feast of Saint James, patron saint of Spain. I recognized the images, the
Pórtico de la Gloria, the *botafumeiro*, the legendary silver censer, which
hangs from thick ropes attached high in the vaulting and takes about
eight men to swing. First they light the incense, then they flex the ropes
gently, the censer begins to swing, they pull on the ropes again and
finally the censer, which is as big as a fair-sized land mine, reaches dizzying heights, and it whooshes through the whole of the transept up to
the ceiling and back again, leaving a long trail of smoke like the tail of a
comet; people duck out of its way and cry out until the men hang on to

the ropes with all their weight to curb the velocity of the holy missile. The brawniest man steps forward in its path and leaps up to catch hold of the monster and bring it under submission. The end. Throughout the spectacle the archbishop of Santiago, with staff and mitre and wearing the crimson of the martyrs, stands among the other mitred men. He looks quite grand, a clothed idol, next to the king's envoy, the Marquis of Mondéjar, old, white-haired, a black tailcoat in a dusky hedge of officers' uniforms. Reformation, capitalism, Enlightenment, industrial revolution, Marxism, fascism – it must be a pretty tough substance to have survived all that. I do not doubt that more sagacious comments might be made here, but pure amazement is excusable.

In that other Santiago, that of Peñalba, reigns the silence of death. I have left my car on the edge of the village, next to the only other car. The high street is a path. It smells of cows. I know where I am; in the domain of sleep. Houses built of the roughest stones, dimly lit stables, slate roofs, the floors of the wooden balconies casting the shadow in which I stand

The roofs of Santiago de Peñalba

and look, a colonnaded arcade. The church is closed and will not open until five o'clock, so a cardboard placard tells me. What I see is the double Arab arch, two delicate horseshoes supported by three narrow columns, the elegance of the oriental world a sudden intrusion among the rough-hewn stones of the same shade as the mountains around. Peaks in the distance, bare, eroded slopes, the coils of the labyrinthine road I have travelled to get here. The slate roofs in the valley gleam as in an old black-and-white film. There is no movement except the shimmer of heat. I climb the slope past the houses and sit down in a meadow with a couple of beehives. *Valle del Silencio.* Very apt. This village hangs in the valley like an eyrie. I leaf through the booklet I have bought and look at the photographs illustrating a way of life that is now sleeping. A knot of men playing a curious game with skittles. A woman churning milk in a sewn-up sheepskin to make butter. Men threshing the meagre wheat harvest. Ancient words, all of them still in service: chaff, flail, hackle, well. The last time I saw a flail on this trip was in San Isidoro in León, in a Romanesque mural representing the month of August. That allegorical scene was painted in the twelfth century, and things are not so different today. There is no sewerage in Peñalba, and no telephone. Electricity was not put in until 1977. In 1978 the road was improved for motorized traffic, but it is not passable all year round. What it must be like here in winter I dare not contemplate.

At about four in the afternoon, floored at last by the heat, I sit amid grass and clover and watch an old man plodding towards the church. He has of course noticed my presence long ago, they have all been peering hungrily through their shutters at the appetizing stranger, but no one has yet moved. Suddenly they're all there: little old women, dead for 300 years but still embroidering, men discussing the dread tidings from France, where the king has been beheaded, two cows laying down a fresh and pungent carpet for my benefit, which I sidestep as I make my way to the church. He is a gruff old man, the church isn't supposed to open until five, but he's holding the key ready in his hand. A gnarled hand. That is how one says those things. A rusty key. He unlocks the door and a double Arab shadow falls on the dusty church floor. It is very beautiful. Inside, other arches carry on the play, although these are closer to the Visigothic. The interior is small, secluded, protected. The distance from this church to the triumphant mastodon of Astorga has to be measured in light years. Faith, too, can modify its taste, or can acquire a specific gravity that verges on conceit. The frame enclosing the two Arab horseshoes projects horizontally at the lowest point and then rises to form a perfect rectangle that is extraordinary. The same goes for the frame around the single arch by the altar. One solitary line enclosing that

The church of Santiago de Peñalba

single and double bow, so elegantly and efficiently. Bravo, I mutter to the artisan in the kingdom of the dead, and suddenly I find I have nothing more to do in Santiago de Peñalba. One final tombstone in the exterior wall, of a "monk of Cluny" lying there quite peacefully, *Sommer und Winter, schlaf wohl,* summer and winter, sleep well, I'm off.

Why a German phrase should come to mind at that point I do not know, but on my way back I feel a sudden urge to be divested of my self, to invent a different persona for my constant presence, a ghost, a double into which I can change myself because I have had enough of me for a while. At home I tend to be less self-conscious, but when I'm travelling I am tough company – away with it. Who shall I become? Frondini is the name that floats into my car. His profession? Engraver and draughts-man, not overly talented. Eighteenth century, to be on the safe side. The great artists have already had their say. I just read the statement "*ich kenne im Stilistischen nur noch die Parodie*" (all I seem to be able to do now looks like parody) in Thomas Mann's diaries, and I'm going to foist that post-modern creed on Frondini, but I shall make it worse, although he doesn't know it yet. Worse? Mann laboured under this notion, but there is no need for Frondini to do likewise. Frondini is a lighthearted, cheerful Italian who enjoys travelling and sketching whatever strikes him. He is not talented enough to feel oppressed by his great precursors, so he can't very well be a Mannerist, he just wants to draw what he sees, he is not the maker of parody, he is himself a parody. How he got here I do not know, and to make things easier I give him this season for trav-elling. On foot, of course, as he can't afford a horse, or has squandered his money on drink, something of that nature. Plump cloud, wood pigeon, harrier, woodpecker . . . Frondini sees what I see, hears what I hear, I even cut the engine at one point because how can I be Frondini in a car? He comes equipped with a *salvoconducto* from Empress Maria Theresa, he has held a respectable and privileged job in the royal *pinacoteca*, but the devil got into his blood, and now he is a traveller.

Everything he sees can become a drawing, such as that plump cloud for a start. Is it possible for the same cloud, with the same volume, to drift along exactly the same slope, high up above Frondini then and me now, where the same amount of snow lies in the same spot, namely there, where the red kite turns the same inexorable arc, swoops down and flies away clutching an animal whose shape I cannot (he cannot) make out? I am just looking, but Frondini has already settled onto a rocky outcrop with his sketch pad; his pencil flies over the paper, kite, cloud, slope, he sketches them all, and he will elaborate his sketch later. He is not plagued by doubts about repetition, he *creates* repetition and brings it to a halt, the not-quite-convincing hawk, the too-steep slope, the too-lavishly hatched cloud. What does it matter to him whether that mossy boulder in the Oca was already there, how much it has eroded since, whether the current is still as strong? Those are not his concerns, they are mine, and that is precisely what I was trying to get rid of. His concern is to catch the ripple in the water, and, more difficult still, to evoke that strange, glistening, elusive transparency that makes everything below the surface vacillate even as it lies still. And now he hears, as I do, the shepherd on the slope shouting at his suddenly emerging flock as it is shaped by the small sheep dog into a ball rolling slowly down the mountain. A flock like a ball, that is my contribution, Frondini wouldn't think of that, he's far too busy with the dilemma facing him now: ought that flock, which was not there a moment ago, to be included in the drawing or not? He hasn't even got round to dealing with the problems of the clefts, the undulations, the shadows and accents, the dappled light on the slope. Frondini is becoming a nuisance, I have enough problems of my own, so I imagine two bandits, I make them attack him, but he is Italian, and, livid at being disturbed in his inconsequential artistic pursuit, he pulls out a knife – that was foolish. Frondini is killed, since the others have knives too. He possesses nothing worth robbing, as I could have told the bandits in the first place. They pause for a moment to glance at his unfinished impression of the landscape. Now they look like art critics and of course the inevitable happens, they throw the sketch into the water; it bobs rapidly downstream, and they disappear, laughing and swearing, into the bushes.

I have picked on Verín for my last stop before crossing the border. From my balcony I can see Portugal, low and distant, bluish, so hazy and blurred that it is as if I can see right across the ocean and beyond, to the Azores, to South America, that organic extension of Spain. One is reminded daily of the sheer immensity of the linguistic expansion, not only by the work of writers and poets like Cortázar, García Márquez, Paz and Borges, but also by the press and television which keep up a steady stream of news about anything relating to the "Spanish family", the countries the Spaniards "discovered" and conquered long ago, and which still suffer the consequences of their colonial origins. The

Spaniards who ventured across the ocean were not known for their kindness of spirit. The conquistadors took with them the right of the strong, and the structured society they encountered when they arrived at their destination supplied them with that other essential ingredient: a people to oppress. Add to that a few other Spanish notions, like *patria chica*, religious absolutism and greed, and you have the makings of a tragedy. *Patria chica* is about extreme loyalty to the native region at the expense of a sense of nationhood. It is thanks to this legacy that the map of Central and South America looks the way it does despite the efforts of Simón Bolívar. It is true that there are frontiers elsewhere in the world that seem equally absurd and surreal, but in this case it was also a linguistic area that was carved in two. That the Indians would have been better off being "discovered" by ethical puritans from the protestant North is unlikely in light of the tribulations of the Sioux, the Hopi, the Navajo and the Apaches, but be that as it may, as a chemical wedding the encounter between the robber barons from Extremadura and the strictly regimented Inca societies was equally disastrous.

The extent of an empire, the expansion of a language. It was soon after I had set out on this journey that Borges died. It was a shock, because you had the weird feeling that he could never die. Either that or that he had died long ago. His own speculations on the subject in his final years made of him a mythical shadow roaming the world, saying he wished to be relieved of "the thing that is called Borges". Perhaps he had had his way at last, or who knows, perhaps he had never existed, or someone had dreamt him up, or someone else had dreamt us all up, including him – since he lived, if he ever lived, in a world of gnostic options.

Newspapers were perhaps not the best medium for finding confirmation of any of this, for although I might encounter him at any time in my life in all sorts of papers as a writer or interviewee, I also remembered what he had said about reading newspapers: during the Second World War he had considered giving up his habit of not reading the papers (because it made more sense to read the classics), but had decided instead to spend some time every day reading Tacitus on a different, early war. In a world like his, in which events repeat themselves ad infinitum, his decision was not without logic and Tacitus had the advantage of a superior style while, in his view, the content remained essentially the same. True or false, Borges enjoyed teasing his readers,

and his contempt was never without a philosophical basis. But I didn't
have Plutarch or Thucydides at hand to instruct me about the demise of
great men, so for the week after his death I bought whatever newspapers
I came across, as if I still needed to be convinced. After all, a man had
died with whom I had had a relationship – and who had had a relationship with me – for thirty years. Those two relationships could only end
when I died, that was another thing he had taught me. It was thirty years
ago that I, driven by instinct, by intuition, bought my first little yellow
books in the *La Croix du Sud* series, with which Roger Caillois introduced Borges to Europe. There is something odd about great writers
dying, for that, to quote Auden, is when they become their admirers.
Auden wrote this when Yeats died. There are two lines in that poem that
I can never forget: "You were silly like us; your gift survived it all" and
"He became his admirers."

Here I sit in my Spanish castle surrounded by newspaper cuttings, and
they are all, after six weeks, deader than any line or page written by the
author himself. It is a pretty wide-ranging collection, considering that
I bought them at kiosks: *Observer*, *Le Monde*, *Libération*, *The Times*,
La Repubblica, *La Vanguardia*, *Frankfurter Allgemeine*. But those are
names, and had he not shown me that I should search for the meaning
behind them? In that case that list can generate another, comprising
Time, Liberation, Messenger, World, Vanguard . . . the names become
allegories and the list a hidden biography. All those pages with photos of
blind Tiresias leaning on his stick surrounded by fragments of the web he
wove during his life, translated now into the slogans of hacks, and even
they read like a strange, exploded poem: Such light in the labyrinth –
Quella luce nel Labirinto. The melancholy minotaur *Il Minotauro
malinconico*. But perhaps he did not exist – *Ma forse non esisteva*.
Innumerable were my forms and my deaths – *Innombrables furent mes
formes et mes morts*. I have been Homer, soon I will be No one, like
Odysseus; soon I will be everyone: I will be dead – *J'ai été Homère;
bientôt, je serai Personne, comme Ulysse; bientôt, je serai tout le monde:
je serai mort*. He has made himself invisible – *Se ha hecho invisible*. The
librarian of Babel – *Le bibliothécaire de Babel*. Death, I want nothing
but her, I want her totally, abstractly. The two dates on the stone – *La
mort, je ne veux qu'elle et je la veux totale, abstraite. Les deux dates
sur la dalle*. A Tireless Weaver of Dreams (*Observer*). And on the front
page of *Libération*, as if that paper had been reporting a match for the

past sixty years: *Jorge Luis Borges a trouvé la sortie* – BORGES HAS FOUND THE EXIT! It is always other people who finish the stories, but only when the stories are worth finishing. That is the true moment of death: when everyone runs off with your words. Then comes the purgatory of utter absence. The press gives up on you. There is no superlative to death, except public death: once the novelty has worn off, the dead person is really and truly dead. Those who never read him will not do so now, and all the rest of us are left with words to which no sequel is forthcoming. Then Auden's law comes into effect: the readers have become the writer, the writer becomes his readers.

Borges has the same effect on me as dearly loved departed friends. You cannot imagine them being dead. At the oddest moments you find yourself thinking: I wonder how he feels about this? Last night there was a programme on television about the fourth-century heresy of Priscillian, a movement that was largely located in the region I am staying in now, that of Galicia in northern Spain, which, like Ireland, is so receptive to all things magic and mysterious. The programme was shot, for the most part, in an immense and splendid library, and it dealt with contemporary Latin commentaries by Sulpicius Severus, with gnostic symbolism and numerology, with death, which, to the Celts, represented no more than a voyage. Suddenly it occurred to me that it could all be fiction, just another of Borges' eclectic fantasies, nothing but prevarication and invention, that Severus never wrote a Latin commentary. In short, pleasant doubts flashed across my mind because it might all just as well be untrue. After all, Borges himself had treated fiction as if it were reality, fitting it out with as many spurious sources and attributions as possible, so that the reality in some of the commentaries was shrouded in invention or at least in equivocation.

In my day the curriculum of the Dutch gymnasium did not include philosophy, all I ever learnt that came anywhere near philosophical instruction were the lessons in religion with those extraordinary casuistic extravaganzas like "if someone is hit by a car and lies dying in the street and an excommunicated priest passes by and the dying man wants to confess, is that confession valid?" (answer: yes) – but neither this kind of scholastic hair-splitting nor the Thomistic proofs of the existence of God prepared me for the onslaught of Borges' reflections, inspired by Berkeley and Hume, on existence and non-existence. You get used to it eventually (but never completely), but I remember well my dizzy confusion at the thought that reality, the objects around us, might exist exclusively by the grace of our perception; the consternation only increased when Borges maintained in another essay that this was not the end of it, that time also did not exist. His argument echoed Sextus Empiricus (*Adversus Mathematicos*, XI, 197), who denied the existence of the past on the grounds that it was no longer extant, and equally denied the existence of the future, on the grounds that it was not yet extant. He also claimed that the present had to be divisible or indivisible in order to exist. But it is not indivisible, because if it were it would have no beginning linked with the past, nor an end linked with the future. On the other hand, neither is it divisible, for if it were it would have separate spheres, one that is already past and one that is yet to come. Hence it does not exist, and because past and future do not exist either, nor does time.

That scared me. Admittedly, Sextus Empiricus also stated that alongside the undeniable despair there was private consolation to be had in the denial of the sequential nature of time, of the I, and of the astronomic universe. What bothered me in particular was that those vaporous thoughts were interfering with my emotions. The sensation was almost physical: I felt as if I might fall off the world, an occurrence that, if both the world and I did not exist, could of course be no worse than I took it to be. The problem was that with Borges and his imaginary citations from real encyclopedias, his invented authors and their non-existent writings, you could never be sure whether Sextus Empiricus, say, had ever existed, and if he had, whether the book from which the master quoted had ever been written. It was not until much later that I understood that although it was all seriously intended, it was a very special kind of seriousness, part of a great literary spell he was casting, that he was using all these elements and musings and self-contradictions to compose his stories and poems. Non-existence, the never-ending compulsion to exist *anew*, the double, the reflection of the other in the mirror, or of a different other, or of no one at all, it was all part and parcel of what he called *perplejidad*, the permanent state of perplexity that is life.

The universe of Borges is one to which, if you are so inclined by nature, you can be easily and irresistibly drawn for a while, and although there are times in your life when your need for "reality" is greater than your delight in perplexities, you always go back to that œuvre with a flutter of vertigo. For the thrill, the flirtation with non-existence and the stimulation of the all-embracing doubt is a stimulus for the denial in which existence is so much more keenly felt.

I saw him once, long ago, in the sixties. Westminster Hall, London. I had travelled to England especially. He sat there, very aloof, an oracle, his head tilted at the odd angles of the blind man responding to sounds. Later on I read Cabrera Infante's account of the event and discovered that the unassailable master had soothed his nerves with a huge balloon of cognac beforehand. We were permitted to ask questions, in writing. The question I submitted was one that had preoccupied me for some time. I asked him what he thought of Gombrowicz, who had been living in Buenos Aires for years as a voluntary exile. He did not bother to reply. Gombrowicz' philosophy of the unfinished, imperfect, immature as the highest goal can hardly have enjoyed his wholehearted approval, I suppose. I was sitting there as a reader, and readers always want the writers they admire to share their admiration for certain other writers, like demanding that Nabokov admire Dostoevsky and that Krol admire Slauerhoff. But life is not like that.

All right. The end. The weaver of so many myths has succeeded, he has spun a cocoon around us, he has become his own myth. Farewell, ancient fan. Those words were spoken by the Japanese poet Bashō on his final visit, a long journey on foot, to an old poet he would never see again. Night has fallen in the place where I am now, the Galician sky is studded with stars. He must be there somewhere, I think, because all these magical thoughts appeal to the most primitive of instincts. He never got the Nobel prize, and that is a pity for the prize, but he deserves better than that anyway. He ought to have a star named after him. He's the only writer that it would feel right to honour in that way, and then at least we would still have one thing called Borges.

XX

I Have Pledged Myself to Spain

Brief respite in Portugal ~ Cáceres ~ Inquisition
The Dædalus of Plasencia ~ Spanish Jews
Lizards for supper ~ Dancing in El Rocío

THE FRONTIER WITH PORTUGAL. As if you were calmly reading a book and turned the page suddenly to find the paper yellowed, and the typeface different, more old-fashioned. No, this is strange, it is another book altogether, one you haven't taken down from the shelf for a long time, that you read long ago and even then it was old. Everything is different, slower, the colours muted, the sounds more gentle. The border guards have uniforms like those of the forgotten kingdoms of Transylvania or Montenegro, the car tyres make a different tune on the small grey cobbles, the language has shed its harshness, the words are muffled.

I am in Portugal, in the region called Trás-os-Montes, or beyond the mountains, in any case I am far from the heart of the country, in what even for the Portuguese has to be a remote province, protected by mountains and poor roads and consequently still unworldly, a desolate region, magnificent, sombre. If I were to choose an instrument for it, it would be the grave and melancholic cello. I am temporarily liberated from the demands that Spain always makes, and somewhat muted, I drive more slowly along the narrow empty roads. I visit some dear friends and the grandeur of their home intensifies the sense of times long past. But it's only for a short while. I must continue my journey since I have, after all, pledged myself to Spain for better or for worse.

I have plenty of time during those few days to reflect on the nature of Iberian dualism and how it has been sustained in other continents. At the border between Bolivia and Brazil there is the same linguistic watershed, the great grid of the Iberian divide having been transported overseas with the colonists. The disparities in accent between the New World and the Old are quite obvious, but the essential division between Spanish and Portuguese goes further. In Manaus I do not think of Madrid, nor in Bogotá of Coimbra. The first time I visited Macao I was dismayed to find so very little Portuguese being spoken there, but I was just coming to the end of a long trip and was suffering from a rare bout of homesickness for Europe. It is reassuring to hear the familiar, mellifluous blur of Portuguese in the vast, tropical profusion of the Amazon basin, as if the heat and the unknown have allowed themselves to be tamed after all. And in a parched region of scorching Costa Rica close to the Nicaraguan border, I once found that the savage landscape which seems to turn away from you could, by the medium of the Spanish language, be tamed, drawn in, subdued.

And what about the Netherlands? It is almost as if all we left behind in our former colonies is a scattering of gravestones and churches. Our language has dissipated, evaporated, blown away above the Indonesian archipelago. Was it all too far from home? Was it that we ourselves, as usual, did not care enough about our language? What if Dutch were spoken today along the shores of the Java Sea and the Strait of Malacca? I envy the Spanish and Portuguese, if only for the literature that has come wafting back from the far west to give the old language a breath of fresh air.

Cork trees, olive trees, brambles, thistles, they occupy my thoughts as I pilot my way along the roads, mumbling the names of towns and villages which, when I reach Spain, will jump from a caress to the crack of a whip when I am out of favour, brought back to my confrontation with the ruthless austerity of Extremadura. The frontier again. When I entered Portugal I had to fill in a variety of forms: returning to Spain I am simply waved on, and one more landscape is transformed. Here I am again. Isn't that what you wanted? I'm in your hands. The temperature in Cáceres will reach 39 °C today.

The moment I set foot on the Plaza Generalísimo Mola I am certain that the last time I was in Cáceres, whenever it may have been, I arrived at the self same hour, the hour of arrested motion, death in the afternoon. I unerringly locate the same café, directly opposite the gateway leading to the old town. On that occasion I did not have time to go into the old town, now I know that all the gates I might wish to enter are closed. The newspaper kiosk is shut, an unshaven old man is dozing at the café table next to mine, before him the remains of a dish of *migas*, food for the poor, stale bread fried in lard. The television drones on about the rest of the world, the slot machine strikes up every five minutes with an electronic jingle to lure gamblers, it is too dumb to see that there's no one around. By rights such a scenario requires the presence of a mangy dog, and the animal world produces one to order: a mangy dog appears stage left, ambles across the square, placing its paws on its own perpendicular shadow. I get up and follow. Cáceres is a town of exteriors, crests, escutcheons, towers, gates, emblems, monograms in stone, cornices, grilles, battlements, stone monuments erected by the nobility in their own honour, relics from the heady days of the Conquista, paid for with gold from the new territories. All I need do is stroll past.

This is real heat. The air is so dry that I want to coin a simile to do it justice. As dry as an afternoon in Cáceres. The old town is surrounded by a wall with twelve towers, inside the wall are churches and noblemen's houses. I am ready for the fray, as I come armed not only with my guidebook but also a dictionary. The guidebook sets riddles I cannot solve without assistance. *Ajimez*, paired windows – but I could have seen that for myself. *Alfiz*, rectangular window, but that cannot be right because it says *trilobulado*, three-lobed, which is hardly rectangular, nor indeed is there a rectangle to be seen on the front of the Casa de los Golfines de Abajo, just a graceful linear ornament winding around the paired windows and encircling the coat of arms borne aloft by winged angels. I take a rest in the shade, alone with my words and the stone messages.

The towers have names, the Oven Tower, the Clock Tower, but also the Tower of *Bujaco*. What can *Bujaco* mean? My dictionary has no answer, but the guidebook is more helpful. In 1173 the Arab rulers, the Almohads, sent their troops to besiege Cáceres. The town was held by the friars of the military Order of Santiago. The friars were rapidly losing ground, and they holed up in this tower to make their final stand. The Moors were victorious and the forty defenders of the tower were beheaded on the orders of Abu Yacoub. Abu Yacoub, the name is corrupted into Bujaco over time. No wonder I couldn't find it.

The next tower is the Tower of the *Pulpitos*, of the little octopuses, so called according to the guide, because "the *matacanes* are shaped like octopuses". I do not know what *matacanes* are and I can't see anything remotely resembling an octopus on the square, robust tower. This is not surprising: the word is written in capitals so the accent is missing. *Púlpitos*, pulpits, lecterns. But what are *matacanes*? Dog-killers, would be my translation, but that doesn't make much sense. My trusty dictionary has better ideas. *Matacán*: poison for killing dogs; poisonous nut; a hare that outruns the pursuing hounds; a stone of the right size and shape to be thrown and caught by the hand; term in a card game. And then, in Murcia: an oak sapling. In Ecuador: a fawn (hunting parlance). In Honduras: a large calf. And finally, just for my benefit, in the plural, *matacanes*: embrasures.

I am filled once again with respect for the translator's craft, which brings me back to the earlier argument: how much richer is the language that travels abroad, to Ecuador, Honduras, that lives in a land so vast that the same word has come to mean different things in different places.

I discover the embrasures, high in the Tower of the Pulpits with its four circular projections, whence the soldiers took aim at the enemy? Here, at the foot of this tower is where Isabella the Catholic swore an oath on 30 June 1477 promising to honour the rights and privileges of Cáceres, the same Isabella who, through her marriage to Ferdinand of Aragón and the reconquest of Granada, would create a united Spain and subsequently break the power of the military Orders of knights.

Whatever the nature of those privileges, they would no longer extend to Jews and Muslims, nor to the *conversos* and Moriscos, the converted, if there was the slightest suspicion of allegiance to their old faith. But that comes later. Towards the end of Isabella's reign 97 per cent of Spain was owned by the nobility and 45 per cent by bishoprics, cathedral chapters and the urban nobility, the rest was in the hands of a few landowners. It is the coats of arms of this few that adorn the walls of Cáceres.

Some of the families have died out, others have not. The system has remained essentially the same despite the Civil War (which was lost, after all). The grand houses bear names, but the names were made by the nameless: a name becomes a Name by devouring the nameless. In the mother country they were serfs, journeymen, small tenants, across the ocean they were miners of tin, silver, gold: the nameless, expendable underbelly of an empire.

Can one say the same of Amsterdam, with the slave traders' mansions, some still decorated with figures of Moors and Red Indians? Not quite. And yet once, long ago, those names and houses stood for human suffering, a circumstance which, on pain of misrepresentation, cannot be relegated to the sphere of demagogic argument but which, on pain of a different type of misrepresentation, cannot be refuted either.

Forgotten, past, nameless torment, but here, in the streets of Cáceres, the suffering lives on in a far from anonymous demonstration of pride, arrogance, self-confidence. The mansions of the Ulloa family, of the Ovando-Pereros, the Torre-Orgaz, the Durán de la Rocha, the Pereros, the Toledo-Montezumas. *Casa-palacio* is the term used in these parts. I walk past their stone fortifications, their massive contours, their closed walls, their might. Gateways with enormous arches of great slabs of undecorated stone, so that all attention is drawn to the gate itself, solid, time-worn, that which you may not enter. Sometimes, as in the Palacio de Mayoralgo, there are no windows at all in the lower section of the façade, at street level there is just the wall, forbidding, tinged orange in the late sun. You have to crane your neck to see the high twin windows flanking the coat of arms: *this is who we are.* And once we are gone, this is who we were. Some escutcheons sit astride a corner, so that they point in two directions, others are accompanied by intriguing mottoes like AQUÍ ESPERAN LOS GOLFINES EL DÍA DEL JUICIO (Here the Golfines await the Day of Judgement). Another family has taken the whole sun as its emblem, wavy spokes radiate from a round face casting a baleful look at the stranger. It was in one of the houses of the Golfines that Franco was proclaimed head of state, and that, too, is somehow fitting.

There is an obscurantist feel to these narrow streets and alleys, as if you are surrounded by mausoleums, as if there, behind the locked doors, whole dead families sit and wait for the angel with the trumpet. If the angel ever comes it will be at this hour of the afternoon, the hour of silence and savage light, an afternoon when the escutcheons with all their symbols and mythic beasts will turn to ashes, indecipherable powder.

Am I the only one to hear the unearthly howling? The sound is coming from some distance away, formless wails fill the air with lamentation. When I come closer I hear not words but syllables in their larval state, basic, groans like words cropped at both ends, mangled, mutilated, clamouring to be heard, but they're all stuck together in a viscous, inarticulate soup. I turn the corner of an alley and spot him, a retarded boy standing against a wall, absorbed in his indictment of the universe, a talking dog trying to howl but prevented from doing so by the rudiments of language in his voice, so that the two sources merge in the animal sound coming from the human mouth, and all the while his unseeing eyes are fixed on me. My presence makes no impression on his distress, I am as transparent as the air, his protest is directed at the institution of life itself, for not hearing him.

It takes some effort to hunt them down, but tucked away in each provincial capital of Spain I find at least one obscure little bookshop, a treasure trove of curious editions which seldom travel beyond the confines of the town or province, local publications mostly, by authors unknown to me, crammed with fascinating information I am not likely to find elsewhere, regional histories, poems by local poets one has never heard of, cookery books with recondite recipes. Tiny, cluttered shops where there is only room for one customer at a time, where I knock over a pile of books every time I reach for a title, where the bookseller's eagle eye follows each movement of this odd-looking, clearly foreign visitor searching amongst the very volumes most people ignore, and where the chances are that the proprietor himself is the author or poet.

Cáceres is no exception. By the time the siesta is over and everyone has undergone the second resurrection of the day (I am the only one still trudging around in the same stale life as this morning), I have found two of these little bookshops, and end up with four items to add to my collection of rare books. Most are indeed rare, and a fair number are weird. I am pleased to have a recipe at last for baked lizard, and another for dried cod with honey "as cooked by monks", and at least now I know how much land is owned by Hilda Fernández de Córdoba, the Countess of Santa Isabella (10,900 hectares); and that the next largest landowners are Manuel Falcó, the Duke of Fernán Núñez (8,825 hectares); and Mrs Cayetana Fitz-James Stuart y Silva, the Duchess of Berwick, the Duchess of Alba (4,423 hectares).

Alba, the very name brings the shiver of the classroom to every Dutchman, an indirect memory of the Eighty Years' War against Spanish domination, rumours handed down from century to century, tales of cruelty and oppression, of the evil that came from the South. The name is so laden with cobwebs that it is hard to believe that there can still be people called Alba in Spain today. But there are, and the current duchess, who looks as though she too, once upon a time, was painted by Goya, merits a Proust to describe the world she lives in. It is a world that refuses to die out. The Albas are still thirteen times grandees of Spain, only the present duke acquired the title not by birth but by marriage to the duchess. Jesús Aguirre is his name, a runaway Jesuit; quite recently I read an article by him in *El País*. It was about Adorno and the Frankfurter Schule. "Jesús Aguirre is the Duke of Alba", it said at the end of the piece, and the series becomes irresistible: Jesús, Duke, Alba, Blood Council, Jesuit, Adorno. The longer the world exists the more it becomes its own anachronism.

Extremadura has other worries on the eve of the third millennium: 40,000 farm workers are unemployed, while vast tracts of privately owned land lie fallow or are rented out for hunting parties.

The power of the nobility has remained, that of the Inquisition has vanished. That loss is regretted by no one, and yet, but for that pivotal episode of heresy, deviance and excess I might never have heard of Fray Alonso de la Fuente, one of those ardent souls that abound in sixteenth-century Spain, a zealot who saw the work of the devil wherever he turned, and chased across these regions like a man possessed hunting down members of the sect known as the *Alumbrados*, or Enlightened. Sometimes it is better not to read the history of a place *in situ*, but the deed has been done now, I have stopped the car in a sweltering landscape to take a break during the hottest hour of the afternoon, I have followed a sandy track away from the road to the stony shade of a few holm-oaks. High above me I watch *buteo buteo*, the buzzard, composing an interminable, slow poem in ever wider circles. Around me I can hear the hoarse whisper of *centaurea aspera*, a rustle of old paper, page upon page all the way to the horizon. This is the land of Fray Alonso, where he pursued his phantoms and where he wrote his *Memoriales* on the degrees of unseemly lust, "a qualitative assessment concerning kisses, embraces and other libidinous touching" ("*calificación cerca de los besos, abrazos y otros tocamientos libidinosos*"). At first he stood alone in his indignation, no one would listen, but he preached, raved, accused and harassed until eventually, after several years, he got through to the Holy Office of the Inquisition in Madrid. An inquisitor was duly dispatched to Zafra, to the displeasure of the hunter of heretics because "the seventy priests of Zafra are all Jews". The inquisitor, too, was disappointed as there was no evidence to be found of deviance from the orthodox doctrine. He had been promised a paradise of heresy and carnal lust, witchcraft and devilry, but proof was elusive.

Meanwhile the zealot continues to write his *Memoriales*. He is quite mad, but he has a way with words – a combination that is not unusual – and this time he gets so carried away that he attacks the Jesuits themselves. He sends his *Memorial* to the cardinal-prince, but the latter is unconvinced. Fray Alonso is taken into custody and summoned before the General Council of the Inquisition to abjure his claims against the Universal Company of Jesus (the Jesuits), whom he has accused of "bringing into the church a pestilent and most detrimental heresy in order to ruin her, of making pacts with the Devil and offering protection to magicians, of betraying the secrets of confession, and of acting in an altogether deceitful manner". To the dismay of the Jesuits, he is banished to Seville, "where the land is better furnished with sins", but Philip II's response to their protestations is simply: "I cannot defy the Inquisition."

Alonso's passion, however, has not waned. In Seville, too, he sees *alumbrados*, profligacy, the hoof-marks of the devil, black magic all around him, and he launches fearlessly into his old diatribes. Inevitably, he is brought to trial a second time, and his defence is yet another rabid indictment. Once more he is released, but this time he is sent to a remote corner of Spain, *ordered* to forget about the *alumbrados*. From then on there is pandemonium in his brain, and he dies soon after. A Spanish life.

Spanish? Is that true? Or is it just a cliché, a prejudice handed down from one century to the next, seeking constant confirmation in history and literature? But isn't the Dutch naval officer's heroic response to a call to surrender "Rather the sky",* or Jan van Schaffelaar's resolve to leap to his death† equally Spanish? There exist certain similarities between the Spanish and the Dutch character. The landscape of La Mancha dotted with windmills is no more rigorously divided into heaven and earth than the Dutch polder. It is an extreme division, unmitigated by temptations, valleys, romantic corners. Most of the *meseta* is as hard for a man to hide in as the flatlands of the Netherlands. A man is always visible between heaven and earth, silhouetted against the sky, and sometimes I think this has something to do with the extremism that characterizes both Holland's Calvinism and Spain's Catholicism. Perhaps that is why our strengths were so evenly matched during the Eighty Years' War.

* Whereupon the speaker, J. C. J. van Speyk, put a match to his explosives and indeed blew himself, his crew and his ship into the sky, rather than surrender to the enemy. This was in Antwerp in 1831.

† Van Schaffelaar was a soldier of Gelderland who jumped from a tower in the fifteenth century.

But in the north it is inconceivable that a regiment should "betroth itself to Death", as a Spanish regiment did during the Civil War, and our literature has yet to produce a man who battles against windmills. The Spanish variant of extremism has irrational qualities that we are not likely to indulge in, or rather which do not even enter our minds. The Jan van Schaffelaar of Spain was a dreamer, he did not leap to his death, he leaped to fly, not from a church tower in Barneveld, but from the tower of the cathedral in Plasencia, which is close to where I am now. His name was Maestro Rodrigo. He, a Spanish Dædalus, was held prisoner in that tower.

A true Dædalus, for he was a sculptor like the first. Rodrigo Alemán had been commissioned to carve the choir stalls in the cathedral, but he failed to deliver on time. Another version has it that the members of the chapter were outraged by the licentious scenes he had carved under the folding seats, the *misericordias*, where "next to an idyllic scene from the life of Jesus or the idealized portrait of a saint or king", one might without warning encounter "a picture of a bishop in the clutches of the devil or of a woman sitting astride a monk, whipping his bare buttocks". It was improper, to be sure, for the canons to be confronted with such scabrous spectacles every time they folded their seats, and so the artist who had carved them was imprisoned in the tower. From which moment on the Dædalus of Plasencia was determined to escape. According to the priest Juan Lis de la Cerda (in the sixth book of his *Aeneide*, 1642), he flew a circuit around the town before crashing to earth.

Antonio Ponz, in his sixth letter in the seventh volume of his *Viaje de España* (Madrid, 1784) offers more scientific evidence. He explains in detail how Maestro Rodrigo built himself into a flying machine. He began by ordering chickens and other poultry every day, and insisted on plucking the birds himself in his chamber in the tower; he had plenty of time on his hands. He did not eat much as he wanted to lose weight. He weighed the plucked chickens and he weighed their feathers and calcu- lated that for every two pounds, *libras*, of flesh four ounces, *onzas*, of feathers were needed to keep it aloft. He saved the feathers until he had enough to raise his own weight. Then he coated his skin with a sticky substance and glued the feathers to his feet, legs, arms, "indeed to his entire body"; he took the two wings he had plaited and tied them firmly to his shoulders. At last he jumped off the tower "and flew away over the town to the far bank of the River Jerte, where he fell to his death".

It is quiet under my tree, and although I know it is I lying on the hard, dry ground, it feels different, as if the parched land itself with its spiky yellow grasses and razor-sharp thistles is getting on top of me, as if the circle of shade cast by the dark-leaved oak is my only shield against catastrophe. I read the Extremaduran stories of flying sculptors and inflammatory fanatics, and they make me smile. They are shot through with a different kind of absolutism which is also to be perceived in this scenery, that of hunger (recipes for lizard, for stale bread soup, dried cod and salted fish) and the attendant scourges of superstition and xenophobia. Cookery books (such as *Recetario de la Cocina Extremeña*) have a lot to tell us. The poverty of a region is written all over the pages. Nowhere can one find more recipes for dried cod than in these parts, and nowhere was there such bitter hatred of Jews or Moriscos. The poorer, more oppressed and backward a population is, the easier it is to find a scapegoat to take the blame away from the oppressors. "Nowhere in Extremadura," Victor Chamorro writes in his *Extremadura, afán de miseria*, "will you find a village without a history or legend linking the Jews with the death of infants, sacrilege, poisonings, corruption of the church". Chamorro, who also wrote a four-volume *Historia de Extremadura* (Madrid, 1981), tells of persecution, torture, confiscation of money and property. He also records proverbs and quotes texts, most of them anonymous, but sometimes they come from sources where, perhaps stupidly, I had least expected them. One of his citations is from Calderón de la Barca, whose wonderful play *La vida es sueño* (Life is a Dream) I saw in Madrid recently, and as Chamorro doesn't give the source of the quotation I don't know whether it is Calderón himself speaking here or a character in one of his plays, and so may well be expressing the *opposite* of the author's opinion. The tone of the excerpt, in any case, is strident:

> *¡Qué maldita canalla!*
> *muchos murieron quemados,*
> *y tanto gusto me daba*
> *verlos arder, que decía,*
> *atizándoles la llama:*
> *Perros herejes, ministro*
> *soy de la Inquisición Santa.**

* Accursed swine! / Many have died at the stake / and such pleasure did it give me / to see them burn that I cried out / as the flames reached them: / Heretic curs, I am minister of the Holy Inquisition.

The whiplash of the rhyme makes it much harsher than my impromptu version can render.

Imagine that history could run against the laws of time, that it could be aware of events before they occurred, then it would no longer be history, it would be something between schizophrenia and irony, and would, in effect, cease to exist as itself. But in that case even ironic historiography is nothing but the negation and misrepresentation of what happened. The very events that, in retrospect, strike us as so ironical, so bitterly absurd, have all the more impact for their apparent logic at the time. Even the word "apparent" here tastes of retrospective irony, and so it is not ironical but understandable reality that the Spanish Jews themselves welcomed the arrival of the Arab troops of the Caliph of Damascus in the eighth century. By that time they already had a long history in Sefarad (the Jewish name for Spain), and had been excluded and perse-cuted by the Visigothic kings since the conversion of Recaredus in 587 and the decrees of Sisebutus in 613.

When the kings turn to the Catholic faith, the Jews turn into heretics. At least, it would seem so, but the matter is more complex than that. In the course of the ten centuries after that first wave of persecution the fortunes of Spanish Jewry were marked by bizarre ups and downs. There were glorious moments, as in Córdoba when the three religions co-existed in harmony, thereby setting an example to the later world, and times of anguish, culminating in the savage persecution and expulsion under Isabella the Catholic at the close of the fifteenth century.

The Jews were indeed better off under Islam, for the Arab rulers were tolerant of the "Peoples of the Book", Jews and Christians alike, because their respective religions were seen as stages on the way to the Revelation that had already been bestowed on Muhammad. Both groups enjoyed internal autonomy, and this example was followed by the smaller Christian kingdoms in the Middle Ages, when Moors and Jews lived in their separate *aljamas*, i.e. ghettos, where they saw to their own affairs and paid taxes to the crown. Things did not go seriously wrong until later, when the conflicts that arose in the economic sphere spread to social, religious and regional issues.

In the early thirteenth century Andalusian Jews – cosmopolitan, sophisticated city-folk – started moving to what they saw as the rural backwaters of the north. Attitudes within the Jewish community were deeply divided. The Aristotelian "rationalism" of Maimonides was far removed from the mysticism that characterized other Jewish circles. In the outlying Jewish communities the orthodox traditions were still strictly upheld, and the religious fervour inspired by the Zohar and other cabbalistic texts clashed with the scientific mentality of the recent Enlightenment; the rabbis in the north were decidedly hostile to the newcomers, and the differences were exacerbated when many of the newcomers turned out to be better educated and consequently to enjoy a variety of privileges on account of services rendered or promised to the local authorities.

It is a well-known phenomenon. You are brooding on a particular subject and suddenly you find references to it all around you. The same evening there is a programme on television from a series on heresy. The subject is *Sefarad*, Jewish Spain. The term heresy is here used exclusively to mean the heresies of the past, and the programme ends on a nostalgic note: not only do the Sephardim miss Spain, but also Spain is homesick for the Jews. I recognize the opening images straightaway, for they show the delicate tracery on the walls of the synagogue in Toledo, *la Sinagoga del Tránsito*, of Transition. Or is it of Exodus, for that is what the programme is about. The notes I make in the dimly lit hotel lobby prove to be indecipherable when later I try to read them, but what I remember most clearly is the *claim* to a Jewish identity. All of a sudden everyone turns out to be Jewish: not just Cervantes but also Saint John of the Cross, and Saint Teresa of Avila, and that great and enigmatic poet of the Golden Age, Luis de Góngora, and if they were not fully Jewish themselves then surely their *linaje* was, their line of descent.

It is undoubtedly all true, and well intended (the programme concludes magnanimously that Jewish Spain is no less truly Spanish than Christian Spain), but if you sympathize with the lineage argument you cannot afford to ignore the virulent anti-Semitism of some of the converts to Roman Catholicism, for they played a crucial role in the indictment and persecution of their former brothers in the Jewish faith. Torquemada, the Grand Inquisitor, was a *converso*, and so was Alvaro de Luna, who persuaded Pope Nicholas V in 1451 to set up an Inquisition in Castile (in the hope of eliminating certain *conversos* who were colluding with the nobility to undermine Alvaro's position at the Castilian court).

That the economic repercussions of the Exodus were disastrous for Spain is also mentioned in the programme, with an eagerness that borders on embarrassment. Isabella herself wrote to her ambassador at the Vatican: "I have been the cause of great disaster and the depopulation of cities, regions, provinces and kingdoms, but my actions were inspired by the love of Christ and His Holy Mother. Those who say I did these things out of greed are liars and slanderers, for not once have I myself touched a *maravedí* of the goods confiscated from the Jews." Was she telling the truth? The Jews were not allowed to take their money with them, and everything that had been seized from them by court order before they were banished for good had been spent on the last military campaigns against the Arabs.

The programme makes me sad. The Sephardic music makes me sad because the song they have chosen is so cheerful and vivacious that, in good Brechtian tradition, it makes everything so much worse: blackmail, extortion, murder, torture and burnings at the stake, the tangled knot of human relations, the lethal chemistry of money combined with superstition, fear with selfishness, distrust with cunning. There is not a sound from the depths of the gloomy armchairs around me; the shadowy figures occupying them emit clouds of smoke, so they must be alive. They watch in silence as their Spain is proclaimed Jewish, and wait for the electronic jingle announcing the news. I go out into the street, and step into the stone backdrop of history, looking for a restaurant.

When I have found it, and have been taken up in the animated chatter of the late Spanish evening, I suddenly hear the word *lagarto*, lizard, being spoken by the waiter at the next table.

"Do you have *lagarto*?" I ask.

He beckons me to follow him to a glass cabinet in the back. Among the silvery heaps of fish and the frozen dainty dance of decapitated frogs I discover two objects that look to me like legless rabbit-trunks, small saddles, wedge-shaped, pinkish.

"*Lagarto*," he announces.

"That?" I ask. "But they're so big. They must be iguanas."

"You're thinking of *lagartijas*, those are the small ones. These are *lagartos*. They're bigger."

"And it's legal to serve them?"

"But of course! That gentleman over there is the local chief of police. What did you think?!"

"How do you catch them?"

"With hunting dogs, they're trained specially."

This is not encouraging, but then I do not usually dwell on the trials of Brother Hare and Sister Salmon either.

After a while I am presented with my *lagarto*, prettily served in a pool of crushed tomatoes flavoured with the herbs of its habitat: thyme, rosemary. A multitude of tiny bones offer protestations, as if playing for time. With that, and an evening stroll past the shuttered aristocratic mansions, I bid farewell to Cáceres. And yet, to the metronome of my footsteps, I conjure up different scenarios for the history I have been occupying myself with lately. Rhetoric, but I know it.

Arab rulers in the ninth and tenth centuries, Christian kings in the thirteenth, fourteenth and fifteenth had all experimented with pluralist regimes wielding authority equally over the three religious groups. Their endeavours had failed. But *who* should have done *what* differently? In the eyes of the masses Jews and *conversos* alike belonged to the upper classes, they were the oppressors. Should they have refused to become involved in fiscal and other governmental affairs? Should they have shown more concern for the so much larger group of their Jewish brothers, artisans mostly, who had remained far from power and with whom they had entered into that debate of enlightenment versus obscurantism, or if you will, of revelation versus ungodly, newfangled ideas?

Perhaps it is best to remain silent about the horrendous bigotry of the Church, but what about those who took such fiendish advantage of its aberrations simply because the past was supposed to have shown (because history had proved!) that pluralism did not work, that Spain could only survive as a single state with a single religion? That a more cosmopolitan, more enlightened and more pluralistic Spain would have enabled the new empire to secure a better future than devastation and ruin on both sides of the ocean, is another of those unprovable, impossible hypotheses.

My footsteps have arrived on the square in front of the cathedral, sounding as if they too are made of stone. In the weak light I can just distinguish two medallions in the façade of the bishops' palace. They are of two heads, one an old man with his eyes closed, his neck mysteriously encircled by a noose of which he himself seems to be a part, the other an equally mysterious-looking Indian wearing a lavish feather headdress.

The latter does not look at me either, but it seems as if he or she is smiling slightly, while the former wears a sad, downcast expression. I am in the kind of mood that makes me look for meaning in everything; here, for example, are two ways of viewing the past, as tragedy or comedy, or, as Hegel put it, the ways of Euripides or of Aristophanes, with a clear preference for the comic because of its well-founded affirmation of the primacy of life over death and furthermore knowing the reason for it. But here irony rears its head again, the irony of wondering which particular fateful error we are committing at this very time, the kind of error that will at some later time look as if it was our destiny. And, wonders the stranger strolling in Cáceres, what if the irony itself were part of that unknown fate?

The full capacity of the sun's laser force is aimed at the earth by the time I drive out of town the following morning. I am heading south, to a region devoid of history, the mud flats of the Guadalquivir, the domain of fishes and birds, no people. Suddenly I am in a hurry to get there; I do not stop in Seville, my head is full enough already, and on the map the area to the right of the river looks wonderfully wide and empty. I get lost, of course, looking for that one ferry I have in mind. I have to drive for hours over non-existent roads. I am greeted by men who intone "God be with you" or "May God protect you" and other sayings that offer a fore-taste of the continent across the water. I drive around in an almost Dutch-looking landscape with little ferry boats, eel nets, waving reeds, and I must be being guided by an invisible hand because after some time I actually find myself, miraculously, as it seems to me, in the village of El Rocío. A friend of mine who was once here has recommended the local hotel. It is supposed to be a quiet place, close to one of the loveliest nature reserves of Spain, the *Parque Nacional Coto de Doñana*, but I arrive to find that several dozen coaches have anticipated me, spilling forth dazzling women in vivid Andalusian costume, clapping and singing.

I look for the hotel, but all I see on the large sandy square are low white buildings. This village, as I find out later, is inhabited only part of the year. The low white buildings house the faithful that flock here each year on the biggest pilgrimage in Spain. I drive to the church, which is filled with loud and moving choir song, but there is dancing and singing out in the square. There are very few men, and more and more

El Rocío

coaches arrive from which all those bright colours catapult into the light. Circles are formed, guitars strummed, drums beaten, it is only women who play and sing – as if the great war between the sexes is over and the women have won.

I escape into a small *fonda*, but there too I find all the tables are smothered in multicoloured plumage and chatter. Two park wardens shift their chairs to make room for me, explaining that this is the day in the year when all the *amas de casa*, housewives from the whole of southern Spain, gather for their pilgrimage, from Albacete and Murcia, Seville and Córdoba, each group with their own songs to make the world reverberate. Outside, in front of the *fonda*, a tape recorder has been planted on top of a Land Rover. A throng of Red Cross nurses whirl around barefoot to the music – I am sure I will never see such rousing *sevillanas* again.

Happiness, that is what this is all about. The air is filled with the clatter of castanets, skirts fly, bare arms twirl and sway against the blue sky. This is not your pilgrimage proper, someone explains, for then the whole of Spain is involved, this time it is only the women. Just women! It's as if they want to kick off the world with their fiery heels, if there was not so much laughter and gaiety you would think they were mænads,

Bacchantes. The few women not wearing traditional costume join in the dancing, too, in trainers and tracksuits, oblivious to all but each other.

In the distance, at the end of the line of white barrack-like houses, a high-noon cowboy on his horse appears in a cloud of red dust, but no one takes any notice, the *sevillanas* and *malagueñas* follow each other in rapid succession, the dancing circles swell and shrink while the dust rises around their stamping feet, happiness in the afternoon. I am standing in the shade of a eucalyptus tree with some old men, we exchange sheepish grins and sway almost imperceptibly to the incessant swirl of the music wrapped in its own Moorish echoes, but I don't want to think of such things, I want all the history to be danced right out of my head, to be snatched up and blown by the wind to the horizon shimmering in the afternoon heat.

But perhaps, perhaps – my brain makes a last feeble attempt at comprehension – that is exactly what Hegel meant. Anyone who dances, dances on the past, and all that laughter belongs to the comic element. Who knows, perhaps this is the primacy of life over death, of which art in all its forms is the confirmation. But different instances govern my inner control system. My thoughts refuse philosophy and dance a flamenco that no one can see.

XXI

The Landscape of Machado

El Cid's Valencia ~ Seven hundred years of co-existence
Castilian dominance ~ French and Spanish chansons
An ocean of olive groves in a blessed landscape

N O NO, I HAVE NO BUSINESS HERE, I haven't come for
Valencia's sake, this is just where my next journey is to begin:
the route southwards, to Úbeda, Baeza, Granada. I will spend
the night here, that's all, I'm not going to abandon myself to yet another
town. I have crossed the bridges over rivers run dry, wandered along
the banks of the non-existent streams, and now I am sitting in a little
park beside a statue of the painter Pinazo. It is summer, the trees are
motionless, I am an agent without a mission here, I'll get started properly
tomorrow, have pity on me, for Spain weighs heavily and the north is
still in my system.

All very well, but didn't you see the purple-robed, white-mitred bishops
on television, Catalan bishops dressed up as if in the Middle Ages in a
Romanesque church? And weren't they discussing the Catalan nation,
and didn't their talk have a vaguely familiar ring, taking one back to the
days of the crown of Aragón, which encompassed the province of
Barcelona and the kingdom of Valencia, independent territories, each
with its own parliament? What is new, what is old? Echoes of the noblemen's oath of allegiance to the king can still be heard in the declarations
of independence issued by the *autonomías* today: "*Nos, que cada uno
valemos tanto como vos y que juntos podemos más que vos, os ofrece-
mos obediencia si mantenéis nuestros fueros y libertades; y si no, no.*"*

And if not, not. So I find myself transported back into the Spain of
history once more, doomed to perceive the old in all that is new: the

* We, who are each one of us equal to you, and who together can achieve more than you, we
offer you obedience if you maintain our privileges and liberties; and if not, not.

Allegorical figure from the façade of the Palacio del Marques de Dos Aguas, Valencia

bishops on television have stepped from the pages of an illuminated manuscript. It is not my fault they haven't altered their outfits in the last thousand years. What's new, what's old? Having left behind the forgotten painter in the park, I stand in front of the medieval Puerta de Serranos and stare at the massive gate that used to seal the entrance to

Detail of the puerta de Serranos, Valencia

the town as if it were a single household (late arrivals had to bang on the doors and shout). Age-old carved wood and wrought iron, dimensions fit for giants or men on horseback armed with tall lances, I see great trusses, nails, iron cladding, hinges, chains, the Valencian royal crown, labyrinthine bolts, a small door cut into the larger one.

Military Gothic, this gate was made two centuries after the time of the Cid, and yet it reminds me of him, because before this gate was built there was another one, and so it was here that he must have entered the town after his victory over the Almoravid Yousuf. Surrounded by his *mesnada*, his own private little army, his *almófar*, the iron head-piece of his coat of mail pushed to the back, he rides straight into his own legend – Rodrigo Díaz de Vivar, the mercenary who sold himself to both sides and who would carve a dominion for himself out of Muslim Valencia, El Cid, Campeador, Sidi the warrior, champion of alternating alliances and consequently the symbol, so to speak, of those confusing centuries during which the quarrelsome Christian lords moved steadily towards the Moorish south.

But there, too, the frontiers of emirates and caliphates shifted so frequently that the map makers could not keep up with them (emirs paid tribute to kings and vice versa – it is perhaps best compared to a gigantic slow-motion war dance with constantly changing partners), until the Christians finally crushed the Almohad military power at Las Navas de Tolosa in 1212. This victory launched the final phase of the Reconquista, although it would be three more centuries before the Muslims were driven out for good. The Christians assembled an army in which the Cid, had he still been alive, would have been glad to serve: the kings of Castile, Navarre and Aragón, contingents of French knights, mercenaries, the friar-soldiers of the new military Orders, they all advanced steadily from the Duero and Ebro to the Tagus across the vast, bare *meseta*. The land here has not lost touch with its past and preserves its memory in the names of the towns and in the strongholds that lie scattered in the land-scape like great beasts, and in the walls and gates of the cities, as here.

Anyone who concludes that the history of fighting between Moors and Christians was the result of simple hatred has not understood. There were vested interests, and there was the grand historical élan of what was, in retrospect, commitment to an idea – the expulsion of Islam from Spain. But it took nearly eight centuries, and in that very long period there had been so much intermingling, so much exchange, that each party had in a sense become the other. Each had caused the other to suffer, but alliances had also been formed and links established. Conversions, toler-ance, mixed marriages, syncretism, all those factors spread out over such a long period had made Spain different from all the other countries in Europe – as it remains to this day. The courts of al-Andalus were centres of learning where Muslims, Jews and Christians studied the works of Plato and Aristotle: when Ferdinand III died in 1252, Muhammad I of Granada sent hundreds of envoys to pay their respects to the king who had joined León and Castile firmly under one crown, and his epitaph was written in Latin, Arabic, Castilian and Hebrew. His son, Alfonso *el Sabio*, the Wise, appointed committees of Jews, Muslims and Christians to devote themselves to two monumental scholarly projects he had undertaken, *Las Tablas Alfonsíes* and *El Libro del Saber de Astronomía*, and all the while this scholarly man steadily continued to wage war, thereby securing Cádiz and Cartagena after centuries of Muslim rule. The realization that the knights of both sides who had to engage in combat made arrangements beforehand for the day of the battle almost transforms the period of the Reconquista into a protracted game of chess.

Alfonso X, the Wise, Madrid

It is quite fascinating to immerse oneself in the practical details of the various societies: in 1250 King Jaime I of Aragón granted the Mudéjars of the Uxó valley a charter stating the following terms:

> all Muslims should continue under their *sunna* [law] . . . they may give public instruction to their sons in the reading of the Koran, without suffering any prejudice from so doing. They may travel about their business through all the lands of our realm and not be hindered by any man. They may appoint a judge and a superintendent of their own accord

and so on. All the issues are covered in that one document. No Christian is entitled to establish residence on their land,

> nor may we [the king], nor any person acting in our name on behalf of the kingdom of Valencia, oblige them to accept such settlement ever . . . Moors both now and in the future will pay over one eighth of all produce to us or to our nominee, and they will not be constrained to make any other payments on produce. Exempt from this tax are fruit on trees and fresh vegetables.

The most striking clause is perhaps the eighteenth, which states plainly:

> Let the Moors remain as they were wont in the time of the Moors, before they departed from the land.

Almost 200 years later the king of Navarre installed a Muslim, Ali Serrano, as notary in Tudela, granting him the

> power and authority to perform and to receive all manner of contracts between Moors or between a Moor and a Christian and also between a Jew and a Moor as befits a notary public appointed by our royal authority according to the *sunna* of the Moors.

I found these details in L. P. Harvey's *Islamic Spain 1250-1500*,[*] one of those books you cannot put down once you've started, because it's just as if someone has been instructed to keep the books of the universe, Section – Spain, Period – 1200. Now I know that according to Islamic law in Aragón the punishment for bearing false witness was forty-nine lashes, four lashes for riding a horse without the owner's permission, eighty for falsely accusing another of being "the son of an adulteress",

[*] L. P. Harvey, *Islamic Spain 1250-1500*, The University of Chicago Press, 1990.

and I also know that the Mudéjars in the village of Ribaforada in Navarre had to pay a tax of three eggs per household on Saturdays and that the Christians catapulted 22,000 stones during the siege of Almería, and all those scattered, fragmented, random details of times past lend an extra dimension to a photograph I come across in *El País* in 1991. It shows the king of Castile and Navarre and Aragón, who is now king of Spain, signing a treaty with the sultan of Morocco, whose kingdom is only a hand's breadth of water away from the al-Andalus of old, from the caliphates and emirates of the past: two twentieth-century monarchs in a setting that could well be the Alhambra, two scions of history, their hands full of *déjà vu*.

What is old, what is new? Thinking about the Cid has reminded me of his epic poem, and because I have thought of his Song I have ventured into Valencia in search of a bookshop, believing (I of little faith) that I will never find one. But half an hour later this end-of-millennium man sits among the white pigeons on the square facing the basilica of the Virgen de los Desamparados, the helpless, engrossed in a poem written *circa* 1140. He vanishes into a region of words, Spanish words that seem as unchanged as the landscape of the *meseta*. He recognizes the thrill he experienced before, so many years ago: the style which is brisk, descriptive, realistic, Spanish, not exalted and mystical like the *Chanson de Roland*, not a high-minded crusade, but the story of a warlord, an hidalgo who is not a member of the class of *ricoshombres* (landowners who could muster a personal army), who has earned rather than inherited his wealth and status, a soldier of fortune who loves money and power, who is banished unjustly by his king, Alfonso VI, and offers his services to the Moorish kingdom of Zaragoza but never turns against his "own" king, indeed who supports Alfonso in times of difficulty, but is only recalled from exile when Alfonso needs his help in the war against the zealous Almoravids, a Tuareg dynasty from Mauritania.

> *Embraçan los escudos   delant los coraçones*
> *abaxan las lanças   abueltas de los pendones*
> *enclinaron las caras   de suso de los arzones,*
> *ivan los ferir   de fuertes coraçones.*
> *A grandes voces llama   el que en buen ora nació:*

"¡ Feridlos, caballeros,   por amor del Criador!
¡Yo soy Roy Díaz, el Cid   de Bivar Campeador!"*

And now for the last time, the old and the new: the *Poema de mío Cid* was the first of the Spanish *Cantares de gesta*, epic poems, and its immense popularity undoubtedly played a role both in the establishment of Castilian supremacy and in the hegemony of Castilian as the language of Spain. The whole world calls that language Spanish, yet there are other languages in Spain. But first things first: only yesterday I heard the elected successor to the ancient counts of Catalonia, Jordi Pujol, explaining the analogy between Lithuania and Catalonia at a press conference, not in Catalan, mind you, but in Spanish, and also the *lehendakari*, leader, president of the Basque country, spoke Spanish in defence of the actions of the *ertzaintza* (Basque police) against ETA. And there's the rub: in spite of all the fuss about independence and nationalism, Catalans buy more Spanish language newspapers than Catalan ones; *La Vanguardia* is the main Catalan paper, but in Spanish – that's the paradox. The same is true of books. And yet we may well live to see Europe soothing her ruffled feathers with a Catalan ambassador in Riga, a Lithuanian ambassador in Zagreb, and a Slovenian ambassador in Bastia – job creation of a sophisticated order. It's a sort of miracle: to become bigger and smaller at one and the same time.

The church bells have started to peal, a voluptuous bride passes by the marble fountain, a clutch of mothers with small children disappear into the basilica as if a great mouth has swallowed them. I don't want to get up from my seat just yet, the pavement around me is rippling with pigeons, but also the pages in my hands ripple: the lines are divided in two, and this not only enhances the delightful cadence as you read, but also draws the eye up and down the page in a most pleasing way. As the lines, and hence the caesuras, are not of equal width, there's an erratic river of white running down the middle of the printed text, capricious and irregular, while the effect of reading out loud is sheer regularity, dance, rhythm. In *The Literature of the Spanish People* Gerald Brenan compares the Spanish and the French *chansons de geste*, and he makes a

---

* They hold their shields close to their hearts, they lower the lances with the pennants, they bend their faces low over the saddle, they, they will strike with resolute hearts. And then he who was born in a favoured hour calls in a loud voice: Strike them, knights, for the love of the Creator! I am Roy Díaz de Bivar, the Cid, the champion!

number of interesting observations: he sees the France of those days (around 1100) as lagging behind Spain. He refers to the Celtic and Germanic influences in northern France, he mentions the spirit of Germanic romantic imagination and, in the same breath, the "barbarian roughness" that gave rise to the "wondrous explosion of creative energy": crusades, cathedrals, scholastic disputes, new epic and lyric poetry. It is a society still in the making, eager for a culture of its own, and consequently making a pretence at a degree of refinement which it does not really possess. The consequences, in those dangerous and uncertain times, were, in Brenan's view, insincerity and exaltation, as in the *Chanson de Roland*, and mass neuroses.

Brenan contrasts the situation in France with the Spanish world of those days, which is so strongly evoked in the poem of the Cid. Spanish society is "healthy and self-confident". There is also harshness, since there is ceaseless warfare among Christians and Moors, but Spain can pride itself on an ancient culture that goes back to the Roman Empire. Not only is the style of the poem sober, uncluttered by unnecessarily discursive descriptions or high-flown mystique, but the demeanour of the hero is composed, self-assured. Here Brenan warns that the idea we have of Spain is all too often influenced by "that century of fantastic but fatal intoxication that is known as the Golden Age, and of subsequent decline". In the Cid's day Castile was in an expansive phase, revolutionary in the sense that resistance against the feudal system was beginning. There is no inkling of such things in the *Chanson de Roland*, that poem's theme is *Paiens unt tort e chrestiens unt dreit*, pagans are wrong and Christians are right (which, as Brenan nonchalantly adds, presumably makes it all right to kill the pagans). His conclusion is that the Spaniards of the Middle Ages, while they may have lacked the intellectual and artistic sophistication of the French, were nonetheless the first people to attain social and political maturity within that medieval context, because the never-ending struggle along those ever-shifting borders between Christendom and Islam gave rise to constant movement and liberation.

Someone scatters grain, causing a whirlwind of pigeons. Finally I get up and walk past the curious fountain with its reclining man and absurd girlish figures on my way to the basilica. My eyes have to get accustomed to the gloom inside. A little ceremony is being conducted, small children are swept off the ground and held up high to the upper world, as high as the priest can reach, and for as long as he can keep it up. This is new to me, I have never seen this before. Confirmation, getting ashes, the blessing of Saint Blaise, first communion, I've been through it all, but I was never snatched from my mother like that and hoisted up in the air, turned to face the altar, held tight, *displayed*, and then swung round for a second display, this time before a temporal authority, the photographer, who bathes me for an instant in his silvery flash, thereby to record the moment for the infant's posterity, in order that I may see myself later soaring through the basilica, the priest in his *capa* beneath me, his hands having me in a hold about my small waist. I'm pinned between heaven and earth, as if the choice must be made already, because first I'm held up to the tabernacle where God resides, next I'm drenched in the light of the flash, and then my feet touch the ground again. Not I, the children, anxious and thrilled. Never will anyone lift them up in a church again in that way. One by one they are chronicled in the sacred light of photography, the mothers look as if they believe their babies might take flight after all, up into the dome and out through the rosette, but they are sucked back to earth to the accompaniment of coins dropped onto a brass platter, the heady aroma of incense, the complicated manoeuvring of small hands struggling to make the sign of the cross, no, not like that, this is how you do it.

Outside the bride is still waiting, like a mighty ship in sails of tulle, the thin peasant beside her is nervous, he seems to shrink from entering that place with its taste of another world, a world of priests, organs and gold, where your own voice sounds different, as if distorted by an unseen agent, which must be the same elusive quality that prevents trees from growing there. I sympathize with this man with the sunburnt face and uncomfortable best suit. The priest, the pigeons, the square have immersed me in Spain again, and I must get away from here, I must leave this town on the coast and head inland, to that other ocean with its luminous, dun-coloured waves, an ocean of olive groves and roads on which nobody drives. That is what I have come for, and I know it is hard to explain what is so seductive about those hours of heat and drought, the formations of olive trees marching up the hillsides like a burning vision, the parched river-beds and the unassuming, often semi-abandoned villages. Time and again a new panorama opens up before my eyes, different and still the same. This is the land travelled by Saint

John of the Cross, mystic, poet; riding his donkey, singing and reading and thinking as a man who needs no one to lift him up to the heavens. Having risen out of his own body, his double hovered like a spirit high above the man with the stick and the donkey making his way across the petrified silence down below.

I am not blessed, but the landscape is, it must be something like that, for again the place names read like a litany: Cocentaina, Villena, Elda, Novelda, Caravaca, Cehegín, Sierra de la Pila, Sierra de Espuña, names with a purpose, rustling and whispering stories of their forgotten provenance, together they are the soul of the sierra, a sea where the waves have names. Don't tell me, I know, those who do not see or hear will find nothing but a sand-pit, a desert, ill-lit taverns, coarse food, land that prostrates itself before you, slow and gaunt, withdrawn, irresistible. I often think I should have been born here, but perhaps it's the other way round: the very circumstance of my birth in the marshy green lowlands has made me sensitive to the temptations of harshness and stone. All that needs to be written was written long ago:

> *¡Encinares castellanos*
> *en laderas y altozanos,*
> *serrijones y colinas*
> *llenos de obscura maleza,*
> *encinas, pardas encinas;*
> *humildad y fortaleza!*

Encinas are holm-oaks, the kind of tree you see growing on the land not planted with olives; *laderas, altozanos, serrijones* and *colinas* all signify sloping ground, hills, small mountain ridges, mounds, mountainsides, separately or in combination; *llenos* means full, *maleza* means undergrowth or weeds in a field, a word with a dark and malevolent ring; *pardas* is the feminine plural of "grey", *humildad* is as humble as it sounds and *fortaleza* as sturdy as a fortress, and all those words strung together the way Antonio Machado has done here produce a singsong effect that is lost when I attempt to translate. But it is what I see around me, the holm-oaks with their stiff, dusty leaves, alone or in groups in the rolling countryside. They are humble but strong, they will endure. "The landscape has made itself a tree in you", he says later in the poem, where he evokes the landscapes of summer and winter, blazing sun and icy cold, *"bochorno y borrasca"*, scorching heat and savage storms, always the grey holm-oak will stake out its rightful claim and, a *"sombra tutelar"*, cast its protective shadow across the landscape, a tree for the traveller who has left his car by the wayside, who has stretched out on a bed of shade and dry leaves and listens to its voice of almost no words.

XXII

From Lorca to Úbeda, Dreams of an Afternoon

From Lorca to Úbeda ~ Silent landscape of campaigns
Thoughts on castles ~ Siesta awakening in Úbeda
Andrés de Vandelvira's palaces

Todo lo corren los moros,	The Moors come from all sides
sin nada se les quedar;	With nothing in their way;
el rincón de San Ginés	San Gines is captured
y con ello, el Pinatar.	And with that El Pinatar.
Cuando tuvieron gran presa	In their rush
hacia Vera vuelto se han,	They went as far as Vera
y en llegando al puntarón	And reaching the hilltop
consejo tomado han	They discussed
si pasarían por Lorca,	Whether to pass through Lorca
o se irían por la mar . . .	Or to go along by the sea . . .

THE BATTLE OF LOS ALPORCHONES was fought in the year 1452, and something of the ferocity of the campaign is preserved in the rush and cadence of the *romancero fronterizo*, the great collection of ballads from the frontier in which the last century of the Reconquista is evoked with such pathos and poignancy. And I read the romances here, in the Hotel Alameda in Lorca, and the names of all the places mentioned are unchanged: towns, valleys, mountain passes, they are all to be found on the map, and I shall traverse the land-scapes where those armies were locked in their eternal embrace. But I live in a different day and age and I am still on my way to Santiago. There are times when the goal I have set myself becomes hazy, as hazy as the distant northern land where my city must be, green, shrouded in mist, so absolutely unlike the time and place of the poem I'm reading. Here in Lorca the blazing July sun beats down just as it did then, when the campaign that had begun eight centuries earlier in the foggy regions of Asturias and Galicia was in its final stages, the slow reconquest of the land that is now called Spain. I am travelling in the opposite direction from the Moors in the song: their desperate campaign was northwards, to the sea. Turning away from the shore I head for the conflagration of the interior, past Vélez Rubio and Vélez Blanco, the golden and the white Vélez, I take a crazily roundabout route through the Llanos de Orce, then via Huéscar and the Sierra de Marmolance to Cazorla in the mountains and across the Guadalquivir to palatial Úbeda.

Chalky, stony ground, crumbling wattle barns, fields of bleached barley stubble, jagged mountain ridges in the distance, hour upon hour in which you don't see a soul, when you stop the car you can hear the silence sizzle. But beware of thoughts of monotony, for on one and the same day you will see stripes of pure gold reaching to the horizon, young bulls frolicking on marshy river banks, oases with little farms which are of a white so glaring that you can't look at them without your sunglasses. The road you have to follow is a mad meander among hundreds of thousands of olive trees, the dream of a madman, and after hours and hours of olives you are grateful for a cornfield or even a lone poplar tree. The people who live here must be as addicted to this scenery as sailors are to the sea. The intensity becomes almost too much to bear after driving for several hours, the heat sharpens the ecstasy, thistles acquire the grace of orchids, and just as you begin to feel your eyes cannot take in any more emptiness there is a gentle curve in the road between fortress-like flat-topped mountains, and you find yourself in a changed landscape, the road drops into what must be a valley in whose depths the river is hidden from view or has run dry.

For hours your eyes have been stinging from the glare, you've given up trying to define the shades of the terrain because your store of words is exhausted. You settle for the shade of *earth* because the temptations of other, more sensual colours have been erased by the nature of the place or by the season. Your field of vision seems to be filled with nothing but earth. And then you notice a shape in the landscape, which at first you take to be a natural mound or outcrop, then it looks like a gigantic inanimate body sprawled on a hill or in the fold of a mountain, camouflaged by the colour of the surrounding rocks, a bastion, a castle, a fortress, pierced by the wind and eroded by time, skeletal or stolid, toothless, eyeless, as closed as the face of a dead man, disproportionately huge. There is virtually no sign of human activity to justify their presence, they are the leavings of an age when men must have been of giant stature, but they weren't.

Vélez Blanco. This must be the wrong season to come here, for it is one of the granaries of Spain. You know this to be so, but it is hard to believe. The image of rippling cornfields has dissolved, the land has disguised itself as a desert crowned by an indomitable castle, a gaunt, Moorish rectangle, linked by a tall bridge to a sharply outlined, massive polygon, high and steep, pale in the afternoon sun. A scooter is parked there, it probably belongs to the warden, but I see no one. No doubt he is taking a nap, only a fool would be about in this heat. Once upon a time there was a splendid bronze Renaissance gate here, but a latter-day descendant of the marquises of Vélez sold the gate and the marble courtyard with it. Anyone with a desire to touch the marble must visit the Metropolitan Museum in New York, only he will never see what I see now from the battlements, a village lodged in a cleft of the mountain like a swallow's nest, an empty square, a house melting into the rock face, a child popping out of its home four times in succession to fetch water at the pump, red roofs so close together that they appear to be connected, as if all the people live here under one and the same vast canopy, a commonwealth.

The courtyard is high and empty, there are some purple flowers I cannot identify. Later, I will come across a dried specimen in my notebook and will find it impossible to imagine just how vividly they stood out against these blind walls.

I climb up to the tower, stand in one of the embrasures that looked from the outside like empty eye sockets and catch a glimpse of a small oasis with a stream, from which the road stretches into the distance, leaving a trail of rocks. Empty, nothing, outside and inside. Inside the walls you feel even more diminutive, you wonder what it is you are after, how to describe the emotion that comes over you. A suspect emotion, it must be admitted. Ortega y Gasset reflects on it in his *Ideas de los Castillos* and comes to a conclusion that I found hard to accept as I stood there on the battlements.

> Fortresses strike us primarily as vestiges of a life completely opposite to ours. We have fled them and sought refuge with the ancient democracies, believing them to be closer to our style of public life, of Justice and the State. But if we then try to feel as citizens – in the

Athenian sense – we notice within ourselves a curious sort of resistance. The ancient State takes possession of the whole man, leaves him nothing for his private use. And in some hidden corner of our personality such utter commitment to the collective whole of *Polis* or *Civitas* repels us. So it seems that we are not the citizens that we so ardently and rhetorically claim to be at meetings and in editorial articles. And then it seems to us that the fortresses reveal, beyond their drama, a treasure of ideas that accord precisely with what we feel in our innermost self. Their towers have been constructed to protect the individual against the State. Gentlemen, long live liberty!

One cannot but endorse his closing plea, but it is nonsense to say that those towers were built for the purpose of defending the individual against the State. The establishment of a bastion was a feat in the centuries-long struggle between Christian and Arab kingdoms and among warring noblemen. They were built in strategic locations to facilitate control over an entire region. But what the excerpt does pinpoint is the shadowy ambience of the Übermensch evoked by this kind of relic: as if there once existed, in and around those fortifications, a better and higher form of life which, had you lived then, would have been yours. But the chances are that, had you been permitted within the bounds of the castle at all, it would only have been to deliver your tithes of corn. It is easy to get carried away when you stand on the ramparts with your eagle's-eye view of the surrounding countryside: before long you will feel as if the panorama displayed before you is your private property, and you will put yourself in the shoes of those who stood here in this high place, not in the shoes of the people they quite literally looked down upon. The individual here seeking protection of any sort (there was no question yet of a state in Ortega's sense) was primarily protecting himself, and the odds against that solitary individual being you, however romantic a figure you cut on the ramparts, are overwhelming. It is far more likely that you and I would have been down below at the mercy of the caprices of whoever stood there as lord of the castle. Only the state that we would found would free us from such dependency, until such time as the state itself became whimsical, withdrawn, and hid itself within the confines of the castle from which surveyors were barred. Nowadays we have our castles of invisible power, with computer screens for watchtowers, and so Ortega might be proved right after all: for a moment, in that theatrical décor of times gone by forever, we are offered escape from the anonymity of our uniform lives. What was it that made me stop here? Was it to indulge a shallow desire for nostalgia? But nostalgia for what? For an age when people were larger than life? But they weren't. For the thrill of art? For the drama of the place, the walls scalded by the white afternoon sunlight, framed against the sky? The site was chosen purely for strategic reasons, aesthetics didn't come into it.

The traveller in these parts has plenty of time to ponder such questions. A few days later I visit another castle, the castle of Lacalahorra. Like the others, this one looms over a village tucked against a hillside, inaccessible but visible from miles away, massive walls, circular red towers, a man-made ensemble of stones on a foundation of stones made not by man but tossed down by the hand of nature, and the same question imposes itself: what is it that makes these structures so irresistible to some people? My suspicions are confirmed in the castle of Jaén, which has been converted into a government-run parador. I can sense it as my anachronistic vehicle (it has shrunk to the size of a toy) negotiates the hairpin bends leading up to the forbidding brigands' retreat: it has to do with drama, exaltation, and not least with ostentation. The men who lived here were no bigger than we are, but we now seem to be bigger. Standing under the huge iron lanterns and high vaulted ceilings, in the rooms with sweeping views of the countryside, scurrying past the gleaming suits of armour in which flesh-and-blood men slaughtered their adversaries, we can for a moment imagine that we have escaped holy equality, we can imagine a life in which we are not doomed to be our brother's keeper, in which we can even contemplate hacking him in two with the sword that hangs beside the granite chimney piece that bears our coat of arms. From the threadbare houses down below comes the sound of cocks crowing, a pack of howling dogs will keep us awake all night, it will take the bikini worn by our next-door neighbour at the pool to bring us back to earth: the likes of her were never to be seen in medieval paintings, nor indeed was the perfidious television set in our air-conditioned room.

Spain is not the only country abounding in relics from days of warfare, but thanks to the climate they are in a better state than in most places. The dry air has not only preserved the carcasses of the buildings, it has usually prevented creepers and mosses from covering the walls, as in more clement and moister climates, and yet people seldom seem to find the land on which the fortresses were constructed an attractive location for building homes today. José Zorilla wrote a wonderful poem on this subject:*

> *Of the feudal splendour, the bare remains*
> *Without carpets, without mural decorations, without arms,*
> *Today there are no roofs, but speechless walls,*
> *Desolation, silence, solitude and shade.*
> *The folktales of such a time*
> *Anonymous, and without date*
> *They would tell*
> *In the vaults, the turrets and the columns,*
> *But there is only yellowed grass.*
> *The birds live under the roof*
> *And the diligent spider's web*
> *These watch the worn grief*
> *Of the towers of Fuensaldaña*

Fuensaldaña, Calahorra, Vélez Blanco . . . Spain has 2,538 more of these fortresses, castles, battlements, ramparts, towers. Many of them are sinking slowly into the landscape, and the question is whether that is bad. I enjoy staying in the paradors, but at the same time there is a degree of insincerity in all those over-restored ruins, if only because you know it will take centuries for the architecture to look properly time-worn again. But this thought has a darker side: it comes painfully close to Hitler's vision of *Ruinenwert*. To the Austrian master-builder the aesthetic of the ruin was fundamental to architecture, and he instructed Speer to design buildings that would still look beautiful when they lay in ruins after a thousand years. This is exactly what has happened in Spain, though no one planned it. Speer could not have succeeded, of course. History has no truck with intentions.

Afternoon, trembling asphalt, a displaced, solitary pine tree like an umbrella over its own shadow. Gesualdo's *"Tenebræ"* on the car radio, snow on the Sierra Nevada, pleated foothills, fields scattered with chalk-coloured stones. Huéscar, Castril, a statue of a saint high above a village,

* José Zorilla, *Obras completas*, Librería Santaren, Valladolid, 1943.

you can imagine the annual procession. I refresh my hands in a little stream and hear a father shout: "*Laura, Laurita, vamos a comer!*" – come home! dinner-time! – and I want to be Laura, Laurita, and I want to be eight years old like that little girl scampering home and I want to go into the cool house and sit at the table and spend the hot hours of the afternoon dozing in a theatre of shifting dreams, but I am not permitted to sleep nor to dream. I drive round and round in the shifting landscape, Tiscar, Quesada, olives and olives and more olives, bend after bend, until the woman with the hoe over her shoulder whom I saw down in the valley steps out into the road before me. She has taken a short cut by clambering up the slope like a goat, and now she wants a lift. She gets into the front seat beside me without a word. Her face rugged and brown, fierce eyes fixed on the road, the hoe still over her shoulder, a basket with a knotted cloth and a pitcher between her feet. It is for her husband. He has been at work in the mountains all day, she always brings him food when she has finished her chores below and he stays there at night, then she walks back home again. It is more than 5 kilometres if she walks by the road, but sometimes she climbs straight up the mountainside, that's quicker. When she gets out of the car I see her husband standing a short distance away, silhouetted against the sun, an outline inked-in, the shape of a man among the shapes of sheep. Here it is 1,185 metres, and for the first time the air feels slightly fresh.

The dreams of the siesta are not the same as those of the night, there's a different, false night embedded in the siesta, the deception of awakening not to a fresh start but to a repeat performance. The day has already been soiled by life and food, by the words of the news and of the world, sunset is nearer than sunrise, and everything has to happen a second time, there is a certain lassitude, a hint of death, shadows in the late afternoon, the slow approach of darkness. I recognize the room but not the sounds. They belong to the closing phrases of the dream, the already unconscionable heaviness of sleep. They are shouts, the shouts of a human being and yet inhuman, a persistent lowing, wordless, an unstructured lament, indefinable grief rushing into the room through the half-open shutter. The sound is also denial, for beyond my shutters the world is all structure, discipline, controlled emotion, and the low-ing sound ought to bounce off the friezes, cornices, columns, the plain, unadorned sandstone walls; a fresh Renaissance breeze comes wafting from the princely towns of northern Italy to the blaze of sixteenth-century Andalusian Spain. For that is where I am, in Úbeda, in the austere palace known as Casa del Deán Ortega, now a parador you are free to enter without a patent of nobility.

The light pouring in through the opening in the shutters etches a belligerent square on my bed, I reread the words I was reading when I fell asleep and think they sound like a song: *Étrange fut le destin de Plotin dans le monde arabe!* and then I get up and push the shutter further open and again I am overcome by a sensation of strangeness as (or perhaps *because*) the lowing persists, for I suddenly remember what I have been dreaming, something to do with lions and bulls, and I am struck by how fine the line dividing dream from reality is in this case, for it was only this morning that I made notes about a relief in one of the pilasters in the façade of the Sacra Capilla del Salvador, next door to the parador: a man, Hercules maybe, wrestling with two bulls. The lion is also at hand: it stands guard before the Palacio de las Cadenas, aloof and watchful, his left paw resting on the Vázquez de Molina coat of arms. If I hang over my balcony and look to the left I can just see the grey stone relief, the naked man standing with his back half turned to me, holding the bulls' heads by the horns under his mighty arms, the bulls kicking their hind legs high, the man's face, ringed by the small Greek beard, turned to the left. I spent hours studying it this morning. The lowing sound goes on and on, and it occurs to me how odd it is that we should find ourselves constantly surrounded by mythic beasts in this kind of town, and that we feel so free to walk about among them. The lion on the pedestal, the eagle and boar in the coat of arms, the unicorn in the stained-glass window: one day they will choose a dream in which they can move, come close, beckon, threaten, in which weathered stone becomes glowing brown skin, in which the eagle hunts its prey, the lion roars, the bull charges.

I go out past shorn privet hedges, lascivious white and pink oleanders with poisonous leaves, I head in the direction of the lowing sound and then I set eyes on him, in the middle of a Renaissance patio: a lonely, self-absorbed imbecile spinning around in circles like a giant, earth-bound butterfly among the columns, shouting incessantly. The palace he lives in is an asylum, the locals are evidently used to the noise because they walk by without a glance in his direction, only I stop and look at him and at the others, who return my look from a world in which mine counts for nothing. But what is nothing? For in my consciousness, too, this lowing noise now belongs to the world, and when I reach the end of the street I still hear it, but it also spreads over the landscape lying below with olive trees in one formation after another advancing from the horizon on the town. Not that the olive trees are screeching like Hitchcock's birds, but the colours of that landscape, the *loma de Úbeda*, scorch the earth all the way up to the sky, if you stare long enough at the trees you can see them spreading out across the hillside, and the shouting is part of it all.

It was to escape the rigours of the landscape just for one day that I had come to Úbeda. The patio in the parador was high and cool, palm trees and light from high windows. I had read about the medieval families here and in Baeza, 10 kilometres away, who had tried to cut each other's throats just as their counterparts in Florence and Verona had done, about how they joined forces to combat the *comuneros* and crushed that popular rebellion by means of swords and gallows, how after the conquest of the Moors in 1227 and 1237 the first two Christian towns in Andalusia blossomed: corn, olive oil, salt, trade. No longer was Úbeda known as Ubbadat-al-Arab, Baeza no longer as Byyasa. Now the families fought over hegemony and money, and the new money required new styles and the latest styles were the prerogative of the richest families. Thus it happened that Charles V's secretary, Francisco de los Cobos, invited the architect Andrés de Vandelvira to Úbeda, and there his palaces stand today. I feel surrounded by the distillation of all the good, clear workings of the man's mind, his sobriety, his poise, his serenity; this creation a classical jewel cut in Andalusian fire, a sanctuary between Arab and baroque, decorative frenzy, exorbitance. A day of all that is exquisitely measured, overwhelmed by the immeasurable infinity of land on every side.

Úbeda is a small town, and so is Baeza, there is little else to do but read, wander around, hunt for shady spots and watch the light photographing the statues, reflect, contemplate. Baeza is the older of the two towns, different echoes, a different silence. Climbing a steep, narrow path behind the cathedral I suddenly find myself face to face with Antonio Machado, and even he is the stuff of dreams, for the poet is a head without a body, a bronze head mounted in concrete atop a low cairn, his eyes are wide open, but he looks over your head. His crown is splattered with bird droppings that weep down the sides, grimy grey-and-white tears of excrement, a stuffed poet's head cradled in concrete, burnt-out, like an idol surveying the countryside of which he wrote, a land of such poverty, such sadness, it *must* have a soul:

> *tierras pobres, tierras tristes,*
> *tan tristes que tienen alma!**

* poor lands, sad lands / so sad that it's as if they possessed a soul!

XXIII

Splendour in the Gardens of al-Andalus

Deaf and dumb in the Alhambra ~ Legacy of the Moors
The gardens of paradise ~ Isabella's tomb
Granada betrayed

T HE WATER CAME UP TO THE lip of the basin, almost
brimming over, the lions with their unseeing faces, their
small ears, their scaled chests whispered with voices of water,
I stood among the slender columns as in a marble wood. I was the
blind man who had seen the fountain in the basin, who had seen how
the wind made the solitary jet of water trying to stay upright curve
gently in the breeze, how the spray dissipated and flew away in a
glistening instant; I was the one who had seen the two small orange
trees in the Court of the Lions in the palace of Muhammad ibn Yousuf
ibn al-Ahmar, and yet I was blind because I did not know that there
was lettering on the rim. I had seen mere decoration, but it was words;
I saw a stream of arabesques pursuing each other and flowing back
into themselves and yet it was writing, but had I come even so close
to the fountain as to run my fingers from right to left over the mean-
dering tendrils, my mouth would not have been able to shape the
sounds of those words. Here between these walls I am both blind
and dumb.

There would have to be someone standing next to me to recite those
verses in the language that has been banished from this land, that dwells
in another continent across the water, and through the gurgle of water I
would not comprehend those words, and at the same time I would
comprehend them because someone else had translated them into
Spanish in the book I was holding, and so I would walk around the fountain and look at those signs and read what I heard:

SO CLOSE ARE THE HARD AND THE FLOWING
THAT YOU CANNOT TELL WHICH OF THE TWO IS STREAMING,

NO, IT IS NOT WATER THAT STREAMS TOWARDS THOSE LIONS
IT IS A CLOUD OF FLUID MOVEMENT . . .

and as long as I stood there alone I could try to formulate a thought and
I would not succeed. Many years ago, in the Winter Mosque in Tehran,
I had written in my notebook that Arab art was inhuman, and by
that I meant that there is no face or figure to focus on. The religion does
not permit images of humans; there is nothing but form, construction,
decoration, geometry, harmony, splendour, grottoes of mother-of-pearl
and wood and stucco and marble, domes of gold and enamel. Nothing to
hold on to, just dizzying splendour, until you discover that there are
letters hiding in the ornamentation and that the space describes itself
through the writing, as in the *tacas* (*tāqāt*, niches) in the passage leading
to the Patio de Arrayanes:

> I AM A MIHRAB FOR PRAYER
> I WILL GO THERE AND NO FURTHER
>
> YOU THINK THAT THE PITCHER OF WATER
> MURMURS ITS PRAYERS FROM INSIDE
>
> EACH TIME IT IS FINISHED
> IT MUST START AGAIN

Thanks to the Spanish book in my hand I am slightly less blind than
the others, but it's no good, for the translations are cryptic and I can't
read the calligraphic Arabic printed alongside. All I can do is pick out the
recurring figurations and try to recognize them in the inscriptions decor-
ating the niches. "You, son and grandson of kings," I read, "you, before
whom the stars humble themselves . . ." But as I read on my mind is
dulled, for not only have the poems been translated, they have been
dissected too: there are six verses, the metre is known as *basīt*, and the
rhyme is *mū*, but I can't hear the music of that rhyme, and to discover
what *basīt* sounds like I would need an extra lifetime, one in which
I would have been someone else, a Muslim in the days of Yousuf I,
someone who would stroll far from the Christian world, would err
through the Alhambra of my king, and would know that the poem by

Alhambra, Granada

the entrance to the Hall of Ambassadors is by ibn al-Jatib, and that the five verses were composed in the *kāmil* metre, and, without thinking, my inner voice would say the words in their proper rhythm and then I would be off again, a man in flowing robes among other men in flowing robes, the shuffle of slippers on marble, the rustle of fabrics as I made my way among the snow crystals of the *muqarnas*, along the mihrabs pointing towards Mecca, through corridors and chambers where a different race would later rove, a people blind and deaf to the words of my poets, all they would see of my time was the décor that we had left behind and that, without our presence, was nothing to them but an ever repeated form in which they did not fit, which might at the most inspire nostalgia or amazement in some, but usually not even that.

My world vanished from Europe for good once the last sultan of Granada, Muhammad ibn Ali (whom the victors called Boabdil because they could not pronounce our words) gave up the keys of the city to the Catholic Kings. We had withdrawn to the land of Ifrīquiā whence we came. What we left were words, buildings, echoes in place names, style, that which was easiest to see, but in the libraries of Granada and Toledo, of Leiden and London, our other heritage would slumber: manuscript no. 539 Or. in the Bodleian Library in Oxford; manuscript no. 9033 Or. in the British Museum; manuscript no. 1411 in the library of the Royal Asiatic Society of Bengal; manuscript *Tabātaba'i* in the library of parliament of Tehran; no. 1143, manuscript *Alwāh* in an anthology kept in the Vatican; catalogue of Levi della Vida, p. 141, with copies in Berlin (no. 4130) and in the Biblioteca Ambrosiana, included in the book of *Sifr Adam*. Scraps of paper, vellums, tattered pages, loose sheets, books and fragments of books. For centuries ahead scholars would sit in a thousand libraries of Alexandria, until such a time as I could not imagine, searching, pondering, speculating, verifying, annotating the writings that we and our fellow expatriates, the Jews, had translated and thus saved for the western world, the *Malfūzāt Aflatūn*, the words of Plato, the explication of Aristotle's *Problemata* by Johannes Philoponus, Plutarch's *al-ara' al-tabī'īyah*, "five maqālāt containing the views of the philosophers on physics" translated by Qusta ibn Luqa al-Ba'albaki, the *tafāsīr*, the commentaries on Aristotle of ibn Rushd (Averroes), the scratch of quills, the shuffle of paper, the transmutation of words into words, script into script.

And what a strange twist of fate it was that all those texts and theories, all that gnostic and scientific knowledge, all those mathematical, astronomical, poetical, medical, philosophical treatises and commentaries, all the cogitation and assessment of axiom and counter-axiom, would bring about the renaissance of their world, not ours. We who had transmitted this knowledge would be barred from it, the forces

The Synagogue of Toledo

that had driven us out would turn away from us to look to the west and would find a new world and riches there, and we, we would be left behind at this watershed, and would never know what kind of Islam it would have been that stayed in Spain and joined with the Jews in escorting the Spanish people into a future that was too big for them alone, a people who, as they overreached themselves fell victim to an isolation which, like ours, would last for centuries. Spain got rid of the Jews first, not knowing that it was amputating a limb from its own body, then it was our turn.

At one time, under different, more enlightened kings, emirs, rabbis, the three peoples of the book had lived side by side in configurations of separation and union such as the world would never see again, as if the

Alhambra, Granada

men of those earlier centuries had sought to prove it was possible. But because of the books we had translated the enlightened West would never again be the world of a single book. It was in such a hurry to move away from itself that in the ensuing anxiety and confusion it could not help becoming alienated from everything that was blatantly different, and thus our paths would diverge, three tongues that did not speak one another. And all the while the Alhambra would be there, as a reminder of the glory of the Nasrids, the final bloom. It would slumber and decay and rise again, and still the words of Ibn Zamrak would be inscribed in the stucco of the Hall of the Two Sisters, words which looked in the moonlight like drawings in crisp snow, and which could never lose their brilliance even in the language of the conqueror:

> Jardín soy yo que la belleza adorna:
> Sabrás mi ser si mi hermosura miras.
> Por Mohámed, mi rey, a par me pongo
> de lo más noble que será o ha sido.
> Otra sublime, la Fortuna quiere
> que a todo monumento sobrepase.
> ¡Cuánto recreo aquí para los ojos!
> Sus anhelos el noble aquí renueva.
> Las Pléyades le sirven de amuleto;
> la brisa le defiende, con su magia . . .*

Ponder, ponder in the Generalife among roses, palms and laurel, dark green pools with nenuphars and unseen frogs, the murmur of fountains under the cypresses, the white mountains in the distance. Théophile Gautier and Richard Ford, Washington Irving and Louis Couperus, they all walked in these gardens where thoughts follow the dictates of a double codex of joy and melancholy, only those wearing plastic armour can escape them.

The pink walls of the Alcazaba are tinged with a different shade each hour, the disciplined gardens around me, the eroded brick of the fortifications which seem to bleed in places, the gates and patios I saw that day, the excruciating intricacy and refinement of the decorations in

* I am a garden, adorned with beauty: / you will know me by gazing on my splendour. / For Muhammad, my king, I will be the equal / of the noblest man who ever lived or will live. / A sublime work, Fortune herself wished it / to surpass all monuments. / Such delight for the eyes! / Here burning desire is ever renewed. / The Pleiads serve as an amulet for my lord; / the morning breeze will protect him with its magic.

corridors and pavilions and then suddenly, in the midst of it all, rises Charles V's Renaissance palace like an intruder clinging to the remains of that vanished Orient, a proclamation of power and conquest.

A severe statement, a massive square enclosing a magnificent circle, a courtyard the size of a town square, one of the most lovely open spaces I know, as if even air could express the advent of a new era and a new might. Columns are curiously akin to trees, the multicoloured chunks of rock that nature once pressed into these marble trunks to make a superior kind of brawn, bear witness to a new military caste deploying its forces worldwide to destroy empires and amass the gold with which armies are fed, palaces built, and inflation generated. Skulls of oxen, stone tablets commemorating battles, iron rings decorated with eagles' heads that once served to tie up horses, winged women of great beauty reclining dreamily on the pediments, their broken wings half spread, there is no more tangible evidence of the confrontation that took place here than those two intertwined palaces: the one extroverted, out to seduce, the other haughty, self-absorbed; over and above the hedonistic bloom of the sultans the imperial edifice points to the might of other, earlier caesars who ruled Europe long before the armies of Islam came and went.

Below, past the popular Albaicín quarter, in the centre of Granada proper, which seems to have nothing to do with the forgotten world on high, stands the cathedral with the adjacent Capilla Real. There are the tombs of the emperor's parents: Joanna the Mad and Philip the Fair, and next to them, in a slightly lower monument, those of the Catholic Kings, Ferdinand and Isabella of Aragón and Castile. It is only when you climb the steps to the high altar (and manage to avoid being sucked into the profusion of gold on the retable) you have a view as over a land-scape, two enormous beds of Carrara marble, so very much larger than the leaden caskets faced with leather down in the crypt where they are truly dead, stored away, dead monarchs in boxes. Not so in the chapel, there they are merely asleep, softly breathing the marble air. Recumbent side by side, they strike a final majestic pose, Joanna with the sceptre on her breast, a forehead and nose forming a straight Greek profile, the lips curved in a smile without a hint of madness, a sleeping Athene with a crown. Philip's hand rests on the hilt of his sword pointing upwards over his shoulder, their faces are turned away from one another, the fifty years separating her death from his erased. Like a keeper going in to feed the lions, a young woman crosses the border between the people of marble and those of flesh and blood and steps into the enclosure. She shuts the little door behind her and runs her dust-cloth lovingly over the petrified faces, the pleated garments, the lion sentries, the folded hands.

The purpose of statues is to remind you of people, studying their likenesses is a way of being close to them, and so this is the third time

Queen Joanna (Juana la Loca), mother of Charles V, Granada

I am close to Isabella. The first time was at the tall statue in the centre of town, which shows her consulting with Columbus, heedless of the busy traffic all around, the second was with Pradilla's crazy painting of Boabdil's surrender: the fifteenth century served up in a nineteenth-century sauce, an anachronistic extravaganza. A cloudy sky, the Alhambra in the distance, on the left the mounted Moor, last sultan of Granada, wearing a slightly too deferential expression, and on the right – always the side of victory – Ferdinand, dressed in red like a page, and Isabella riding a grey horse, an actress wearing a crown. Boabdil holds the key of the city in his hand, but there is a measure of deception here, for Islamic Granada had for many years been open to the noblemen and merchants of Aragón and Castile, León and Andalusia; there was a steady flow of men and goods from Christian Spain through the harbour of Malaga, which was part of the sultanate, members of the military caste of Castile had fought as condottieres in the Muslim armies when it suited them, and until the coronation of Ferdinand and Isabella the two sides had lived in peace for fifty years. But all that was over now, Boabdil's key would serve not to open doors, but to lock them. The machinations of the church were to ensure that the kings would never keep the solemn promises they made when they signed the *capitula-ciones*. The truth behind the painting is a story of parting and deceit. Louis Couperus believes in the front, the bittersweet extravaganza:

> In the early hours of the morning the Bishop of Ávila arrives with a small retinue at the Gate of the Seven Storeys, at the foot of the Alhambra, in the forest of holm-oak. And as he approaches Boabdil rides down from the castle, surrounded by his loyal nobles. And he says: – Go, Lord, and take possession of my citadel, for it is granted to you by Allah to punish the Moors for their sins . . . Then the unfortunate man rides on. He is met at the next curve in the road by the Catholic Kings, Ferdinand and Isabella on horseback, and attended by splendidly dressed and mighty courtiers. In the distance, in the *vega*, wait the troops, their weapons glittering in the sun among the white tents of the encampment. The ceremony accompanying the surrender of the keys has been carefully planned. Boabdil is to remain on his horse, to spare him the humiliation of being obliged to kneel. He draws near. He greets his victors, and the victorious kings return his greeting as if they have never been enemies. Civilities are exchanged from the saddle, as if the occasion were of no particu-lar significance. But Boabdil's voice catches in his throat. Now he reaches the keys of Granada to Ferdinand, who accepts them with gratitude. Isabella, too, is moved, and offers some words of consolation to Boabdil. And even we are moved by the spirit of chivalry, also in that proud woman, after the intrigues of politics, after the bitterness of the long war . . .

The story behind the picture, the deceit, is recounted by another, far older voice from a manuscript in the Biblioteca Nacional in Madrid (*vitrina reservada* 245, fol. 87–8). It is the voice of Yuce Banegas, member of a prominent Muslim family in Granada:

My son, I am aware that you have little knowledge of what has happened in Granada, but do not be surprised when I remember it all, for not a moment passes without those troubles twisting my heart; there is not a minute, not an hour when they do not gnaw at my gut . . . I think no one has ever wept over a misfortune so great as that of the sons of Granada. Do not doubt my words, for I was a witness, I saw with my own eyes how the women of our families, married women and widows, were held up to ridicule and how more than three hundred young girls were sold at a public auction; I will say no more, it is too much to bear. Three sons I have lost, all three died for the faith, and I have lost two daughters and my wife, my only consolation is that one daughter has been spared: she was seven months old at the time. I do not weep over the past, for there is no way back. But, my son, I weep over what will yet befall you in this life, and over the future you may expect in this land, in this peninsula of Spain. May it please God, because of the holiness of the Quran, that what I have to say will prove to be unfounded, that things may not turn out as badly as I think, but our religion will inevitably suffer. What will the people say? Where have our prayers gone? What has happened to the religion of our forefathers? For a man with feeling there is room only for bitterness. And what hurts most is to think that the Muslims will grow to be exactly like the Christians: they will eat their food and adopt their style of dress . . . If it is already hard to survive after such a short time, how much harder will it be for people at the end of these times? If parents are already turning away from the faith, how will their great-great-grandchildren uphold it? *Si el rey de la Conquista no guarda fidelidad, qué aguardamos de sus sucesores?* If the king of the Conquest does not keep his word, what can we expect from his successors?

History has given him the answer he expected: the king and queen asleep in their capilla, Boabdil growing old at the court of Fez or being killed in the battle of Abu Aqba, defending a kingdom that was not his, expulsion, forced conversions in Spain, suspicion, the fanaticism of *limpieza de sangre*, "ethnic cleansing", of persecution and inquisition.

There's a saying that wisdom for the Chinese is in the hands, for the Greeks in the head, and for Arabs on the tongue. The *sound* of the text was almost holier than the text itself, and the sound was evoked by the appearance of the words. One more time, by way of farewell, I walk through the palace complex, through those seemingly endless strings of visualized sound, Kufic letters entwined in the tendrils of vines, peacock feathers, pineapples, serrated leaves catching on each other, by the dizzying effect of the repetitions, the starry skies of the ceilings, the lions' heads, the water, the script. Never again would the mihrabs of the Alhambra ring with the sounds of:

> *Bism illah ar-rahmān ar-rahīm*
> *Al-hamdu lillah rabb al-ʾālamīn*
> *Ar-Rahmān ar-rahīm mālik yawm ad-dīn*[*]

It is early in the morning, I have the gardens of the Generalife to myself, I am alone with the birds and the fountains, the red towers, the green of the trees touching the hem of the city down below. The *copla* is right, being blind in Granada must be the worst punishment of all, so give the blind man some alms:

> *Dale limosna, mujer,*
> *que no hay en la vida nada*
> *como la pena de ser*
> *ciego en Granada.*[†]

---

[*]In the name of God the compassionate the merciful / Praise be to God, Lord of the two Worlds / The compassionate the merciful, Master of the day of Judgement . . .
[†]Give him alms, woman / for in life there is nothing / to compare with the hardship of being / blind in Granada.

XXIV

On to the End of Time

Medieval performance in Madrid
Madrid on a cold evening ~ Departure for Gomera
A night in Tenerife ~ Gomera

I T'S COLD IN MADRID IN FEBRUARY, cold and clear. From the plane I can see the city lying beneath me, captive in that stony landscape that expresses the soul of Spain better than all else. There are two countries that inspire in me a special poignancy of arrival, Spain and my own country, the Netherlands, because the same thing happens there: anyone who flies in an ever lower circle around Amsterdam after a night on a plane and sees the white morning sun sparkle in the ditches and the soggy, low-lying, so very green meadows, knows that even after the hundredth time there is something more to be learnt about that country's relation to water, and hence about its history. It is between those two countries that I divide my life, I am at home and not at home in both. It is best to cover the distance between them by car, so you have plenty of time to adjust your sights, as it were. Flying is only a good idea when you're not too familiar with the country you're going to. So now my whole system needs to be readjusted, and I have learnt to do so radically, to plunge right in. A few hours after landing I find myself in a small, somewhat obscure chapel buried in the old part of town, where a mystery play is to be performed.

The Capilla del Obispo, chapel of the bishop, gradually fills up with people. The play is a success; the actors have toured half of Spain with it, and it has been running here for four months already. I read about the production recently in *El Público*, the Spanish theatre journal. The photographs illustrating the article showed a certain neo-Catholic crudeness, like Catholic art from the thirties: a joyful return to what was believed to be the simplicity of the Middle Ages. But the text itself dates from the thirteenth century. It was written by Gonzalo de Berceo, one of the first Spanish authors to express himself in the vernacular, although until now he meant little more to me than a street name. He wrote his *Milagros de Nuestra Señora* sometime between 1246 and 1252, and that alone is reason enough to be here. Preserved language coming out of living mouths, what more could you wish for! The décor is primitive, or basic, if you prefer: golden, ecclesiastical. An echo of Gregorian plainsong helps, too. It is very cold in the chapel, an age-old chill rises from the flagstones, and for an instant, absurdly, I feel drained and utterly displaced, as if I don't belong here, or, worse still, as if I'm not really here at all, but then suddenly a medieval figure stands before me and, in one of those harsh Spanish voices that must have sounded exactly the same seven centuries ago, recites:

> *Amigos e vasallos / de Dios omnipotent*
> *si vos me escuchássedes / por vuestro consiment,*
> *querríavos contar / un buen aveniment:*
> *terresdeslo en cabo / por buene verament.*
>
> *Yo, maestro Gonçalvo / de Verceo nomnado*
> *yendo en romeria / caeci en un prado,*
> *verde e bien sencido, / de flores bien poblado*
> *logar cobdiciaduero / pora omne cansado . . .*

"Friends and vassals" (I will give a rough translation). "Permit me to tell you a good story . . . I, master Gonçalvo, named Berceo, lay in a green meadow full of flowers, a most appealing place for a tired man . . ." There is a lengthy pause before the fateful "*and then*" but the diction draws you irresistibly towards some market square. The 2,000 kilometres I have travelled earlier in the day must be added to the seven centuries that have gone by since somebody wrote those lines; I am muddled by these impossible reckonings of disparate entities of time and space, and abandon myself to the wonders of the cleric and the flower, the pregnant abbess, the priest who could read only one mass. The scheme is always the same: something goes terribly wrong and great injustice is done, the victim appeals to the Virgin, after which the situation is reversed. It is a puppet show with life-sized dolls that are made to move and speak by the young actors. The dolls make a somewhat sugary impression, there is none of the menace and potency of Japanese Bunraku puppets (which are about the same size), but the immobility of their features accords with the emblematic nature of early Romanesque sculpture: grief, rage and innocence, it's all there, and it is because of this and also because of the Gregorian chanting, the strange, elongated and swollen string and percussion instruments, the Arab-Andalusian songs, the little portative organ played by astonishingly feminine, chaste-looking hands, the pale tunics, the high voices, the dry crash of the tambourine interceding in each line, that I notice I am being drawn into something that has not forfeited its validity, an archaic form of narrative poetry full of imagery and rhythm.

It is a victory of the vernacular over the decaying lingua franca of Latin:

> *Quiero fer una prosa / en romanz paladino*
> *en qual suele el pueblo / fablar con so vezino*
> *ca non só tan letrado / por fer otro latino . . .*

as Berceo himself put it – I wish to write in the language people speak to their neighbours, in Romanz. That's where the romance crept in – *roman*, a story written in the Romance language. I go out and buy the text edition of the *Milagros* the next day and discover that I can quite easily follow the early Spanish, more easily perhaps than Middle Netherlandish, I am ashamed to say. I soon come upon passages that were cut out of the performance, pure unadulterated medieval anti-Semitism of the kind that later, under Ferdinand and Isabella, would have such dire consequences. The Dark Ages is what they are called – an apt epithet if you yourself haven't lived in an age when that same darkness commandeered the enlightenment of technology, to set off a chemical reaction that culminated in the most appalling pogrom of all time.

As evening falls, the cold air of the high plateau and the cold of winter blend with the cold of the Plaza Mayor, high, the colour of granite, a square like a royal hall. Only the perimeter is thronged with people walking under the arcades, no one crosses the centre of the square, as if it's too empty, too awesome. The La Toja restaurant has a window display of flatfish, lobsters giving a slow terminal wink, living lampreys with triangular teeth glittering cruelly in their jaws. From a basement nearby comes the sound of old-fashioned piano music being played on an out-of-tune instrument, I go down the steps past counters laden with shellfish, sausages, chunks of lard and the foolish faces of sucking pigs. The waiters wear the breeches and slanting velvet berets with pompoms of the Andalusian bandolero, but they don't look as if they are in fancy dress – their faces are too broad, too rugged for that, their voices too harsh, and the looks they give the women entering the place too brazen. The piano is a mechanical one, and the man operating it knows the instrument's moods, for it is disposed to play a paso doble, but only on the condition that the man wearing the grey tweed jacket, red neckerchief and checked cap turns the handle with exactly the right rhythm, giving it an extra swing during the rests and speeding up and slowing down to make the tune sound just that little bit false, but still danceable. He has the features of Manolete, the greatest Spanish bullfighter of all, who was killed by a bull in 1947, the pale face of a saint with watchful eyes that would fail him when he needed them most.

The old carnation seller in the bodega next to the electronic slot machine with its warped Beethoven-jingle, the gypsy children begging for alms, the old women in black sitting on the pavement selling single cigarettes and cigars in the freezing cold of Madrid by night, those are the images I take with me as I fall asleep. The next morning I am woken by the hoarse shouts of a lottery-ticket seller, which come wafting up the five storeys of my hotel. *Tira para hoy*, result-drawing today, the *tee-ee-ee* is drawn out, the *hoy* like the crack of a whip, and I lie in bed and think of Proust lying in *his* bed and describing all those vanished street vendors' cries (artichokes, I seem to remember, mackerel, cheeses, each in its own distinctive singsong). Sometimes it is as if Spain is out to preserve the past for the rest of Europe; sounds, smells, occupations which have long since vanished elsewhere but which were once so much part of everyday life as to be considered part of nature, human voices uttering long-drawn-out cries, exhortations reverberating among the houses, fruit and fish and flowers in carts and donkey baskets, all those things that have been rendered obsolete by social justice, technology and big business, leaving the world both richer and poorer.

The day I leave for Gomera it is bitterly cold out in the street, as if the pavements are actually harder than in summer. It's about ten o'clock when I step outside, but the sun's rays are those of early morning, there is a thin, wispy haze in the air that makes the highly polished brass (gold's poor relation) gleam like a counter-sun. I must confess to being a magpie, I like things that glitter, and in Spain all the brass, like the ornaments here on the gate of an important bank on the Calle de Alcalá, is still rubbed to a high polish by pixies during the night. Of course there's plenty more to be seen in that pale morning light, but the first thing to strike me is the brass. Veiled in the morning mist, it is a proclamation

Monument to Alfonso XII, Buen Retiro Gardens, Madrid

of unseemly wealth, as if the vaults of the bank are filled with Moorish gold which, like the sun itself, will glow more brightly by the hour. What is the future of brass, I wonder. Will it die out for lack of hands to polish it? There is no brass to be seen in the modern architecture of northern Europe, and perhaps one day people will go to Spain just for the brass door knockers and stair-rods – mirrors of congealed sunlight in which your reflection is gilded and crazily distorted, and which, if you wait long enough, could be changed in the evening by a thousand fingerprints.

Sometimes you can tell by the look on people's faces whether you ought to buy a newspaper or not, you haven't listened to the radio, you haven't watched television, you step out of your hotel into a pristine day, and walk across the wide pavement to the newspaper kiosk. There are two ways of approaching a newsstand. One way is carefree: you don't know what news the paper will bring. The other way is more involved: you know something has happened, you have heard the news, and now you want to read about it. Newspapers no longer *are* the news, but they remain the only confirmation: here it is, the news, black on white. I can tell from the face of the woman coming in my direction that something is wrong. I can't tell what it is. She walks down the pavement wreathed in intimacy, holding the half-unfolded newspaper up in front of her. From the format I can tell it is *El País*. She's only 50 metres away from the kiosk, but she is engrossed in her paper, reading as she walks, her gaze fixed on the newsprint; and her expression is one of private grief. There is a certain intimacy in watching other people read, and it is intensified when they do so in public and are lost to the world. I go to the kiosk, buy the newspaper and read that Julio Cortázar is dead. I walk away from the kiosk, find a bench to sit on and turn to the inside pages for the obituaries. Meanwhile my thoughts drift to the books by Cortázar that I have read, I stare at the photographs of a man who looks surprisingly young for a seventy-year-old, and am reminded of the book I bought just a few days ago, in which he describes his last journey with his lover before she died of leukaemia. Now, barely a year later, he has died of the same disease. I have not yet read the book, but I've looked at the photographs of a man and a woman in or next to a Volkswagen van along the *autoroute*, for that was the extent of their trip: from Paris straight to the south of France without leaving the motorway. A strange parting, a story about himself, staged by a writer. It has become part of him, like the expression on the face of that woman whom he never set eyes on and who has vanished into the crowd with her paper. Her expression reminds me once more of Auden's poem on the death of Yeats: the writer vanishes into his readers.

During the next few days I see Latin sentiment working overtime. Perhaps it's just nostalgia, or indeed envy, but it does seem to me that writers are truly cherished as public property in this country – Mario Benedetti, Gabriel García Márquez, other, less famous names – pouring in from the far corners of the Spanish world come mourning, memories, grief. And again I am overwhelmed by the enormity of that linguistic domain stretching from Tierra del Fuego to Los Angeles, and the pivotal function therein, even today, of Spain and Madrid.

Then I allow myself to be lifted up from the wintry *meseta* and put down again in Tenerife, the giant's stepping stone to South America. The Spanish spoken there is more mellifluous, the vegetation leans towards the tropics. The Canaries signify goodbye to Europe. My destination is Gomera, but I won't be able to get there today. The island can only be reached by boat, and the ferry has left by the time the plane from Madrid arrives.

The hotels around the airport and the harbour 20 kilometres away are all booked up, but a taxi driver finds me a bed for the night in a film set: a small, white, unilluminated building that looms in the shadowy night. I can hear the ocean, the wind blows the sand in drifts along the deserted street. I bang on the door and after a while a man appears; without speaking, he takes my suitcase and puts it down in a bare stone hall. Up above there's a balustraded landing all around the hall, giving access to several small rooms without running water. This is the Spain I used to know. I ask myself what can be the purpose of the stone hall down below? I will never know. There is no furniture, there's nothing at all, and then the antithesis presents itself: the empty space is in fact full, full of nothing. This is not just wordplay. A space that is so outspokenly empty makes you stop and think about emptiness, which you would not have done had there been one or two chairs. As when your mind is utterly *blank* as the English say, and you want to think but can't think of anything to think about except the one thought that was already there to start with: that you want to think. I climb the stairs to the landing, inspect the room, count the two narrow iron cots, count the one, small picture of a non-existent chapel in a non-existent landscape. Looking outside I count *one* night and *one* storm, and for a long time I stand at the window and gaze at that most magical of nocturnal spectacles: a moon like a frenzied horseman charging at stolid, motionless clouds.

I have been to Gomera several times before, this is familiar ground. The island is steep and poor, you have to take a ship to reach it. That there is only one way of getting there intensifies the ritualistic aspect of the journey. It's always the same boat, the *Benchijijua*, white and quite big, the same Canary faces, so different from those on the Spanish mainland, the same two-hour crossing, in the course of which

Tenerife dwindles and the horrendous sprawl of tourist accommodation disfiguring the bare south coast fades from view, until only the white summit of the volcanic Teide is left hovering like the sail of a ghost ship. There's something peculiar about this crossing, and it is to do with memory. You've made that boat journey before, but you have also seen the ship arrive and depart so often that it is easy to imagine yourself floating on high like the Teide and surveying the world from aloft. An hour after disembarking I lean on the parapet in the parador's tropical garden overlooking the harbour and see the ship below, shrunken to minute proportions, enchanted. To be able to get on board I'd have to become as small as a thumb. It is lying there quietly for the moment, but soon it will cast off its moorings and I will follow its progress with my eyes. I often do that, and I know what I'm after: the moment *in between*. Best of all is when, on a clear day, the water takes on the oily sheen of satin. The ocean reflects the sunlight, the ship heads across the empty stretch of water, I will be able to see it until just before it reaches the other end. About fifty minutes after departure it enters that meta-physical zone that belongs neither to Gomera nor as yet to Tenerife, a speck drifting in the great gleaming expanse, and the traveller recalls the sensation of being half-way between two shadows rising from the sea. The shores of the looming phantoms are not visible from that point, there are just the two grey giants as a reminder of nature's fit of earth-shaking rage at some time during the Tertiary period. The traveller, in this case me, tries to imagine the din generated by that cataclysmic event, but in vain, for the ocean is too serene, while the volcano crowning the far island is like a monk seeking to blot out the memory of past violence. I see it all from a high vantage point and know that, if I were on board, I would turn at that precise moment to face Gomera, to watch it draw near just as Christopher Columbus did five centuries ago, but all you see is a great cairn of spewed-out rocks, congealed rage on which man cannot live. But I am not on board now, I am standing among jacaranda trees and bougainvillaea high above the town and the world. I can't recall quite when I was here last, and I am filled with a false sense of timelessness when I find that I recognize the trees as if they were people I have known, that the palms have not interrupted their conversation with the sky and the breeze during my absence. It's only I who have drifted away and drifted back again, and if that were not the case everything would be the same. To travel is to lead a fleeting existence, and that is still to my liking; each parting is a natural rehearsal, one shouldn't form attachments, for they jar with fate. I want to return here just as I return to other places, to measure my own transitoriness against the apparent *permanence* of my surroundings, until it's all over and someone else stands here in my stead, gazing over the town and the sea, another man who at this same moment (albeit in another day, a day not meant for me) harkens to the bronze bell of the restored church where Columbus once knelt to pray, and hears, above the peals of bronze, the rasp of a handsaw cutting off a piece of the afternoon and hence of time.

The town lies in a hollow which acts like a sound box, making it seem as if every intimate sound comes towards me. A tempting thought – I'd like to be sent to a world where no mortal had ever set foot. I would not come equipped with visual material, I would have only this one sound-track to illustrate my explanation of life on earth. Would it be possible? Gomera, the dull chop of a hoe in the earth, the sound of children laughing, an old motorbike chugging up the mountainside, the chatter of people on the quay, the mournful elephant's call announcing the arrival of the ferry. I ask myself what made me think these things and I know the answer: all those humble sounds represent the essence, the perfume of life on earth. How long would I need? Pretty long, my lecture would take a couple of years. I would have to explain what Spanish is, why different languages are spoken on earth and also why the same languages are spoken in different parts of the world. God knows, I might have to explain the whole process of evolution, how a motorbike works and the purpose of a hoe – no, perhaps they had better send someone else instead, and leave me here so that I can contemplate the little town lying below like a poem which, as poems do, sums up the life of man. I can see the black pebble beach and the dusty palm trees pretending to line a proper boulevard, the wooden *kiosco* where Francisco keeps his falcon and parrot in cages and where you can eat a poor man's lunch for a few pesetas – a plate with a chunk of fresh tuna with onions and potatoes in their skins and sea salt, served with *mojo rojo* or *mojo verde*, a sauce of red peppers or fresh *cilantro*, or a plateful of leftovers from previous days, a hodge-podge, *ropa vieja*, old clothes, as they say in Spanish – and where you will be served by one of Francisco's pretty daughters, who are named after three continents: Africa, Asia, America.

The town is so small from up here that I can take the Torre del Conde between forefinger and thumb, the tower where Beatriz de Bobadilla received Columbus who was on his way to America, although the name had yet to be invented, and who berthed here for his final *aguada*, to replenish his store of food and water. I see the narrow, tumbledown streets and the houses with their hand-made colonial shutters, the gleaming square with the elm trees, which are so old that the conquistadors themselves may well have sat in their shade. I see the newspaper kiosk where you can buy only *El Día*, which the *Benchijijua* brings over from Tenerife every day, no foreign newspapers, not even any papers from mainland Spain.

The sun will soon sink behind the mountains, which at this hour are being nuzzled by inflated clouds like water buffaloes. A flock of pigeons flies past *pizzicato*, their wings transparent against the sun. Turning to face inland I can see the roads, still in the sunlight, winding up the mountains, one leading to the top of the Garajonay and from there to the villages further down the coast, the other going across the island all the way to Hermigua in the north-east. But it takes a while to get there as there is much climbing to be done, there is no road along the coast linking the villages because the mountains are too high and the clefts too deep. Over a distance of no more than 30 kilometres you will encounter an array of different landscapes and climates, as if nature is offering samples of the various challenges she poses to mankind. The map of the Instituto Geográfico Nacional makes that quite clear. The round island, which is only 378 kilometres square, can best be compared to an old apple, first wrinkled and then petrified, a hard stone fruit with grooves and sharp edges, something you might cut your hands on.

Hundreds of names are scattered across the map of the small island. Roque del Herrero, Crux de Cirilo, Casas de Contrera, Cabeza de Pajarito, Lomito del Loro, Playa del Inglés, Charco de los Machos, Cueva de las Palomas, you can recite the names like a song, and in some of them you can hear an echo of the first inhabitants of these islands, the Guanches, a legendary race of tall, fair-haired folk whose blood has been absorbed into the successive waves of Spanish colonists and immigrants arriving in this archipelago over the centuries.

In the open patio of the parador, over which the darkening sky hangs like a living ceiling, there is a severe, monastic bench with an extra panel you can unfold to rest your book on, which leaves just enough room for a glass of sherry. The clouds paint a shifting roof overhead, the palm fronds stirring in the faint breeze trace their tremulous calligraphies, always different, the parrot in its gilded cage reels off a phrase in English with an undertone of homesickness, and there I sit, as if it has been thus ordained, on that curious bench with my unread book at my side, swathed in the tropics, thinking back on the old gentleman, long since dead, who taught me that "sherry ought to taste like a rusty nail". I think of my dead friend's white hair, his regimental tie, the slightly too garish ribbon of his obscure knighthood on the lapel of his outsize blazer. I drink to his memory, savour the rusty tang and think how right he was, then I wander down the lane from the parador towards the churchyard. With its vista on the ocean and the Teide in the distance, it is a fine place to rest.

Why on earth should anyone in this wind-blown spot in the ocean be called Walkiria? Her full name was Doña Walkiria Arteaga Herrera. Was her father an admirer of Wagner? No answer. Why did Señorita Carmen O. Hernández Padilla, who lived to be fifty-six, never marry? Her mother and her brothers will cherish her memory forever. Forever? And was Don Rafael Oliver Padilla, sergeant in the Guardia Civil, who lived to the ripe old age of seventy-eight, her father? The enamelled photographs from the kingdom of the dead reveal nothing. Some of the crosses lean sideways, others are broken or have toppled over. The names on most of the headstones are barely legible. The soil is red. The flowers are of plastic. The ocean is vast. Death means nothing, or at any rate very little. Meanwhile the sun must have set behind my back, and indeed without my permission, but the moon, flushed pink and full-faced like the sun, is attached to the same rope and is now being hauled up the slope of the volcano in the distance. And there it pauses for a moment, as if reluctant to take to the sky. What I see next is the following: the road at my feet, then a dip in the landscape, then the barracks of the 19th Infantry Division, then the ocean shimmering in the moonlight, then the Teide, and finally the celestial body which is now unceremoniously hoisted off the gentle slope into the heavens and instantly set alight in a silvery glow. Someone blows a trumpet – a beginner, by the sound of it – which is, given the time and location, deeply moving. Sunset, the rising moon, a clarion call in the dusk, military footsteps on the asphalt, the dead turn in their graves, children's voices float up from the barranco, the darkened flanks of the mountain behind me move gently, but they are sheep. Peace! Peace and cicadas sending out coded messages about Then and Now.

There are also human cicadas on the island, but they don't chirp, they whistle. Communication between one deep valley and the next was so difficult that the Gomerans, if that is their name, invented a special whistling language known as *silbo*, for sending messages across the mountains. The phenomenon attracted the attention of scholars in the last century, someone wrote a book about it (*El Silbo gomero, análisis lingüístico*, by Ramón Trujillo), which contains not only some crude (and hence all the more impressive) photographs of the dizzying heights the whistles had to scale, but also X-ray-like diagrams of the whistled words, sound waves forming wonderful abstract patterns, except that they aren't abstract, for those strange oriental-looking calligraphies represent common words such as rock, table and mass. There are still some *silbadores* left, the most famous being Don Gilberto Mendoza Santos, Don Olivier González Hernández and Don Vicente Herrera Ramos, and it takes persuasion for these human birds to give a demonstration of their mastery of this language, which is doomed to die out before long.

What will not die out is the geographical problem of Gomera itself. Immediately after leaving San Sebastián you enter a high, forbidding landscape where nothing can grow. Stone. The scenery stays the same until you reach the Garajonay National Park, but then the change is dramatic. Often there is a thick fog during the day. You drive through a phantom world to the rhythmical accompaniment of your windscreen wipers, and then you plunge down the other side of the island via the sharpest hairpin bends you have ever seen. Suddenly the sun bursts upon you with the force of an explosion and you are in the tropics, in a Balinese landscape dotted with palms, a domain of enchanting beauty ending in a valley with banana plantations, fields, a fishing village and an indigent population that must scratch a living from the soil and the sea, under the eyes of a tribe of German hippies who, like those Japanese soldiers in the jungles of Borneo, still haven't heard that the war is over, and who lounge around in the folkloric uniforms of a bygone philosophy.

On my last day on the island I find myself on a deserted stretch of coast. There are no people in sight, there is a football field sprouting two sets of goal-posts but not a blade of grass. Sand, and more sand. A crumbling fortress, quite macabre, Piranesi-sur-Mer. Two imploded houses. Leaden mountains to the left and right, and on the beach, where during heavy rainfall a stream gushes into the ocean, a couple of dead cats lying on their sides, their lifeless bellies agape. There is something deeply gratifying about the place. An artist has obviously been at work here, only he has forgotten to sign the picture. Beauty and decrepitude, the surf pounds and scrapes the fortress, dislodging invisible flakes of basalt with each surge, the lurid green wallpaper in one of the ruined houses droops like flayed skin, each time the surf recedes to gather momentum for the next onslaught the water swirling around the dark pebbles makes a sucking, clattering noise, the empty windows beat an indeterminate rhythm. The end of time is near.

XXV

Arrival

RITES OF INTROSPECTION. I catch myself muttering this silly, old-fashioned phrase under my breath. Sometimes the words come before the thoughts, or so it seems. Needless to say, everything contributes to invoking those thoughts, the place I am in, the sweeping landscape, the abandoned Cistercian monastery I am looking at, the icy February wind tugging at my clothes, the age-old iron cladding on the gate I am about to enter. Catalonia, Monasterio de Santes Creus – it is the umpteenth time I have been diverted from my planned route by a name, a word. Was it not my intention to drive to the monastery of Veruela, where I once began my wanderings over a decade ago? My goal was Santiago, but the roads frayed like rope, the years piled up, I drifted off course and became increasingly immersed in a Spain that is changing and a landscape that is constant.

Introspection – could it be that you turn further and further inward so that, even if the roads lead south or west, you feel as if you are plumbing the depths of a country's soul, and that you will find something there that you will never find anywhere else, however widely you travel? This affair spans forty years and, along with writing, it is the most constant feature of my life. And it is physical, too: a year without the emptiness of this land, without the colours of the earth and the rocks, is a year lost.

Ten years ago I resolved to drive to Santiago, and so, eventually, I did – not once but several times – but because I had not written about it, I still hadn't really been there. There was always something else that needed thinking or writing about, a landscape, a road, a monastery, a writer or a painter, and yet it seemed as if all those landscapes, all those stories of Moors and kings and pilgrims, all my own memories as well as the written memoirs of others pointed steadily in the same direction, to the place where Spain and the oceanic west come together, to the city which, in all its Galician aloofness, is the true capital of Spain.

I am about to undertake the journey one more time, and even now I know that I will be side-tracked, a tour being synonymous with a detour in my experience, the eternal, self-contrived labyrinth of the traveller who cannot resist the temptation of side roads and country lanes, of a branch road off a main road, of the sign pointing to a village with a name you have never heard before, of the silhouette of a castle in the distance with only a track leading to it, of the vistas that may lie in store for you on the other side of that hill or mountain range.

Perhaps it is best compared to a love affair, in all its elusiveness and imponderability. And this lover will never abandon you, which is a comforting thought. What am I looking for? The same sensations I felt thirty years ago, or ten, and I know I shall find them. The changes have usually occurred in the cities: they are fuller, more modern, the country-side has emptied. You see the signs of modernity there too, but the villages are besieged by the unchanged plateaus, the table mountains, the valleys. I am still in Catalonia now, tonight I will be in Aragón, and as I drive towards the interior the landscape will widen, unfold, become more parched and less tolerant of humans, until the traveller turns into a solitary swimmer in an ocean of earth stretching up to the horizon, and the earth will take on the colour of bone, sand, crushed seashells, rust, decaying wood, but even the deepest shades will be overlaid with a luminous glow that looks from afar like a veil, as if to protect the eyes from so much vastness and light. In the distance rise churches and convents which commune with visible eternity, they have something to say about the unconscionable past that has been conserved, for whoever comes looking, in the heat and cold of an extreme climate.

Long ago, before I was aware of such things, these landscapes must have invaded my consciousness, an answer to my youthful longing for the kind of infinity that is to be found only in the ocean or the true desert. I know the locutions are outdated, but that doesn't bother me, I don't mind being misunderstood on this point. After all, who can one talk to about fulfilment, or enlightenment? In *A qué llamamos España* (What We Call Spain) Pedro Laín Entralgo examines the effect of the colour of the Castilian landscape on those who look carefully, and Ortega y Gasset in *Notas de andar y ver* (Notes on Walking and Seeing) refers to the geometry of the plain, a "sentimental geometry for the benefit of the people of Castile and León", in which the poplar tree is the vertical element and the hunting hound the horizontal, and in a flash you recognize them, sliced out of the emptiness: horizontal and vertical demarcations to guide the eye and save it from losing its bearings in that boundless space.

My home is not Castile, nor is it León. One does not choose the country of one's birth. The country I come from has its own brand of geometric absolutism – the plane of the polder overhung by the rectangular sky. Mondrian could not have been born anywhere else. No distractions, no temptations, utter visibility. That's where Calvinism and certain forms of Spanish Catholicism come within touching distance. But Holland has forfeited its space and as a consequence, oddly enough, its time too. When I go there nowadays I taste a certain transitoriness, a neurotic instability, as if everything and everyone is in a hurry to shake off their own past in order to be or to become different. Spanish friends of mine feel the same way about their own country since the death of Franco. They talk about *transición* and *movida*, and I would be a miserable traveller indeed if I did not see how much has changed; sometimes the change is so dramatic that I forget that I also lived and travelled in Franco's Spain in the days of censorship and bigotry, of Falange uniforms, death sentences and executions, holy masses for the Blue Division, which fought beside the Germans in Russia, the banished writers, the bitter reticence of those who had fought on the losing side.

All that has vanished, save from the heads of those who suffered – sometimes it seems as if that vast country has sucked it all up like a sponge, has let it dry and evaporate along with the memories and the blood, a few more scars in the tanned bull's hide, scratches in a history that refuses to end, the saga of Romans and Moors and Jews and Visigoths, of foreign invasions and the slow reconquest, of discovery and colonization, of oppression and civil war. I don't suppose you can reasonably make this connection between space and time. Yet it seems to me that Spain, still the emptiest country in Europe, has preserved a different sort of time, as if topical issues, however vociferously debated, have less relevance, and so lapse into an infinitely slower measure. Perhaps it depends on where you go, because what I'm after is deceleration, and regardless of the laws of the land, I find what I am looking for. In a landscape where a solitary tree is visible miles away, time is measured by different standards. It is that disparity that I have come for.

No, I didn't ponder all these things in the biting wind outside the gate of the monastery. Sunshine in the sheltered courtyard, the dead who have rested here for close on a thousand years know more than I do. When I stand still the light etches my shadow on the wall between those multi-lobed Gothic arches, when I walk my footsteps measure the distance from one grave to another, from Ramón d'Alemany to Guillem de Claramunt, both killed during the capture of Majorca in 1230.

In the silence I hear a woman's voice talking in Spanish about an "English sculptor" who came to live here, but when the hand that goes with the voice is raised to point out the capitals in the cloister I understand that she means not now, but ages ago, in the time of once upon a time, and it is from that time that the undamaged sandstone figures gaze out at us, the lion with the sun's head, the images of Creation, of Eve emerging from Adam's rib, of original sin and the expulsion from paradise, of monsters and taunters and of Cain the farmer and Abel the shepherd, the eternal panopticon to which we are becoming progressively blind, until our dwindling knowledge reaches the point where the whole show means as little to us as a symposium of Greek gods.

The ever accelerating mutations of progress have eroded the idea behind these images, leaving no more than a fable that you may or may not have heard. During my journey these thoughts have to be pondered over and over again. This is not intended as an exercise in nostalgia, but such encounters always lead to confrontation, something collides with something else, the definite past is still present in the stones, its age alone is enough to lend it gravity. But what does a thing mean when it has dropped out of its meaning, when it no longer means what it meant? Does that leave simply art, which is both accessible and not accessible? Or is it the very confrontation, the realization that you do not recognize the ideas of your own kind, that makes you so sure that one day your own thoughts too will fail to be understood? In that case what have I been looking for during all of my travels? Perhaps it is the thrill of danger that such musings inspire, the sensation of the carpet being pulled out from under you, the desperate diachrony of those who venture further into the past than is good for them, not because they want it back so as to reinstate it as a never-ending present in the way fundamentalists do – quite the contrary, it is "because they", as Ortega y Gasset says, "love the past for its own sake", that which has ended and yet will never end because it lives on in the present.

A Romanesque arch and Gothic gate usher me into the church. "It is with landscapes as with architecture," Unamuno said, "nakedness is the last aspect you learn to appreciate." The interior is bare, austere, light, the walls high and undecorated, the kind of space in which you yourself become a mathematical focus with lines constantly being projected from your moving body to the planes, rectangles, sources of light around you. It is not until the twentieth century, with architects like Adolf Loos, that the functional forthrightness of the unadorned Cistercian style returns, and although the functions have changed, the ideal is the same: renunciation of superfluity. The fact that I am all alone here adds to the austerity. Aragonese kings rest here, Pedro el Grande and Jaime II with his wife Blanca of Anjou, the great king from the thirteenth century in his never-desecrated porphyry tomb, conqueror of Sicily, excommunicated by the pope who gave preference to a Valois in Sicily. They lie still, they have danced their dynastic dance to the end, conquering Sicily, Corsica, Sardinia, Majorca, losing those territories and recapturing them, monarchs of a kingdom with 800,000 subjects. This monastic church is the extension of their tombs, their paladins lie buried beside them, their names and ranks chiselled in the freestone alongside the marble oriental lions bearing the royal casket. When they slide the stone lids off their resting places they will recognize everything around them, except me.

Outside there are orange trees, a mossy fountain in a stone arbour, the whisper of water, wine cellars with empty barrels, a deserted library, the tombstones of abbots in the chapterhouse floor, names and dates. By the year 1830 it was all over, the monasteries were taken over by the liberal government, the monks moved away, the decay, which is now, very slowly, being repaired, set in. From up here I have a sweeping view of the landscape with the road curving northwards, to Huesca and the snow-capped Pyrenees beyond.

Just one more time. Churches, landscapes, nostalgia, the passion for ruins. Someone once asked me why I am so fond of the *meseta*. Taken aback, I said: "Because I think that's what I look like inside", which is precisely the kind of subjective aestheticism that Goytisolo holds against Unamuno, but Goytisolo himself is uncertain, because he too acknowledges that industrialization and tourism are corroding the soul of the *meseta*. He can't make up his mind. On the one hand he says that Unamuno and, to a lesser degree, Azorín saw the deserted landscape through the eyes of the aesthetic-religious military caste of Castile (significantly, Ortega's *Tierras de Castilla* contains a passage where the author muses about El Cid having once ridden across the same landscapes where he, Ortega, now travels with his donkey), but on the other hand he acknowledges that the bleakness of the land, when you have escaped from the spiritual bleakness of the corrupted coast, possesses a majesty of its own.

Once there were forests in Spain, there are paintings and stories enough to prove it. The trees were felled and uprooted in a secondary, negative act of creation: no rain without trees, no trees without rain. I suppose I should regret this deeply, but I cannot. This is the last refuge from the fullness of Europe. And it is by no means dead. I see flocks the colour of the earth, a bird of prey tracing its slow letters in the sky and dropping like a stone before winging away with a snake in its beak. Only the people have gone, leaving their houses behind. It's very strange, as if a war has raged here. At first you can't believe it, surely not everyone has gone? However, when you come closer you know, you step gingerly, you think there might still be a corpse lying in one of the houses.

This is the north of Spain, I am driving along the road from Boltaña to Broto. I was here in 1957, perhaps this village was still alive then. I walk over a muddy path leading to the first low houses, the wind tugs at the loose shutters, a moaning sound. *Prohibido el paso*, it says, *pueblo en ruina*, and so it is, a whole village in ruins, balconies of rusty, twisted iron, windows without panes, lamps dangling from their sockets, everything demolished, emptied, withered bramble bushes sprawling across flaked windowsills, ilexes growing crookedly into the houses, I clamber over the debris of stones. It is sad, this world without people, the useless, broken objects, bits and pieces they could not or would not take with them. Did they all leave together? Were there children among them or were they all old? No voices, no footsteps, just the inaudible rhythm of the infinitely slow process of decay, collapse, pulverization. If I come back in a hundred years' time all this will never have existed.

My arrows are incapable of flying in a straight line, something always crops up – the temptation of a map, a sentence I have read, a photograph, a reproduction, the sound of a name – to lure me off my course which will in retrospect look like a single straggling journey, the detour as itinerary. This time it was all these things at once: a book (*Elegía*) on Antonio Saura, containing illustrations of the ceiling he painted for the *Diputación* (provincial government) of Huesca. So I had to go to Huesca, but also to Roda de Isábena, because of the early mural paintings that inspired Saura. Two artists, eight centuries, Aragonese continuity. I look up Roda on the map. It is situated in the foothills of the Pyrenees, which can be reached by white roads only, and it's quite far, the road goes all the way across the Sierra del Castillo de Lugares.

That the village has not yet been totally abandoned is probably due to the church alone. The place is as quiet as a crypt. A very old man sits dozing in the sunshine with a dog curled up at his feet. There is no one else to be seen, and the church is locked. But a woman emerges from nowhere and lets me in.

The church dates from 1018, she tells me as if she herself witnessed its construction, and she talks of counts and bishops and founding fathers as if they were still alive. She draws my attention to the funerary inscriptions along the capitals and walls of the cloister, a flow of obituaries in twelfth-century letters so crisp that the artisan who chiselled them must have finished his work only yesterday. The sarcophagus of Raimundo, who was prior here, and who would later be canonized, an angel with the head of another angel resting on his arm, the story in pictures along the sides of the stone casket, annunciation, visitation, birth, flight into Egypt, faint murals in faded colours, the woman describing what I see before me and at the same time telling me that the village population is shrinking rapidly, that the young people no longer want to stay.

There is a certain transparency about such stray hours: the inscriptions and images take their place in the long row of other impressions, the detour has cost me half a day, I could have driven straight on, I will forget the details, confuse them with others, but I will not forget the essence, which is becoming increasingly associated in my mind with silence, although I am not yet sure where it is leading me.

Towards evening I arrive in Huesca, a slate sky hangs over a park with tormented plane trees, in winter the strangest trees of all. You see them everywhere, in Burgos, Logroño, San Sebastián, naked, stiff armies in long formations, at night they march in your dreams. There's a concert going on in the *Diputación* that I have no desire to attend, and I ask if I may slip in to see Saura's painting. Yes that's all right, someone switches the lights on for me, and to my surprise the room actually contains three leather couches specially for visitors to lie on and stare up at the ceiling, and that is how I see it – supine, with a wild planetary swirl overhead, a vast confluence of colourful bodies which have broken free of their own contours, in a far corner the spidery signature of the artist. For a moment I try to imagine a distant future 800 years hence, in which someone lies staring at this very ceiling, just as I looked up at an 800-year-old painting earlier today, but I don't succeed, so much permanence is not for the likes of us, no more than are carved sarcophagi. We are in too much of a hurry to remain dead for so long.

Torla. In 1957 there was only one solitary inn. I had arrived by bus, an ancient bus with cardboard boxes on the roof, and wooden crates with chickens. Farmers smoking *Ideales*, a heavy, pungent aroma. Trout, and goat meat and great loaves of bread. I wish I could glimpse myself as I was then. I would not recognize myself any more than I recognize the village, what with the hotels, pensions, and the entrance to the National Park of Ordesa. I drive up the mountain until the snow gets too thick and I see the high peak of the Monte Perdido, the lost mountain. The map of this area is dotted with deer. There were still bears here in the fifties, and I remember thinking then, that one day I might see a bear. Perhaps I still think so. I have cut the engine to hear the silence, and I sit down on a rock in a snow-covered field. An ensemble of birds is busy playing its eighth symphony, and if I listen carefully my young man's ears will hear the bears playing the bass.

Jaca lies on a high plateau bordered by two rivers, the Gállego and the Aragón. The pilgrims coming from the north could choose either Jaca or Pamplona, Aragón or Navarre. If you opted for Navarre, then you would travel through the mythic setting of Roland's defeat by the Basques, through the forest of the blossoming lances, where 53,066 armed girls stood in for the dead soldiers of Charlemagne's army. But I am not coming from the north. The mountains that the pilgrims risked their lives to cross lie white and glistening to my right, I am heading for the low, broad shape of the cathedral of Jaca as purposefully as a sailor steering for home.

It does exist, love for a building, however difficult it may be to talk about. If I had to talk I would have to explain why it should be this particular church that, when I can no longer travel, I will want to have been the last building I have seen. It was the first Romanesque cathedral to be built in Spain (1063), but it is not just its venerable age that inspires awe – it certainly is ancient, but it doesn't *feel* old. The building is alive,

Detail of a capital in Jaca Cathedral

you can slip it on like a coat, when I go inside I draw it tight around my body, as if it is made not of stone but of another, recondite material which is a blend of stone, light, proportion, sheen, intimacy. And each time I return here, no matter how long my absence has been, the same joyful emotion comes over me.

The floor is wooden, the stone from which columns were hewn and capitals carved came from Castiello nearby, and is slate-grey. Not my favourite shade, but here it works special wonders: the columns appear to recede, yet they seem capable of reversing that movement at any moment to incline forward, and this is why they seem to breathe, to be alive.

The shade of the exterior is more like red sand, the church has draped the city around itself, as a natural environment. Shops, a small square, a woman selling vegetables and fruit, the triple-lobed apse, the

Jaca Cathedral

dromedaries and lions, the basilisk in the cornice, mythic beasts. In the south portal Abraham raises his knife to sacrifice Isaac, while King David and his company make music: the king holding his stringed instrument upright on his knee and resting his long, narrow feet on the base of the column, his courtiers playing the horn and the harp and other instruments unknown to me. A death announcement has been nailed to the wooden door; every few minutes someone stops to read it.

The main entrance is situated on the west, a forecourt, an atrium in which to pause and talk or take shelter from the snow. Over the doors a semicircular tympanum with two lions as in a Mozarabic manuscript, beneath the one a recumbent figure of a man and a snake, beneath the other, which is keeping a bear at bay with his right paw, a basilisk. They flank a wheel containing the Christogram, but they themselves are Christ in his apocalyptic leonine guise. Animal tales! Gods as animals, sons of gods, devourers of monsters, if I am not careful I will, under this stone relief, gradually turn into a Babylonian, a man who recognizes the double feline apparition as a divine being, but who is unable to read the later Latin words of warning under the lions' paws:

> *Vivere si qveris mortis lege teneris*
> *Hvc svplicando veni renvens fomenta veneni.*
> *Cor viciis mvnda, pereas ne morte secvnda.*[*]

The passage leading to the Diocesan Museum is guarded by a sallow-faced priest. He is muffled in a black scarf, knitted for him by his ancient mother no doubt, and wears the pale, long-suffering expression of a prospective saint. He asks me where I'm from. Ah, Holland! The Eighty Years' War! The Reformation! And he sets about explaining his view of the affair, how the Dutch never did understand the Spaniards, which is why we are still angry with them, and I tell him I'm not angry with them, that we stopped being angry a couple of centuries ago, and that I'd like to go in now, to see the Romanesque murals. I leave him behind, mumbling, all alone with Luther and Calvin and Alba and Egmont and Hoorne and Philip, but I must go much further back, past him and his sixteenth century, to the faded, crumbling remnants of paintings, fragments, hands, half-vanished faces. Time itself has become the artist here, a painter who knows that less is generally more so far as beauty goes: time has scratched the surface, erased contours, retained the one and rejected the other, and that is the way I see it all, a charred figure in the shape of a woman, a negative crucifixion, an image you recognize because of what is missing. The absence of shoulders, heads, attitudes, makes the scenes abstract, enigmatic, evocative, empty spaces among the members of a saintly tribe, each with his own golden nimbus, as if there once lived a race of men born with a radiant disc of gold fixed to the back of their skull.

---

[*] If you wish to live, you who are subject to the laws of death, come here and implore, refuse the poisoned food of the world, purify your heart of vice lest you die a second death.

It is Friday evening in Jaca, and I see the same sight here that I will see in Logroño, Burgos, Santiago: streets thronged with young people, there seem to be hundreds of cafés and they are all overflowing. It is cold, but no one stays at home, a confounding mêlée of wriggling spermatozoa. Disco music ricochets against the old walls, the contrast with the daytime scene could not be greater. What are they after? You do not see this kind of crowd in Berlin or Amsterdam, this blend of desperate laughter and boundless boredom, they stream in all directions, surging in and out of the cafés, catching each other's glances, searching, flirting, drinking, shouting, forming chains and disengaging again, stampeding, deaf to the clamour of their own strident voices. Anyone still at home has to be mad, anyone reading a book is banished, ostracized, the ecstatic faces with the glinting eyes jostle to the thump of the music, the electronic whine of slot machines, the non stop blue shimmer of television sets no one is watching now. Over all those heads hangs a cloud of unfulfilled or unfulfillable craving, and at the same time a premonition of a reckoning that will be presented to someone in the not too distant future.

I am reminded of a different ecstasy, that of the crowd in Madrid, so many years ago, when it was clear that the socialists had won the elections and the women were chanting: "*Felipe, capullo, queremos un hijo tuyo.*"* The time seemed to have come at last for Spain, confined for so long within the walls of its own house, to struggle free and turn to face Europe, to drive out the shadows of the past. There was a lot of catching up to do, and it was duly done, with a zest that left the land gasping for breath, and it is with the same euphoria that people take almost everything in their stride, rising prices, ostentatious materialism, the loss of things that will be hard for later generations to recover. And behind that memory of election day lurks another memory, of a much older Spain, beset by other disparities, when men paraded the streets wearing German helmets. They were the same helmets I had seen in my own war only ten years earlier, and somehow I felt they didn't look right on those young Spanish heads.

But then I see an even earlier crowd, so different from the crowd today, and also different from the joyful crowd on election day and the crowd watching the marching soldiers: an intimate, swirling mass of people, a sight never to be forgotten. It was in Salamanca. I was staying

* "Felipe, rosebud, we want to bear your son."

in a pension on the Plaza Mayor, a square like a stone-built living room. It was 1954. From the balcony I looked out over the perfectly square arcaded plaza. No pavements, no distractions – and within that geometric figure revolved another figure, a circle formed by students and teachers, some walked backwards while others walked forwards – however odd it sounds – talking to each other. I had never seen anything like it, and I was filled with the same emotion as when I saw, that same year, Catalonian exiles dancing the *sardana* in Perpignan: communal spirit that is still moulded to a form, the form of dance, of the likewise circular discourse, the sound of which reached me on the balcony in a blur of words, like a long, unintelligible poem.

The *sardana* is a tempered dance, which only flares up now and then, and when it does it is always kept in hand. The same could be said of that peripatetic discourse taking place down on the square, there was no trace of urgency or tension, and I stood there in my Nordic, autistic persona on that balcony and I was jealous. Has that Spain vanished? I don't know, surely the constants of history cannot be discarded quite so speedily? Perhaps the old Spain is just lying low until the sudden squalls of misconceived modernity blow over. Or perhaps I am just hopelessly old-fashioned and sentimental about the wrong things. Through a light snow I walk to my hotel, the flakes resting like weightless flowers on my coat, a decorated pilgrim. In my room I take one more look at one of the reproductions I bought from the pale priest earlier in the day: Adam and Eve, a thirteenth-century fresco which should have been left where it belonged: in the church of Urríes. Instead of the uniform gold that was once the background there are now two pink figures dancing or standing in front of a cracked, scratched wall, and this gives the scene, which is in itself unintentionally lugubrious, a sting of modernity. Our earliest ancestors are obliquely portrayed as long, pink, naked bodies. Eve's breasts point downwards, they are a different colour to the rest of her skin, faint white lines indicate the ribs of both figures, the bellies are strangely distended, the sexual organs elongated. She is busy feeding him that wretched apple, so robbing us of eternity, and her smile is as sly as a witch's.

The next morning banishes all those images. I drive into the mountains, towards the monastery of San Juan de la Peña. The road winds through

Giant stone oak on the way to San Juan de la Peña

the Sierra de la Peña, vistas, ilexes, peaks on the horizon. There is no place of refuge between the monastery and Jaca, and I wonder how the pilgrims fared here.

The last time I was in these parts was with a Dutch television crew; I had set off from California, where I was then living, to be the presenter in a film about the pilgrimage to Santiago. Something had gone wrong after take-off in Los Angeles. Once we were airborne the pilot was unable to get the landing gear to retract. We had to turn back, but before we could do so we had to shed 140,000 litres of fuel, and so we flew around spurting four plumes of terrifying white foam, and for a while thoughts of death hovered about the plane. Confusion when we finally landed, my suitcase was lost, the camera crew were expecting me in Pamplona, it was December and I had no proper winter clothes. So there I stood, from one moment to the next so it seemed, in that deserted monastery clinging like a swallow's nest to the dizzying high bluff, and everything that had happened in the preceding 24 hours, from the too-calm voice in which the pilot had announced the problem up to and including those ominous chalky jets of fuel shooting past my window, and the Japanese tourists with their cameras crowding around me because my seat afforded such a good view of it all, the pell-mell change of planes and the subsequent flight via Miami to Madrid, and then the abrupt silence of that mountain eyrie, the blind, bulging eyes of the figures on the capitals in the cloister, the graves of the Aragonese monarchs, the rock face that seemed to tower into the sky, all of it conspired to make my standing there absurdly unreal, as if I had become transparent and as if the words I was saying (about Jerusalem the heavenly city, the theme of one of the capitals) were nothing but air that could never be caught by a microphone.

But again there is something in the offing here. These monasteries lead the traveller quite a dance. The further I drive the more ice there is on the road, the alternating patches of sunshine and shade have made the snow melt in places and freeze over in others, the car begins to slide, it slithers downhill crosswise. Instinct tells me that I should turn back, but I am too stubborn. When I finally draw up in front of the monastery it is closed "for the winter".

It is the same rock face as ever, and I gaze up at the few capitals I can glimpse from here. All around there stretches a forest of pine trees. Their rustling needles are laughing at me, and when I try to drive back I get stuck in the snowdrift on the first bend, and then I start sliding backwards, slowly down the steep slope, until I come to a standstill facing the verge. There is nothing for it but to wait. In the silence I will be able to hear people coming. And then I do hear a purring sound, very faint at first, then swelling and fading by turns, a car is approaching, and the sound of the engine is muffled by each bend and released again as if it were its own echo. But it is not what I thought, for there are two cars coming from opposite directions towards the idiot from the lowlands who thought he could drive here without snow chains. They've got chains, of course, and the two drivers set about rescuing the stranger with a courtesy that is not of this age. Judging from the licence plates, we are all strangers here. One of the men has a spare set of chains, and together they secure them around my tyres. I drive my car out of the danger zone and walk back to my saviours. By a blessed chance I have two copies of the Spanish version of my novel *In the Dutch Mountains*, and I can see them thinking surely there aren't any mountains in Holland, but it is too complicated to explain, and besides, what can you expect of a man who goes driving in the mountains in February without chains?

I know I must drive west, towards Navarre, towards Santiago. I know which places are on the route and which I will have to pass by if I am ever to get there. I must be strict, it would take me a year to revisit all the places I have been to before. I keep my transgressions to a minimum. For a brief moment, as if just to be sure everything is still there, I stand in the mysterious, low crypt of the monastery of Leyre, among the wide, chalk-coloured columns with their Visigothic motifs. This is crazy, one should take the time to let it all sink in, and the same is true of the magic of the priory which, by dint of the perspective feat of three successive high arches inclining towards the apse, seems to gather itself up and take flight.

I ought to have a parallel life, a sea of time in which I would be able to remake those earlier journeys in the course of my present journey, to Silos, to León, to Oviedo. As it is, I must distil that reservoir of time from my own memory, but even if the appropriate images are evoked they can never be enough – it is all about proximity, tangibility, running your fingers over the stone, and about the impossible, because what you really want by now is not another life but a longer life, one in which you go round and round in the same circles of leave-taking and revisiting until such time as you feel so sated and tired that you lie down in a nook of one of those chapels, and slip into a dream of stone.

However, that time has yet to come. Parallel time is not part of my mental luggage. I possess but one mortal body, which cannot be in two different places at once and which now takes me outside to look out over the *embalse de* Yesa, a large artificial lake of steely blue still water in which are reflected the dark outlines of the surroundings hills. This region was fraught with danger in the old days; Aymery Picaud, a monk in Poitiers and co-author of the *Codex Calixtinus*, the first pilgrims' guidebook, issued dire warnings about the savage inhabitants of Navarre. He warned against all manner of other dangers, too, the only people not under suspicion being those of his own native region, it seems. He had undertaken the journey himself, so he knew what he was talking about, but his experiences did not inspire love for his fellow men: the ink in which he dipped his pen was concocted of sulphur and gall in some squalid corner of hell. "For one sou and a half," he wrote,

> a man of Navarre will stab a Frenchman to death. The people of
> Navarre are full of malice, swarthy of complexion, ugly of appear-
> ance, depraved, perverse, despicable, disloyal, corrupt, lechers,

drunkards and past masters of all forms of violence, wild, savage, treacherous, deceitful, blasphemous and foul-mannered, cruel and quarrelsome, incapable of honourable behaviour. All vices come easily to them.

In short, charming folk.

Yet the pilgrims of old, trekking from hospice to hospice, separated by an eternity from the security of their homes and having another thousand kilometres to go, were undaunted. Picaud's admonitions concern "the barbarian language of the Basques" and "ferrymen who try to drown you", robbers and swindlers, wolves and ice and snow, not to mention the myriad perils preying on the soul. There is hardly a tympanum that does not feature the damned: as in Sangüesa, they tumble head over heels into the netherworld of hell, trumpets are blown, demons with great jowls await the moment when they can sink their sharks' teeth into all that soft, decaying flesh. The horror of these images is always just a fraction more eloquent than the ecstatic glow of eternal recompense.

View of the artificial lake at Yesa

Who on earth goes all the way to Uncastillo? The village is tucked away in such a far-off corner miles from anywhere that it must have been the sheer blankness of that area on the map that lured me there in the first place, or was it the name? I can't remember which.

Each time I arrived at the wrong hour for the church and the right hour for the butcher. Perhaps the church was permanently locked, and I contented myself with the small triple arch above the southern doorway, the animals holding their heads above the door frame and their paws underneath, the man holding open the jaws of a monster, the little figure with the pitcher, the twosome sharing the same saucer of food, stone fairy tales first observed many years ago, the sun at its zenith, a fire without flames. I was hungry, that first time, and as I stepped into a butcher's shop the butcher himself emerged from his kitchen, a steaming dish of blood pudding in both hands.

Rio Riguel is the name of the river that flows there. I looked for a place to sit and arranged my prizes around me: white glistening cheese, bread of the kind you see in a still life by Meléndez, the blood pudding a

Detail of a capital, Uncastillo

deep purple close to black. It is made with cinnamon and rice, the grains sparkle like tiny chips of enamel. I remember a flock of sheep on the far side of the almost dry river bed, whispering poplars, the motionless shepherd and his dog tracing wide, nervous circles around the flock. Shepherd, flock, river, bread – when I visited Uncastillo again years later it was for the sole purpose of reliving that experience.

It must be a form of presumption, this desire to weave a strand of eternity into your own life, but my presumption went unpunished this time: when I stepped into the butcher's shop the butcher was just emerging with a steaming dish of sausages as he was on the first time, and the thought struck me that he and I could continue this *pas de deux* for centuries, he the butcher and I the customer, and that the church would forever etch the same shadow on the pavement with pebbles arranged in a pattern of little squares. So this is my third time here, and it is winter. The butcher is still there, but his sausages are cold, like the ground by the river. The flock and the shepherd are gone, but the stone man still holds open the monster's jaws, and that is the only form of eternity there is. The butcher smiles when I tell him my story, but perhaps he thinks I'm soft in the head, and then I succumb once more to the vast plain.

Logroño, Navarrete. Enigmas that belong to this road: suddenly I glimpse something without seeing it, something in a wall, words, flowers, something that asks for attention. I park the car and walk back. "*Peregrino, reza una oración en memoria de Alice de Graener, que falleció el 3 7 1985* – Pilgrim, say a prayer in memory of Alice de Graener, who died here on 3 July 1985 on her pilgrimage to Santiago de Compostela, and in memory of all pilgrims who died on the way." The text is given twice, in Spanish and in Dutch, and underneath it someone has chalked, in Spanish: "Alice – good luck on your new road." I see that the wall belongs to a cemetery, but I can't find her grave there. Two small reliefs have been placed in the wall, one of them shows a young man with a pilgrim's staff walking towards Santiago, the other shows a young woman, little more than a girl, sitting on a stone bench, and she too turns an anxious face towards Santiago while her feet rest on Saint James' pilgrim shell. Here and there against the wall lean plastic flowers, a thought, a memento for someone who was on her way, someone who would not arrive, who was destined to go elsewhere. The traveller proceeds

Art nouveau scallops in Santiago de Compostela

Tomb of Doña Urraca López de Haro, Cañas Monastery

on his journey with the mystery of who she was and what had happened to her.

Burgos, Castrojeriz, Frómista, Carrión de los Condes, Valencia de Don Juan, León, the Panteón de los Reyes, each name a temptation and a memory, like sirens they rise up on either side of the road to seduce me – but I have adopted Odysseus' ruse and sealed my ears with wax, I will not hear them and I refuse to see them. One day I will sell my soul to the devil in exchange for an extra year of Manichaean pilgrimage, but for the moment it is forbidden.

Once only do I allow myself to be lured from the road, the song from afar being so ancient and so oriental that I cannot resist. At the River Esla I turn right onto a narrow, winding road. Oxen, carts laden with manure, people everywhere at work, the land is fertile in this valley. The wintry clothing gives a northern aspect to the scene, a man behind a plough, a woman carrying a bundle of red alder twigs on her head, a hunter with his dog. I know that what I am about to see does not accord with the almost Dutch-seeming landscape: the grace of the Orient that has lost its way in the north, but that is precisely what brings me back here, the shock of inconsonance.

Nothing in the landscape prepares the eye for the vision of the twelve so graphically defined arches of the deserted monastery of San Miguel de Escalada, which was constructed in 913 by Mozarabic monks from Córdoba as a jewel in the necklace of churches around León, the royal city of Alfonso III. With my eyes closed I know how the monastery will loom in the landscape, always unexpectedly, I know, and yet I must go there. It is Monday, so the church is shut, it is the solitary warden's day off, but that doesn't matter, my object is the *pórtico*, the forecourt, the site, the way it rests on the hillside, the wide circles of silence all around. And it is as it should be, there is no one and no one is coming. The same, or other, crows carry on their thousand-year-old conversation as they wheel around the massive square tower and I see what I wanted to see, the twelve delicate columns which turn to ivory in a burst of sunlight, the horseshoe arch above, multiplied eleven times, which I glimpse for the last time when I climb to the top of the hill and peer through that small, unglazed paired window, *alfiz*, an Arabic undulation, petrified a thousand years ago, an echo of the mosques of Córdoba and Kairouan, a form the builders brought here from a world that had excluded them, from the Caliphate of the Ummayads. I know the

San Miguel de Escalada

capitals and reliefs with Asturian and Visigothic memories featured in the interior, but above all my thoughts go to the repeated floral motifs, the tropical birds with their barbed beaks, the stylized palm fronds, the bunches of grapes, the shells, the whisper of Islam in that small Christian plantation of columns, an oasis where the deer come to water unseen.

The closer you get to your goal, the more milestones you encounter. Tall ones, stone ones, the old metal plaques with names which in Galicia are crossed out and written anew in Gallego, the new standard European Community signposts carrying a stylized shell quite unlike the old scallop shell emblems everywhere else, the signs indicating a section of the original pilgrim's way, usually no more than a path. And suddenly it gets to you, you want to be rid of your car, you want to walk, you've been doing everything wrong, you are no match for the others, the true pilgrims, those who have made the entire journey on foot, the only ones who really know what it's like. "I'll do it one day," you tell yourself, and you hope it's true, and to get the feel of it you leave your car idle for a day to walk. Without a staff and without any luggage, without a shell because you are not entitled to one, but you walk, and by walking you become someone else.

Only now does the enormity of the undertaking sink in, suddenly you are compelled to adopt a measure that has to do with you alone, with your own thoughts in which you try to think those of all the others, in the past. The signposting being erratic, you often don't know where you are, there is only the clock of your feet. Now it is you counting the hours yourself, observing the lethargy of the landscape, walking over a dusty plain with occasionally the shape of a house in the distance, or later, another day, another time, walking along a river or in a forest, there where the land becomes wilder and begins to ripple. The images of all those churches have long since merged into a wondrous, long ribbon running from Haarlem or Paris or Cluny and rising and falling with the land, other voices are speaking now, magpies and owls, different sounds, someone else's footsteps, water dashing against a bridge, invisible, nocturnal animals, a voice singing in a house.

You watch the light fade, but you have no torch of your own to light and so you can imagine what they, once, in another time, thought and felt when they had fallen behind and had to walk alone in the dark. The Galician countryside is the setting of fairy tales and fables, witches and wizards, of sudden apparitions and enchanted forests, roaming spirits and Celtic mists, even if you walk in the gathering gloom of nightfall for just an hour or two you will be caught in an illusion, the path is not a path, the bushes are horses, the voice I hear comes from another world. It is also getting cold, and when I reach the top of the Cebreiro it is snowing. I step into one of those prehistoric stone huts they call *pallozas*, low-ceilinged, dimly lit, an earthen floor, a few sticks of tree-like furniture, blackened cooking pots that used to hang over a fire in the middle of the hut, the lingering smell of smoke, the roof pointed and thatched with reeds, like the huts of the Dogon in Mali. Twenty years ago they were still inhabited, nine of these hovels are still standing, but there is no one left to make a fire. Yet once upon a time the whole of Europe passed through here, because of a miracle that had taken place on the mountain top: a devout farmer, a doubting monk, the true flesh, the true blood which was kept in the chalice that is still there. Even the Catholic Kings came to see it.

The monks of Cluny, too, established a hospice which was here until the last century, and then, quietly, they left, like someone who has been reading a heavy tome for a thousand years and now turns the final page and shuts the book for ever, a tale of power and influence, piety and politics, which dominated the history of Europe for centuries, finished. It is still standing, that hospice that looks as if the mountain itself erected it, there's a gleam in that rough cold stone, the ninth-century church next door is equally forbidding, one final hardship the pilgrims had, and still have to endure before setting eyes on their ultimate goal. This is the watershed between the Atlantic Ocean and the Cantabrian Sea, it is the highest point on the surrounding sierra; the land, bleak and sombre, slips away to the west.

The *Codex Calixtinus* directs me across hares' fields (*Campus Leporarius*) which are now called *Leboreiro*, the bridge in the medieval village can be crossed only on foot. Nothing can have changed here, the sun has come out and sparkles in the swift water, the meadows blanketed in a snowdrift of tiny white blooms, an old woman crying out in a language I do not understand. The circular granary full of corn cobs was plaited by hand – what kind of world am I in that makes my own world so dingy and shadowy by comparison? Another footbridge, some more cottages, that meadow must be velvet, I want to lie there and listen to the bird imitating the other birds, but the guidebook is adamant:

"after marker 558 we leave the country road and turn left, and then straight ahead".

Wrong! You perhaps, but not I, I must make a detour just one last time, irrational, foolish, I am not ready yet, the city is too close, the whole of Galicia is its garden, I am coming, but not just yet. I draw a wide circle around the city, unsure whether this is serious or just child's play, instinct or whim. First I must go to La Coruña which marches on the ocean like a balcony, a city of light and wind and large windows where it feels so very different from the rest of Spain, as if she belongs more to the sea than to the vast, stony mass of mainland behind her. Ships and markets, swaying statues, but I cannot stay here either.

Onwards to the west the land is lush and Irish-looking, but where it meets the sea it is called Costa de la Muerte, coast of death, and today the wind is doing its utmost to explain why: when I arrive in Muxia I am almost blown off my feet, the fishing boats have come into port and the fishermen huddle together in the cafés on the quay. On a rocky promontory stands a church, the storm rings the bells, but it can't keep time, it clamours at random with its bronze voices, the fishermen take no notice. Coast of death, the rusty carcass of a ship wedged between the rocks is lashed by thongs of white, tufts like a burst of chicken feathers, the churning water glitters in the harsh light, the glare hurts the eyes.

Further south lies Finisterre. It was on this coast that the small ship carrying the body of the Apostle drifted ashore, covered with scallops. Someone would find him, a king would build a church for him, he would fight as Santiago *Matamoros* (Moor-killer) on the battlefield, he would perform miracles and his name would be broadcast along all the roads to the east and north, and would return amplified by the pilgrims who would wear the shell from this sea on their clothes, and then the stream would become a river, as far away as Scotland and Pomerania people would abandon their homes to visit this place where the earth came to an end. Many of them saw the dangerous, lustrous infinity of the sea for the first time in their lives here, at Cape Finisterre, *finis terræ*, and their constant, seething presence in the north of what is now Spain, in the last Christian kingdoms of Navarre and Aragón and León and later Castile, would force Islam to retreat to the pillars of Hercules, to the Africa where the first Muslim armies gathered before flooding al-Andalus like a spring tide.

Now I can complete my circle and lay siege to the city. I drive along the *Rías Bajas*, the great fjords that cut so deep into the green land, along the island of La Toja (La Toxa) where women stand in the mud at low tide to gather shells, then I head inland over climbing roads lined with white and yellow broom. In a month's time the fields will be full of poppies, clover, foxgloves, until a sweeping curve eastward through a forest of eucalyptus and past fields and terraced slopes brings me back to the pilgrim's road, there where *inter duos fluvios, quorum unus vocatur Sar et alter Sarela, urbs Compostella sita est*, between two rivers, one called Sar and the other Sarela, rises the city of Compostela. Now I must climb the mountain from which, on a clear day, you can see the city, the Monxoi, Monte del Gozo, Mons Gaudii, mountain of joy.

I stand and look, but the eyes that see are not mine, they belong to the others, to those of the past. It is their gaze, the view is their reward for walking, risking their lives, believing, they had given all they had just to be with the saint for once in their lives, with his relics, and now they sighted the city, the towers of the cathedral, later the same day they would enter the Puerta Francígena, they would climb the steps to the cathedral, rest their hands in the hand-shaped hollow in the central column of the Pórtico de la Gloria which they had heard so much about, they would pray at the Apostle's grave and receive full absolution. They were different people, with the same brains thinking different thoughts.

Some places do that to you, they have a certain magic whereby you find yourself partaking in the thoughts of others, unknown people, people who existed in a world that can never be yours.

There is no one to be seen on that high mound, nothing at all, a somewhat bare field, a closed chapel, a few boulders. I climb onto one of them and stare into the distance, and then, slowly, as if a veil is lifting, I discover the cathedral, almost hidden behind a ripple of green hills and a transparent screen of trees, three fragile towers drawn in infinitesimal detail, a vision in a dream, and whether I like it or not, an indefinable chemistry floods my heart with their joy, and I sit there until the dusk creeps up the slope and the cars down in the misty valley turn on their lights and beam towards the city in sinuous ribbons of light. Here I am at last, now I can arrive in Santiago.

In old Spanish cities you are woken by church bells. Santiago is not a big city, but there are forty churches, and now and then each of them has a request or an announcement to make which reverberates between the stone walls. Walls are usually made of stone, you might protest, and yet it is as if the core of this place is stonier than elsewhere, you walk on great blocks of granite, and granite is also the material of the houses and churches. When it rains, like yesterday, it gleams and comes alive. I walked among black umbrellas and they were like a colony of migrating bats. Narrow streets, spacious squares where the fine drizzle shrouded the looming shapes of the buildings. No cars, so that the human measure prevailed, voices and footsteps, and once, from an alley, a strain of sorrowful music, a story without end, *la gaita*, the Galician bagpipe. It was coming from a tavern where I had eaten a meal and drunk deep purple wine from a white bowl.

Everything was just as it should be, I knew now about the ocean and the landscape, I could look at the faces and gestures and feel the pride of the city and its aloofness from the rest of the country, the self-absorbed confidence, the splendour this winter evening masked by the misty rain which made me glad and the city melancholy. I looked at *La Voz de Galicia*, with local news that was no business of mine although it would be if I lived here. I read the items about a Spain that was far off and a Europe that was even more remote, I overheard conversations in a language that resembled Portuguese and yet was very different. I surrendered to the languor of arrival after a long journey, for this journey had been the sum of all those other Spanish journeys, whatever I might wish to say about Spain in the future would have to take a different form, my abiding amazement could never be described like this again. I was a stranger and would always remain so, but I had also become a stranger who had come to recognize what he already knew, and that was another story.

Julien Gracq has written, in *La Forme d'une ville*, that when people think back on a city they have visited they take their mental image of a few buildings as reference points, the way a sailor searches out the beacons that will guide him to port. Yesterday, however, the city itself became my seaman's memory, it was memory and reality at once, and I had drifted aimlessly along the beacons. Perhaps that is the traveller's deepest melancholy, that the joy of return is always mixed with a feeling that is harder to define, the feeling that the places you have ached for since you first saw them simply went on existing without you, that if you

Santiago de Compostela

Santiago de Compostela

really wanted to hold them close you would have to stay with them for ever. But that would turn you into someone you cannot be, someone who stays at home, a sedentary being. The real traveller finds sustenance in equivocation, he is torn between embracing and letting go, and the wrench of disengagement is the essence of his existence, he belongs nowhere. The anywhere he finds himself is always lacking in some particular, he is the eternal pilgrim of absence, of loss, and like the real pilgrims in this city he is looking for something beyond the grave of an apostle or the coast of Finisterre, something that beckons and remains invisible, the impossible.

In the dim light I had looked at the carvings in the south portal. God was still creating his bashful Adam, King David's bow was still poised on the strings of his lute-like harp. Not a single fold had shifted in the royal cloak rippling down from the neck to the narrow crossed feet. Christ with a medieval royal crown and the blind eyes of a Greek god, the adulteress with the oversized face and Gorgon's locks, with the small round breasts and the contradictory skull in her lap, everyone had kept the appointment, and everyone, including me, waited for the king to play, in another life, another millennium, later, in the distant future, when the world still has not perished and you will return as someone you would fail to recognize.

The enormous gates at the bottom of the steps to the cathedral were shut, but I knew what was up there, behind the similarly closed doors and the soaring baroque façades. I knew what it was like to enter through a grotto full of statuary, and that among all those carved figures there was one of pink granite that I would seek out as soon as I had laid my hand in the absent hand: the smiling Daniel – because it is as if a new era is dawning in that uncanny smile. This figure by Master Mateo dates from the twelfth century, but the forbidding archaic holiness of the statues in Silos or Moissac has been set aside, here something else is at hand, this expression, this smile, the wonder and surprise, the irony, are familiar to us, they mark the transition from the mythic to the psychological, they belong to our world. The people, needing a story to attach to the figure, say he's smiling at the statue of Esther across the way, and that's it, there has to be an explanation that ties in with the real world, because this figure represents itself and no longer symbolizes an idea. Here someone's

The Prophet Daniel on the pórtico de la Gloria, Santiago de Compostela

face broke into a smile 800 years ago, and his smile was as riveting as ever.

And now? Now all the bells were pealing. I had reached my destination, but I was still delaying the moment of arrival. It was twenty years ago that I began this pilgrimage, if you could call it that. Twenty years of travelling and writing, of leaving and returning, of detours and side-roads. Things changed, politicians disappeared, but the essence, the soul of the country, I thought, remained the same. My travels carried me to Aragón and Andalusia, to Castile and León, to Asturias and Galicia, to the eleventh, the sixteenth, the twentieth centuries, to Visigothic and Mozarabic churches, to books, paintings, monasteries, landscapes, cities. The way I travelled might look erratic to some, as if I were following secret paths through a labyrinth. But all the time I knew where I was going, and now I was there. I was guided by a scallop, and now I was going to put my hand into that other, empty marble hand. Yes, I had reached my destination. First some air, first the Alameda where the trees were, the spacious park of Susana by the hotel, perched high above the surrounding landscape which seemed to flow away to all sides. I walked down the Paseo de las Letras Gallegas, past the statue of Rosalía de Castro, the sun was shining, oak trees, cypresses, palms, eucalyptuses towering skywards, the poetess of Galicia sat with her head resting on her hand and listened to the other poets among the rose-bushes, blackbirds, doves, thrushes whistling the song Eugenio d'Ors composed for her:

En la Ría	In the Ría
un astro	A star
se ponía:	Arose
Rosalía	Rosalía
de Castro	de Castro
de Murquía	de Murquía

This was a park in which to grow very old, but I would not stay; you could read the thirty-eight volumes of the collected writings of a forgotten Icelandic master here, but I would go to the city; you could write a poem of four lines that would take a lifetime to complete here, but I would sit on the stone steps of the Plaza de los Literarios and watch the people cross that huge space and disappear round the corner to the Plaza de las Platerías. Somewhere up there had to be the shabby little office where I once visited the priest who kept the great ledger of pilgrims.

Everyone who had completed the journey on foot or on a bicycle could, if they wished, obtain a rubber-stamped document from him and have their names registered in the great book. "Many times people burst into tears right here," he had told me, pointing in front of his desk. He had shown me the ledger, too, a sort of account book, written in longhand. He had turned the pages until he spotted a Dutchman, a chemistry teacher, "not a believer", motive: "thinking". He had appreciated that, he said, people came up with the oddest motives, but "thinking" was seldom among them. Three months, it took at least that long for someone to walk all the way here from the Netherlands, he didn't think he would be up to it himself. But there were more and more pilgrims now every year. Those who persevered received a sort of certificate, which entitled them to three days in the Hostal de los Reyes Católicos free of charge, not in the best rooms, to be sure, but still. Anyone who stays there feels like an actor in a royal drama, or at least under an obligation to pull an aristocratic face when he emerges from the Plateresque portal into the street. Gothic, Renaissance, baroque, they all come together in that edifice, and the hotel guests, most of whom feel underdressed for such splendid surroundings, buy off their embarrassment by overtipping the liveried doorman.

But once they have passed that barrier they step into one of the loveliest squares in the world. Standing with their backs to the labyrinthine treasure-trove of their temporary hostel, they can see the severe, classical Palacio de Rajoy on the right, and next to that the church of San Fructuoso with its baroque statues teetering on the roof-ledge, to their left rises the Palacio de Galmírez and the ascension into heaven of the great cathedral, and looking ahead, to the far side of the empty stone space, they see the low, archaic Colegio de San Jerónimo. The impression is one of vastness, in that town square, a granite plateau bordered by granite jewels, at such altitude that you can see nothing but sky beyond. And it is *always* beautiful. Snow, night, hail, ice, moon, rain, mist, storm, sun, they all have the run of the Plaza del Obradoiro, they alter people's gestures, attitudes and gait with one stroke of their cold or heat, with the lashes of whips or the fluttering of veils, with their light or their gloom, they clear the square or fill it with people, creating an ever-changing drawing in which, as soon as you set foot on that rectangular plane, you are as much a participant as the statues dancing against the western sky, a movable element in a work of art conceived by someone else.

And then once more I plunge into the book that I will never finish because I don't want it to end. Nor can it end: the more you read, the more pages there are ahead of you. Beyond the triumph of the soaring steps and the eighteenth-century façades with their pilasters and pinnacles waits the so much older Pórtico, with its sculptures and the

Apostles and prophets on the pillars of the pórtico de la Gloria, Santiago de Compostela

column with the hand and the tree of Jesse and the Apostle on high. I stand there and look at all those faces and at that one face wearing the smile and the small, crouching figure that is the sculptor's self-portrait. I watch mothers gently shoving the heads of their children against the head of Master Mateo in the hope that some of his genius will rub off, and then I walk on, into that other church, *his* church, hushed and Romanesque, not the kind of space you would expect to encounter after all the vanity and ostentation of the baroque exterior. This building is its own anachronism, but it doesn't matter. As Ernst Jünger once said, "It is not the churches that are venerable, but the invisible that exists within them." The invisible, that of which you cannot speak, perhaps because speech does not provide the tools, perhaps because you have no desire to, because you want to leave well alone. You can slip nonchalantly from one era into another, walk in beams of light past side chapels harbouring recumbent knights, hear the murmur of Spanish prayers, see the unseeing faces returning your gaze and marvel at the double presence of people in motion and motionless statues.

I stand behind the stiff-backed statue of the apostle, who looks out from the golden insanity of the Capilla Mayor into the church, an idol transposed to later times. I can see three of his shells: a golden one behind his head like the nimbus of a latterday Poseidon, and two more on his back of burnished gold which I touch, and there's no one around at the moment to prevent me from gazing over his mighty shoulder into the church, which looks from here like a clearing in a misty wood. Glancing up the twisted columns of the main altar I see the red marble, the gilded wood, the shades of an autumn that will not end in winter. The *putti* hovering above are many times your size, they're monstrous, tied to their gigantic ankles are the chains of the oil lamps and the sheer madness of the place makes you realize how triumphalism and sentimentality crept up on Spanish religious art over the centuries. At the same time you know it's going to be all right, the architecture can easily stand up to all this glitter and opulence because it is governed by a different system of measurement, a different definition of space, in which a prophet can smile like a man besotted with love and a tide of ever different, ever the same pilgrims ebbs and flows.

The day passes, museums, streets, shops, newspapers, evening brings out the moon and racy clouds. Again the chiming of bells, first three strokes, brief, the clang of metal on metal, dry, no frills; then twelve resounding strokes dashing the hours on to the square and breaking the night in two, the ghostly hour. The Plaza clothes itself in light and darkness by turns and so it, too, appears to be in motion, it turns into a sea and the church into a tug, bearing westward, a boat dragging a country, the country a vessel as big as a country. Antonio Machado once asked the Duero (poet questions river) whether Castile, like the Duero itself, did not always flow in the direction of the sea, which means towards death and what comes after. If it's true, it is to be seen at this hour; at Puigcerdá, at Somport, at Irún it is not just Castile but the whole of Spain that has broken away from Europe, Saint James is the captain on his own tugboat, the dark shape of the cathedral pulls the ship of Aragón and Castile and all the Spanish lands into the ocean, and gathered at the railing, playing and drinking and waving, is the Grand Theatre of Spain, Alfonso the Wise and Philip the Second, Teresa of Ávila and John of the Cross, the Cid and Sancho Panza, Averroes and Seneca, the Hadjib of Córdoba and Abraham Benveniste, Gárgoris and Habidis, Calderón de la Barca, the banished Jews and Moriscos, the victims of the Inquisition and the exhumed nuns from the Civil War, Velásquez and the Duke of Alba, Francisco de Zurbarán, Pizarro and Jovellanos, Gaudí and Baroja, the poets of 1927, the puppets of Valle-Inclán and Goya's drowning little dog, anarchists and mitred bishops, the stocky little dictator and the nymphomaniac queen, the castle of Peñafiel on its sulphur-coloured hill, the pink Alhambra and the Valley of the Dead, friends and enemies, the living and the dead. The place where the *meseta* once was is now a seething ocean, the noise is deafening, and then, suddenly, as if time itself has come to a halt, it is over. The traveller hears his footsteps on the flagstones, he sees the moonlight flooding the towers and the awesome palaces and knows that behind the ramparts of history there must be a different Spain, a Spain that cannot, or perhaps does not wish to, recognize his. His detour has come to an end. His Spanish journey is over.

INDEX

Figures in italic refer to illustrations